D1528949

Changing Keys

Changing Keys

Keyboard Instruments for America
1700–1830

Jᴏʜɴ R. Wᴀᴛsᴏɴ

The Colonial Williamsburg Foundation
Williamsburg, Virginia

ɪɴ ᴀssᴏᴄɪᴀᴛɪᴏɴ ᴡɪᴛʜ

Scarecrow Press
an imprint of the Rowman & Littlefield Publishing Group

© 2013 by The Colonial Williamsburg Foundation
All rights reserved. Published 2013
25 24 23 22 21 20 19 18 17 16 15 14 13   1 2 3 4 5

Library of Congress Cataloging-in-Publication Data

Watson, John, 1952-
  Changing keys : keyboard instruments for America, 1700-1830 / John R. Watson.
      pages cm
  Includes a catalog of the thirty-eight keyboard instruments in the Colonial
Williamsburg Foundation collection.
  Includes bibliographical references and index.
   ISBN 978-0-87935-258-5 (hardcover : alk. paper) -- ISBN 978-0-8108-8485-4
(hardcover : alk. paper)
1. Keyboard instruments--Catalogs and collections--Virginia--Williamsburg.
2. Colonial Williamsburg Foundation--Catalogs. 3. Keyboard instruments--Virginia--
Williamsburg--History--18th century. 4. Keyboard instruments--Virginia--
Williamsburg--History--19th century. I. Title.
   ML462.W45C65 2013
   786'.197554252--dc23
                                              2012049277

ISBN 978-0-87935-258-5 (CW)
ISBN 978-0-8108-8485-4 (Scarecrow)

Designed by John R. Watson

Colonial Williamsburg is a registered trade name of The Colonial Williamsburg Foundation, a not-for-profit educational institution.

The Colonial Williamsburg Foundation
PO Box 1776
Williamsburg, VA 23187-1776
www.history.org

Published in association with Scarecrow Press
An imprint of the Rowman & Littlefield Publishing Group

Printed in China

For Dordy and Charlie Freeman,
passionate educators,
generous patrons of the arts,
and faithful champions of the harpsichord

Contents

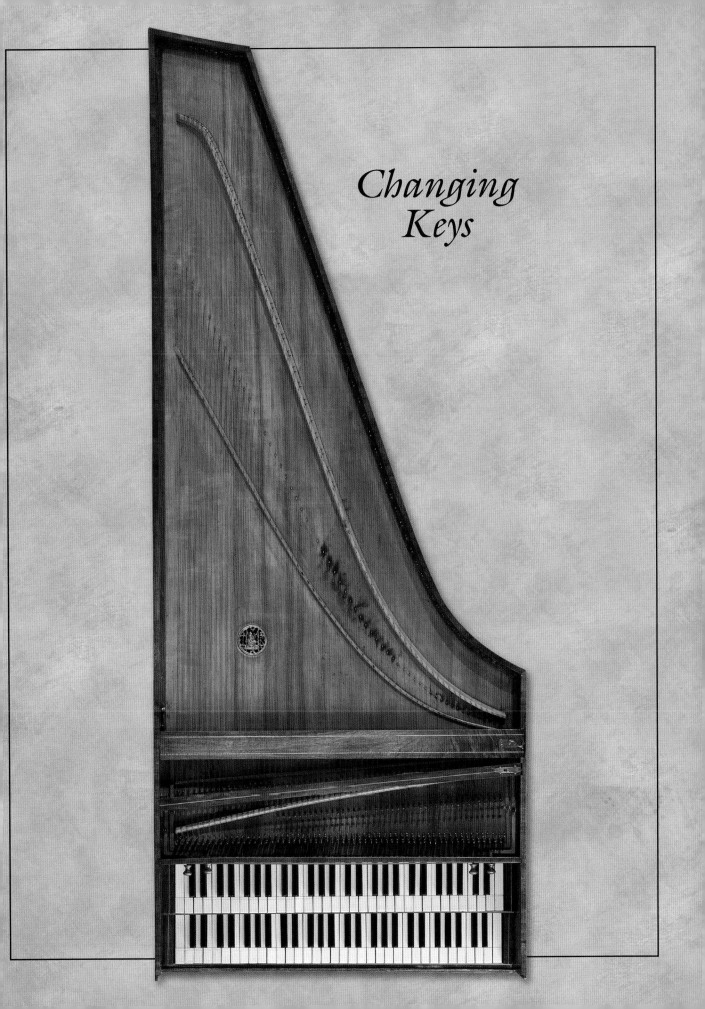

*Changing
Keys*

INTRODUCTION

A minimally structured tour through the Colonial Williamsburg collection of period keyboard instruments, this book pauses on each instrument to consider whatever theme or topic it seems best suited to raise. All of the period keyboard instruments in the Colonial Williamsburg collection, plus three that are on loan from other institutions, are included. Twenty-nine of these instruments were selected for a special exhibit by the same name that opened at the Art Museums of Colonial Williamsburg in November 2012.

The title of this book, *Changing Keys,* has multiple meanings. The exhibit and book are so named in part because they seek to demonstrate how the keyboard musical instruments familiar in early Virginia changed over a 130-year period. The transition from harpsichord to piano is a major theme, but developments over that formative period had almost nothing to do with an evolution from primitive to complex.[1] Rather, changes in instrument design followed constant mutations in musical taste and furniture design, regional and political influences, market and demographic shifts, developing manufacturing technologies, reversals of regional economics, and the rise and fall of instrument manufacturers.

Changing Keys also refers to the way individual instruments were changed over their long history

of use. We may like to think that a museum object accurately represents the period of its making and first use, the most favored examples being free of later remodeling. But, just as colonial period houses became Victorian houses (and usually were modified accordingly), eighteenth-century keyboard instruments were called on to fit into nineteenth-century interiors, and, if a musical instrument remained in use, it had to manage later musical styles and new technical demands. Often, this need prompted a "restoration," in which the goal was not to return to an original or past state but to recover currency through remodeling. Indeed, even restoration to a past state often reveals more about owner and restorer preferences than about the actual and largely unknowable past.

An artifact can serve as a picture of a moment in time with physical evidence in old surfaces revealing in remarkable detail the hand of the maker and first users. As the instrument passes through ensuing eras of use, signs of wear and evidence of alterations of form and decoration accumulate on its surfaces, and it becomes a motion picture of a longer history. It was in part due to the high cost of keyboard instruments that they, like the buildings that housed them, were often updated rather than replaced.

Some alterations carry fascinating clues about

A watercolor drawn in 1939 by restoration architect Singleton P. Moorehead showing the west border of Palace Green. Bruton Parish Church on the far left and its first organist, Peter Pelham, figured prominently in Williamsburg's musical life throughout the last half of the eighteenth century. When Thomas Jefferson was a student at the College of William and Mary, his mentor, George Wythe, living in the brick *house center left, introduced him to Lt. Gov. Francis Fauquier. The governor included Jefferson in private music making at the Governor's Palace, located outside the drawing at the far right. The large white house on the right was located next door to the Palace and was the home of Robert Carter, an amateur musician and musical theorist who owned a spinet, harpsichord, organ, piano, and glass armonica, among other instruments.*

the spirit of an era. If the square piano purchased by Williamsburg's Robert Carter in 1771 had survived, for example, it would illustrate the potential of alterations to intrigue and inform. Carter was a prominent Virginia plantation owner and skilled amateur musician who lived in Williamsburg in the house shown below at the far right from 1761 to 1773 while serving on the royal governor's council. A true product of the Enlightenment, Carter considered his piano, one of the first in the colony, to be both a musical and a scientific instrument on which to experiment as much as to play.[2] Carter ordered a drawplate to draw his own harpsichord wire, and he experimented with musical pitch and temperament.[3] He lamented that the sharps on his new piano were not split to allow separate tuning for the sharp and flat versions of each accidental, as advanced by Dr. Robert Smith in a then-recent theoretical treatise, although Carter did convert the piano to single stringing as advocated by Smith.[4] When his piano was thirty years old, Carter instructed Baltimore instrument maker William Harper to replace the hammers and action, making the hammer rail movable, presumably to enable transposing.[5] Had it survived, the piano would be a document with chapters covering the years 1771 to 1802, revealing one of the most searching musical minds in early America.

A harpsichord attributed to Cusseneers, Düsseldorf, 1726 (entry no. 4). The nameboard is inscribed "REBUILT BY JOHN CHALLIS 1950."

For an example of alterations to an instrument that does survive, consider the harpsichord attributed to I. N. Cusseneers of Düsseldorf, Germany (entry no. 4). The harpsichord was restored in 1950 by John Challis, a significant figure in the early music revival and the principal keyboard specialist in America at the time. Challis embodied a philosophy that is in dramatic contrast to today's but is of its own era and worth study. His addition of pedals and other mostly internal "improvements" to the Cusseneers harpsichord were radical departures from the materials and construction choices of the original maker, yet they are true to Challis's mid-twentieth-century credo of historical stewardship. In his restorations, as much as in his new harpsichords, Challis sought to revive the historical harpsichord and fortepiano while also believing the technological advances of the intervening industrial era could vastly improve them. In this 1726 harpsichord, technologies and values of the mid-twentieth century are imprinted over the old. The instrument is a study piece for both periods. Amnesty is sometimes extended to altered artifacts such as the Cusseneers harpsichord. Our present-day goal, however, is to preserve all remaining historical evidence as unchanged as possible.

COLONIAL WILLIAMSBURG AND THE EARLY MUSIC REVIVAL

The twentieth century opened with disillusionment over the dehumanizing effects of industrialization and a frightening world war, setting the stage for a revival of interest in the past. For Americans, nostalgia for the colonial period in general and the time of the Revolution in particular had begun to take root during the centennial in 1876. Efforts to preserve and restore the physical remnants of the past, and even to step into the reconstructed landscape of the founding fathers and mothers, was an idea whose time had come.

Williamsburg was the capital of Virginia, Britain's largest American colony. Among the representatives in Virginia's House of Burgesses were Thomas Jefferson, George Washington, Patrick Henry, and others who would build the foundations of the new nation. Unlike Boston, Philadelphia, and New York, the capital of Virginia moved to another city after the Revolution, leaving Williamsburg relatively untouched by the urban growth of a political center.

Through the vision of Bruton Parish Church rector W. A. R. Goodwin and philanthropist John D. Rockefeller Jr., restoration of Virginia's colonial capital began in 1926. It would become one of the first living history museums. Teams of researchers set to work collecting volumes of information about political and cultural life in one of the most important and well-preserved colonial towns in America. The result is an extraordinary museum city, preserving and, where necessary, reconstructing not only buildings with their furnishings but also the day-to-day lives of its early inhabitants, including free and enslaved, genteel and middling, patriot and loyalist. Museum staff restored buildings, re-created historic trades, and illuminated all facets of culture among the early inhabitants.

Among the cultural enrichments and diversions essential for the capital city were music and dance. From the beginning, keyboard musical instruments were part of that emerging picture of life in colonial and post colonial America.

In 1930, the first musical instrument was purchased for use in the restored city. It was an early nineteenth-century grand piano by Muzio Clementi. The instrument had come from Lotta Van Buren, grandniece of U.S. president Martin Van Buren

A 1939 performance in the newly reconstructed Governor's Palace with harpsichordist and Colonial Williamsburg consultant Ralph Kirkpatrick and friends.

and pioneering jack-of-all-early-music-trades. Having studied with Arnold Dolmetsch in Haslemere, Surrey, England, she collected and restored period instruments, especially clavichords and harpsichords, and presented costumed performances in New York. Van Buren was the first to advocate that the ballroom of the newly reconstructed Governor's Palace should be enlivened with music. The celebrated harpsichordist and fortepianist Ralph Kirkpatrick was brought in as performer and consultant.

Kirkpatrick located many historical scores for the fledgling collection, most selected on the basis of a 1938 research report, "On Music in Colonial Williamsburg" by Helen Bullock. The sixty-five-page report documented numerous eighteenth-century references to music making and musical scores in Williamsburg and vicinity during the colonial period.

From 1938 to 1946, Kirkpatrick and various associates presented several series of Palace concerts. The success of the 1938 series prompted short-lived thoughts of hiring a resident musician. Restoration

Twenty-first-century Colonial Williamsburg musicians continue a tradition of music making in the Palace ballroom, with roots that go back three centuries. The performance practices, instruments, costumes, and interiors are informed by decades of research.

architect William G. Perry wrote, "I wonder if it may be possible to use these more formal concerts as a background and to introduce music more frequently into the buildings in a much less formal way. . . . I therefore suggest that a musician be engaged to play at the Raleigh Tavern and the Palace alternately. This person might have other duties such as helping Mrs. Fisher with the flowers."[6] Interestingly, Perry's idea echoed a request from Thomas Jefferson to a friend in Italy: the Virginian asked for a few Italian musicians who could double as servants at Monticello.[7]

Pianist and conductor Cary McMurran established a Palace orchestra that would offer concerts from 1948 until the early 1980s, when a growing emphasis on historical accuracy rendered it obsolete. A few of the instruments, including some Italian stringed instruments, were acquired during that period for the orchestra's use and remain in the permanent collection. The first harpsichordist for the Palace orchestra was Bruton Parish organist Arthur Rhea.

The year 1953 brought the largest single growth spurt for the collection. Mary Goodwin prepared a research report titled "Musical Instruments in Eighteenth Century Virginia" that would guide the collection for several decades. Arthur Rhea then spent

six weeks in England acquiring thirteen instruments, including the Foundation's earliest keyboard, the 1700 Stephen Keene spinet (entry no. 1), and a large chamber organ then thought to be by John Snetzler (no. 6). Rhea also collected xerographic and microfilmed materials in the music division of the British Museum and purchased period scores in London, Oxford, and Cambridge.[8]

A 1960 restoration of the 1762 Kirckman harpsichord (entry no. 9) by respected English scholar and restorer Hugh Gough was the beginning of a new era for the care of the collection. Kirkpatrick had played most of his Palace concerts on his own modern Chickering harpsichord, saving the less dependable antique Kirckman harpsichord for the occasional encore.

Spinets are made today in Hay's Cabinetmaking Shop in Colonial Williamsburg's Historic Area, as its historical counterpart on the same site advertised in the Virginia Gazette *in 1767.*

Gough had moved to New York, renting space in Wallace Zuckermann's new workshop, where he would restore four more instruments two years later: the piano by Frederick Beck (no. 17) and the spinets by Keene (no. 1), Cawton Aston (no. 3), and John Woolfinden (no. 5).

The well-known musicologist and collector of folk music Alan Lomax was hired in 1960 to help create the film *Music of Williamsburg*. The fictional story depicted much of what had been learned about the musical cultures in the colonial capital, with its near equal numbers of black and white residents. In the following year, Bruton Parish Church hired a new organist, James S. Darling, who eventually played as many as eighty recitals and concerts annually in his duties as church organist and Colonial Williamsburg consultant. In 1968, Darling assisted in the selection and acquisition of one of William Dowd's popular French double harpsichords. The state of historical accuracy at that time was such that Dowd was asked to veneer this reproduction French harpsichord in the English style.

The next watershed for music at Colonial Williamsburg came in 1971. Musical activity expanded in Williamsburg's Historic Area beyond the Palace

with the hiring of Charles Hardin as music master at the recently established Music Teacher's Room on Duke of Gloucester Street. The Foundation subsequently hired a small staff of full- and part-time musicians. A new aspect of music also sprang back to life in that year with the hiring of George Wilson as master musical instrument maker. At first, guests watched many types of stringed instruments being made in the shop, but the work eventually narrowed to spinets, which the shop had advertised in 1767.

Keyboard instrument maker Peter Redstone had begun restoring keyboard instruments for the Foundation by 1974 and, while continuing such work on a contract basis, took a one-day per week position in the 1980s to tune and monitor instruments on-site. The author joined the new conservation staff as conservator of instruments in 1988, becoming full-time in that capacity in 1995 and adding the title of associate curator of musical instruments in 2008.

Thousands of Colonial Williamsburg guests were first introduced to harpsichords at the Music Teacher's Room. In this 1983 photo, James Darling plays a 1971 reproduction Kirckman harpsichord made in Williamsburg by George Wilson.

THE COLONIAL WILLIAMSBURG COLLECTION OF KEYBOARD MUSICAL INSTRUMENTS

The goal of the Foundation's historical and decorative arts collections is to illustrate the material culture of Williamsburg, the colony of Virginia, and, to a diminishing degree, regions extending outward to the middle Atlantic and southern states. The time frame for the keyboard collection begins at 1700, which is about the earliest that keyboard instruments might have begun to appear in the English colonies.

The Foundation's historical and decorative arts collections extend through the early Republic era to about 1830, a convenient ending date for the keyboard collection as it marks a turning point in piano history. The advent of iron framing around that time accelerated the technological revolution that produced the modern piano.

The succession of keyboard specialists serving as musical consultants from 1938 onward predisposed the Colonial Williamsburg collection to its particular strength in period keyboard instruments. This book describes all thirty-four of them plus three that are on loan from nearby institutions and one historic revival harpsichord made by Arnold Dolmetsch in Boston at Chickering & Sons in 1908. The total includes six spinets, six harpsichords, three organs, five grand pianos, and a vertical piano. The remaining seventeen instruments—nearly half of Colonial Williamsburg's overall keyboard collection—are square pianos. This ratio of keyboard types is not far from what might have been found in Virginia from

1700 to 1830, with the possible exception that spinets would have been better represented. The period of popularity for spinets in the first half of this time frame means they have survived in smaller numbers.

The dominance of London-made instruments in the collection (there are twenty-seven) also reflects accurately the keyboard culture in early Virginia. Only near the end of this time period did the great American piano industry begin to develop, so the collection includes just six American-made examples. The collection also includes examples from Manchester and Edinburgh in the United Kingdom and Düsseldorf in Germany.

Not included in these figures but also part of the collection are ten reproduction keyboards: five spinets, four harpsichords, and a square piano. Six of these are copies of instruments in the collection. Reproductions played an important role from the beginning of Colonial Williamsburg when Ralph Kirkpatrick used his own Chickering harpsichord for most of the early concert series. The lack of skilled caretakers at that time rendered antiques less reliable as functioning instruments. As the Colonial Williamsburg Foundation and other museums became aware of the value of historical evidence and its vulnerability during restoration, reproductions were used increasingly to take the brunt of wear and tear from daily use. This book mentions reproductions from the collection when they have a particular relevance to featured historic instruments.

A rehearsal on period instruments, most from the Colonial Williamsburg collection, in the auditorium of the Art Museums of Colonial Williamsburg.

Keyboard Musical Instruments
in British and Anglo-American Society

Gentlemen, Music, and Industry in the Eighteenth Century

London was Europe's largest city in the later part of the eighteenth century, yet its importance is often overlooked in histories of music of that period due to the small number of native-born composers. British and American attitudes about music and industry in the eighteenth century, however, were optimized not for the composition of music but for the production of musical instruments.

Stated simply, social values in British and British-American society were based largely on the productivity and business skills of men and the domesticity of women. Those ideals placed restrictive conditions on the role that music could play in the lives of both sexes. However, what was lost in producing native-born composers was gained in the technology, science, and production of musical instruments.

People played music on an amateur basis at home and enjoyed music in the theater and in public entertainments. Professional performers were often foreign. To members of the upper levels of British society, too much musical proficiency often was associated with intemperance and laziness, especially if the musicians were male. Writing at the end of the seventeenth century, John Locke, who profoundly influenced the philosophical underpinnings of the Enlightenment, presented a point of view about music that was to characterize British and American attitudes in the century that followed:

> Musick is thought to have some affinity with Dancing, and a good Hand, upon some Instruments, is by many People mightily valued. But it wastes so much of a young Man's time, to gain but a moderate Skill in it; and engages often in such odd Company, that many think it much better spared: And I have, amongst Men of Parts and Business, so seldom heard any one commended, or esteemed for having an Excellency in Musick, that amongst all those things, that ever came into the List of Accomplishments, I think may give it the last place.[1]

Similar warnings appeared throughout the eighteenth century in tracts on virtue and conduct.[2] A 1788 London publication offered the following words of guidance for a young man thought to be spending too much time learning music:

> [Your pursuit of music] may tend, which it naturally does, to enervate the mind, and make you haunt musical societies, op-
eras, and concerts; and what glory is it to a gentleman, if he were even a fine performer, that he can strike a string, touch a key, or sing a song, with the grace and command of an *hired* musician? . . . I am far from dissuading you from these amusements, so long as you consider them only as such.[3]

The disparagement of more than modest musical proficiency for Britain's brightest young men had predictable side effects, not all of them negative. The list of prominent eighteenth-century British composers and performers is short. Instead, these roles typically were relegated to foreigners who had taken up residence in Britain, such as George Frideric Handel, Johann Christian Bach, Karl Friedrich Abel, Muzio Clementi, and Johann Baptist Cramer, or spent short periods there, such as Franz Joseph Haydn, Jan Ladislav Dussek, and Johann Nepomuk Hummel. Despite the unwritten rules against male proficiency in music, some men did excel in the profession.[4] Thomas Augustine Arne's devotion to music was irrepressible in spite of social norms. William Boyce's role as organist at St. Paul's Cathedral and composer for the church exempted him from conventional secular limits. Charles Burney's accomplishments in musical journalism legitimized his role as a skilled organist and harpsichordist.

To dismiss British musical culture in the eighteenth century because of the lack of native composers is to miss the flip side of those same British values. The emphasis on business and industry allowed first Britain and later America to emerge as world leaders in technology and the manufacture of many commodities, not the least including musical instruments. Using innovative manufacturing and marketing methods, John Broadwood did for keyboard instruments what Josiah Wedgwood did for ceramics and Matthew Boulton did for metalware and steam engines. The London firm of Longman & Broderip was an international leader in all aspects of musical merchandising. Their massive catalog of music included their own publications and those of leading Continental publishers.[5] The firm also supplied a full array of keyboard and other musical instruments and accessories for wholesale and retail sale. Indeed, London-made pianos were better known on the Continent than were Continental instruments in Britain, and innovative designs by London piano makers were widely appropriated by Continental makers, especially in Paris.[6]

A 1790 print highlights the importance of dress and musical accomplishments in the lives of young women in British society. The publisher's Wardour Street address was doors away from piano makers Robert Stodart, George Garcka, and James Houston. Published by Gallery of Fashion; CWF acc. no. 1971-2993

most becoming of a young woman.[7] Frequently a part of the core curriculum in girls' boarding schools, keyboard lessons taught discipline and coordination. In that male-oriented society, long hours of practice were considered a constructive way to occupy girls within the home, away from worldly temptations.[8] This role for keyboard instruments helped to justify their considerable expense.

Considering that 80–89 percent of keyboard instrument users were young women, they—through their fathers who purchased the instruments for them—constituted a vast market contributing to the success of keyboard instrument manufacturers.[9] Highly valued among the so-called accomplishments that marked a young woman as worthy of her place in polite society, music took its well-earned place next to painting, needlework, various decorative handicrafts, and the French language, all taught by itinerant tutors or in established academies.

Music's long association with romance undoubtedly encouraged fathers to invest in keyboard instruments to give daughters every advantage for favorable marriages. The efficacy of the scheme is evident in a poem published in Williamsburg in 1768: "When Nancy on the spinet plays / I fondly on the virgin gaze, / And wish that she was mine."[10] That music could engender feelings of affection also prompted concerns about the moral, and not just musical, qualifications of male music masters, who were often depicted by caricaturists as lecherous and unsavory.[11]

Musical pursuits often stalled after a girl's marriage as new domestic responsibilities took priority. As a girl in the 1790s, Eleanor "Nelly" Parke Custis was said to practice many hours a day on the harpsichord bought for her by her step-grandfather, George Washington. Twenty years later, Nelly wrote to a young bride her hope that the girl would "not give up music & painting, for pickling, preserving, & *puddings* although I have done so in great measure."[12]

Some uses of keyboard instruments were not musical. Of all musical instruments, spinets, harpsichords, pianos, and organs were expensive enough and large enough to serve as bold declarations of the owners' wealth and taste. Their large surfaces covered with

THE YOUNG LADIES AND THEIR ACCOMPLISHMENTS

The prejudice against professional musicians and the lack of native-born composers did not prevent the British from valuing music and instruments for domestic music making. For those who could afford them, keyboards were the most versatile tools for re-creating cherished music from the theater and other public entertainments. Published transcriptions brought within the keyboardist's grasp the entire instrumental and vocal repertoire. Arrangements were often published in separate versions for diverse levels of skill. The role of keyboard instruments as accompaniment for voice and other instruments not only added to their own versatility but it also helped to cultivate the larger body of domestic vocal and instrumental music.

Keyboard musical instruments served as essential equipment for the education and refinement of adolescent girls of the gentry. Musical proficiency on keyboard or guitar was a social ornament considered

9

figured veneers and brass hardware made them the ideal trophy furniture in a status-minded society. Such a use for keyboard instruments has hardly changed. Grand pianos—whether they are played or not—still serve as symbols of taste and affluence in domestic interiors.

For some in the Age of Enlightenment, musical instruments functioned also as instruments of science suitable for mechanical and acoustical study and tinkering. Experimentation with instrument design or tuning schemes was a particularly honorable form of musical activity for gentlemen in British-oriented society. Francis Hopkinson read papers pertaining to "An Improved Method of Quilling a Harpsichord" to the American Philosophical Society in Philadelphia between 1783 and 1787.[13] Thomas Jefferson exchanged letters with Hopkinson about the quilling question and engaged instrument makers or their agents in conversations about details of design, leading Charles Burney to write, "You, Sir, are [a] speculative musician."[14] Robert Carter of Williamsburg experimented or encouraged others to experiment with alternatives to crow quills for harpsichord plectra and to try delft earthenware in place of glass for the bowls of his armonica. He described an experiment in his daybook about a type of monochord in which the sounding portion of the string was between bridges set five inches apart and tensioned by a specific weight, all calculated so the string would sound "in unison with D-in alt, of my Forte Piano – that Instrument being then in Concert Pitch."[15] Carter also attempted alterations to his fortepiano to implement the mathematically complex tuning theories published by Robert Smith. When ordering his chamber organ, Carter, relying on the advice of Williamsburg organist Peter Pelham, specified an improved type of bellows.[16]

In the colonial and early Federal eras, music was as pervasive as it is today, finding expression in the rhythm of everyday life in the work fields, the campsites of the militia, the slave quarters, the church, the theater, the tavern, the ballroom, the parlor, and the nursery. Unlike today, music usually was self-produced or came from the hands and voices of friends and neighbors. Landon Carter wrote in his diary during a visit to Williamsburg in 1771, "From every house a constant tuting may be listned to upon one instrument or another, whilst the Vocal dogs will no doubt compleat the howl."[17]

Tunes from public entertainments could be enjoyed at home but only through the purchase of sheet music and instruments. Beginning in the late eighteenth century, the popularity of some stage personalities greatly stimulated sales of sheet music. Favorite songs from the musical theater were often published with the names of the singers who popularized them rather than the composers', and, of course, the accompaniment required a keyboard. This market for popular sheet music and pianos continued to increase until the mid-twentieth century when, for better or worse, the ubiquity of sound recordings meant people no longer had to sing and play the music themselves to hear it at home and throughout their day.

THE PROFESSIONALS

Professional musicians were rare in eighteenth-century Virginia. Most were itinerant music masters who made their rounds teaching the children of wealthy plantation owners or settling for brief periods in Williamsburg, Norfolk, Fredericksburg, or, later, Richmond to offer lessons and provide musical accompaniment for dance. In America, as in Britain, the role of music master often was relegated to French or German immigrants, for whom the prospects for employment were better here than in their native countries.

Other professionals came through American towns in traveling theater groups that typically included only one or two musicians, relying on local amateurs for instrumental support as needed. America's first professional theater group was the Murray-Kean Company, which arrived from London in 1751 and performed first in Williamsburg in a new theater prepared for them.[18] The troupe moved on the next year and was followed a few months later by the London Company of Comedians, variously known over the next few years as the Hallam-Douglass Company, the American Company, and the Old American Company.

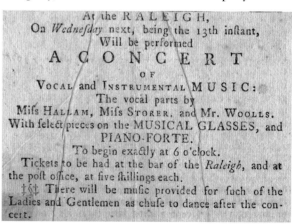

The Williamsburg public was introduced to the pianoforte within months of its debut in Boston. Members of the American Company featured it in a 1771 concert at the Raleigh Tavern. Rind's Virginia Gazette (Williamsburg), November 7, 1771.

One concert by the American Company took place on November 13, 1771, at the Raleigh Tavern in Williamsburg. A momentous occasion for keyboard history in the central colonies, the program introduced

Minuet in C attributed to Peter Pelham from a 1744 keyboard tutor used by one of his students. Peter Pelham manuscript, MS 2003.7, John D. Rockefeller, Jr. Library, CWF.

the pianoforte to Williamsburg audiences. The concert occurred soon after the first known public performance on a piano in America, organized in Boston by James Juhan in March of the same year.[19] Appearing with another novel instrument, the musical glasses, the piano played in the Williamsburg concert could have been the one brought to Virginia by the royal governor Lord Dunmore, who arrived only two months before, or it could have been that belonging to Williamsburg resident Robert Carter.

Popular support for musical activity was sufficient in Williamsburg to attract a respected member of London's musical establishment to take up residence there. Cuthbert Ogle had been a harpsichordist, impresario, and conductor who organized concerts in London featuring celebrated performers from London and Europe prior to his 1754 move to Williamsburg. On his arrival, Ogle advertised in the *Virginia Gazette*, proposing to teach organ, harpsichord, and spinet. There must have been instruments and students enough to make Williamsburg a promising destination for someone of his profession and reputation. Only four months after his arrival, however, Ogle died. Adding useful historical context to Ogle's presence is a surviving inventory of his sizable collection of music and instruments. The compiler of the inventory was Peter Pelham, himself a musician and recent arrival.[20]

Peter Pelham was a rare resident professional keyboardist in eighteenth-century Virginia. Hired as organist of Bruton Parish Church after setting up its first organ in 1755, Pelham remained a central figure in the musical life of Williamsburg for nearly fifty years. He taught lessons and advised townspeople in the ordering of instruments. He drew detailed specifications for a chamber organ for Robert Carter and a barrel organ

for the Upper Parish of Nansemond County.[21] Pelham also played concerts and conducted and played harpsichord in the theater, including a 1768 performance of *The Beggar's Opera* by the Virginia Company of Comedians.[22]

Neither Williamsburg nor any other Virginia city had a population sufficient to fully support a resident music professional. Even though Williamsburg was Virginia's capital and its cultural and political center prior to the capital's move to Richmond in 1780, the town's only professional musician nevertheless relied on supplementary income from nonmusical enterprises. Peter Pelham served as a clerk for royal governors Fauquier and Botetourt. He was also appointed to supervise the printing of currency for the colony, and he served as the city's jail keeper, for which lodging was included as part of his compensation.

THE REVOLUTIONARIES

Several of America's Founding Fathers were gifted amateur musicians, and, while their influence had little to do with American musical culture, their voluminous and well-preserved papers shed a useful light on the broader role of musical instruments. Francis Hopkinson, a signer of the Declaration of Independence, was a published composer, organist, and harpsichordist who tinkered with adapting a keyboard to Benjamin Franklin's glass armonica.[23] Patrick Henry played violin, flute, harpsichord, and piano.[24] Thomas Jefferson famously played the violin and joined other Virginia luminaries for musical gatherings at the Governor's Palace. Francis Fauquier, lieutenant governor of the Virginia Colony, had known Handel while he was a governor of the Foundling Hospital in London.[25] The last of the royal governors of Virginia, John Murray, fourth Earl of Dunmore, also kept instruments at the Palace, including a piano, a harpsichord, and an organ.[26]

Thomas Jefferson was the foremost architect of the new American Republic, yet, even during intense periods of his professional life, he found time not only to maintain competence as an amateur violinist but also to engage in many ways with keyboard instruments. Although Jefferson did not play them himself, keyboards were a source of fascination for him, and he thought them to be essential for the education of his daughters. His papers include sporadic observations on keyboard instruments. In a 1786 letter to Francis Hopkinson, for example, Jefferson described with enthusiasm a newly invented pedal-operated "Foot-bass" piano, which he had seen in Paris.[27]

Jefferson's papers are peppered with references to keyboard instruments he owned, rented, or considered buying. He ordered a clavichord from Hamburg

With Revolutionary tensions rising, the royal governor, Lord Dunmore, fled the Governor's Palace in Williamsburg leaving behind a harpsichord, a piano, and a chamber organ. The residence had long been host to msical gatherings. As a student at the College of

William and Mary, Thomas Jefferson joined then Governor Fauquier and other leading figures in the political and cultural life of the colony for musical and conversational engagement. Fauquier's musical friend Robert Carter lived in the house next door.

through a London agent in 1770 for his fiancée Martha Wayles Skelton. Although clavichords were rare, they were not unknown in Britain and its American colonies. Jefferson may have seen one among the Pennsylvania Germans on his visit to Philadelphia in 1766. Jefferson later wrote to Thomas Adams, "I must alter one article in the invoice. I wrote therein for a Clavichord. I have since seen a Forte-piano and am charmed with it. Send me this instrument then instead of the Clavichord. Let the case be of fine mahogany, solid, not vineered. The compass from Double G. to F. in alt." This letter secured for Jefferson a place among the examples for the term *forte-piano* in the *Oxford English Dictionary*.[28]

Martha Skelton presumably brought a spinet into Jefferson's household when they married in 1772. References to a spinet in the house are scattered through the records thereafter, such as when Jefferson paid for his wife's spinet lessons and ordered strings and repairs for the instrument. In 1778, Jefferson made an unsuccessful attempt to buy Robert Carter's organ. While they lived in Philadelphia in 1782, Jefferson rented a clavichord for his daughter Martha. The next year, in a letter via Francis Hopkinson to publisher Robert Bremner of London, Jefferson inquired about a double harpsichord with John-Joseph Merlin's forte-piano

stop. On March 31, 1784, Hopkinson replied, "Mr. Bremner agrees with me in Opinion respecting Forte Pianos. He says there is one Merlin who has contrived to unite the Forte Piano and Harpsichord, but he adds the one Instrument injures the other so that neither of them is good, and that they are frequently to be had at Second hand for half Price."[29]

After moving to Paris in 1784 with his daughter Martha, Jefferson rented a piano for her use.[30] Martha was taking lessons from celebrated French harpsichordist and composer Claude Balbastre when Jefferson ordered a two-manual harpsichord from Londoner Jacob Kirckman for her. Against Kirckman's recommendations, Jefferson arranged that a celestina stop be added by its inventor, Adam Walker. The stop enabled the sound to be sustained as long as the keys remained depressed, which was accomplished by an elaborate mechanism consisting of a rotating belt of rosined ribbon that excites the strings in the manner of a violin bow.[31]

Thoughts of an organ for Monticello were revived in 1786 when Jefferson asked Charles Burney of London for advice about who made the best organs. Burney recommended Samuel Green, but no organ was ever ordered. A second harpsichord ordered from Jacob Kirckman in 1798 was for his younger daughter, Maria. Jefferson voiced reservations about Maria's choice of a harpsichord, presumably because harpsichords had fallen out of fashion by then. Two years later, Jefferson ordered a so-called portable grand piano made by young John Isaac Hawkins in Philadelphia. The instrument lacked tuning stability, so Jefferson asked Hawkins to swap the piano either for another of his diminutive upright portable grands or for one of his newly invented claviols. In an 1802 advertisement, Hawkins described the instrument as producing its sound "from gut strings by horse-hair bows rosined, it is played on with finger-keys like the organ or Piano Forte."[32]

Finally, four months before his 1826 death, Jefferson received one last piano at Monticello. It was a square piano by Currier & Gilbert of Boston, which he purchased for his granddaughter Virginia Randolph Trist.[33]

In addition to these well-documented keyboard instruments in Thomas Jefferson's life, a square piano by George Astor & Company, presently at Monticello, has an oral history of ownership by Jefferson. Jefferson's daughters also had partial use of a piano owned by his neighbor Dr. Watkins, who stored the instrument at Monticello for a time. For someone who did not play keyboard instruments himself, these instruments nevertheless appeared with surprising regularity in Jefferson's papers.

Jefferson was one of several well-known gentleman amateurs who were skilled in tuning the instruments in their possession. Robert Carter of Williamsburg and Nomini Hall even invented a means of tuning using a set of whistles to produce the pitch of each note in the octave. Most impressively, Carter purchased a drawplate for sizing wire for his harpsichord. Pulling wire through holes of diminishing diameter in the drawplate produced wire of various sizes.[34]

The Tuners and Makers

Not all owners of stringed keyboard instruments were so resourceful, however. The tuning and maintenance of keyboard instruments were often among the diverse services advertised by itinerant music masters. An 1804 newspaper advertisement in Richmond, for example, announced "P[hilippe] A. Peticolas & his Son August, *PROFESSORS OF MUSIC*,

Respectfully inform the ladies and gentlemen of the City of Richmond and its vicinity, that they intend to teach MUSIC on the PIANO FORTE or HARPSICHORD." After the contact information, Peticolas added, "TUNES INSTRUMENTS." Many traveling music masters diversified their services in various other ways. The Peticolas advertisement, for example, also offered "MINIATURE PAINTING; good likenesses, warranted by himself." In addition to working in Richmond, these two artist-musicians spent time in Petersburg, Alexandria, Baltimore, Philadelphia, and Lancaster, Pennsylvania.[35]

At least two itinerant jacks-of-all-musical-trades who spent time in Virginia and vicinity advertised the manufacturing of keyboard instruments. James Juhan, noted above for organizing America's first known public performance on a pianoforte, moved to Richmond in 1792 and advertised grand pianofortes of his own manufacture. These he claimed were better and cheaper than imported models.[36] At various times Juhan also advertised making violins and tuning, repairing, selling, and leasing various types of instruments. For a while, before moving to Petersburg in 1787, Juhan also worked in Williamsburg.[37]

Christian Veltenair was another itinerant handyman who provided an array of musical services in and around Virginia. Besides being an inventor and artist, Veltenair advertised tuning, repairing, and making pianos, organs, and harpsichords. In Baltimore and Norfolk, he advertised concerts to be performed on a keyboard violin of his own invention.[38]

Williamsburg cabinetmaker Benjamin Bucktrout was not primarily known as a musician or instrument maker, but he advertised in 1767, "N. B. SPINETS and HARPSICHORDS made and repaired." Bucktrout had arrived from England the previous year. He may have been employed and received experience at a keyboard workshop in England, or he could have hired a journeyman who had emigrated from a London shop. Four years later, one such workman did arrive, according to an announcement in the *Virginia Gazette*: "Just arrived, the *Scarsdale*, with about a Hundred and twenty healthy SERVENTS, Men, Women, and Boys, among which are many Tradesmen, namely, . . . a Harpsichord Maker, and several others."[39]

Tracing of an inscription by Christian Veltenair inside the bellows of a combination organ and upright grand piano made in 1799 by Longman, Clementi & Co. probably for St. George Tucker of

Williamsburg.[40] Veltenair was a Richmond-based itinerant inventor, artist, and keyboard instrument maker who repaired the instrument in 1805.

THE OTHER REVOLUTION

The patriots of 1776 boldly declared American independence from Britain. It would be another quarter century, however, before an economic and technological revolution would begin to free America from near total dependence on Britain as its source for musical instruments. Until then, it was London in particular that supplied the great majority of musical instruments for America. The largest city in Europe and the center of technological innovation and world trade, London promised greater prosperity for skilled instrument makers. German craftsmen were particularly attracted to Britain's hub of musical instrument making.

London's near total dominance of the market continued past the Revolutionary period into the early Federal era. As George Washington was being elected to his second presidential term, it was from Longman & Broderip in London that he ordered a new harpsichord for Mount Vernon. Thomas Jefferson was vice president in 1798 when he placed his second order for a harpsichord from Kirckman of London.

By the time the American keyboard industry was ready to significantly challenge the London monopoly, spinets and harpsichords had fallen out of fashion. Only four American spinets and one harpsichord, representing four makers, survive.[41] Prior to 1790, American production of pianos was also sporadic and struggled along on a small scale. During the 1790s, however, Charles Albrecht, Charles Taws, and Charles Trute—all working in or near Philadelphia—began producing pianos on a larger scale, leaving a combined legacy of about thirty surviving square pianos.[42] In the first decade of the nineteenth century, piano manufacturing picked up also in New York and Boston.

From the perspective of the American musical instrument industry, the embargoes against British goods leading up to the War of 1812 accomplished what the American Revolution had failed to do. As British instruments became less accessible, a growing number of American makers stood ready to fill the need, setting the stage for a period of dramatic growth over the next century. About 370,000 pianos were produced in 1919 alone, more than the leading piano-producing countries of Germany, England, Austria, and France combined.[43]

THE SURVIVORS

In the twenty-first century, the few keyboard musical instruments that have managed to survive from the colonial and early Federal eras have become something more. They are no longer simply utilitarian tools for personal expression, status symbols for wealthy owners, subjects for scientific speculations, or equipment for educating young girls. These venerable musical instruments have become historical documents. The lost craft tradition that produced them is now revealed through scientific identification of their materials and interpretation of tool marks, wear patterns, and other types of surface evidence. Historic instruments now serve as conduits to the past, continually raising new questions and revealing answers about why and how they were made and about their makers and early owners.

Musical instruments differ from all other historic artifacts in having much to say not only to modern eyes but also to modern ears. Restored instruments are an invitation to step into the historical landscape to experience the past in sight and sound. Yet silent musical instruments are no less revealing when they have been preserved without the losses of historical evidence that are unavoidable during restoration. Their untouched historical content serves musical purposes by informing accurate reproductions to satisfy the appetite for musical heritage.

Movement toward independence from Britain's monopoly over the manufacture of musical instruments did not gain momentum until the end of the eighteenth century. Charles Albrecht (see entry no. 25) was among the early leaders, many of whom were Pennsylvanians of German heritage.

PART ONE

KEYBOARDS WITH PLUCK
SPINETS, HARPSICHORDS, AND ORGANS ENTHRALL
1700–1765

For the first two-thirds of the eighteenth century, spinets and harpsichords were the most common keyboard instruments in England and America. With both, as well as with their seventeenth-century cousin the virginal, depressing the keys causes bird quills to pluck the strings to produce their sound. Unlike the piano, which can be played louder or softer by how hard the key is pressed, a spinet or harpsichord remains the same volume no matter how the key is approached.

Harpsichordists achieve musical expressiveness by their skill and dexterity in using other techniques. Some of the methods have to do with timing, such as the choice and variation of tempo or articulation, the overlapping or separation between notes. These methods allow harpsichordists to shape the character of each phrase of music, much the way painters create effects by the nuances of their brushstrokes. After mid-century, harpsichords and organs more commonly offered a choice of stops, which provided the musical equivalent of a painter's palette of colors.

1 Spinet

Stephen Keene
London 1700

SPINETS REIGN

The spinet was the predominant keyboard instrument in England and America from the 1680s to the popularization of the square piano a century later. Unlike harpsichords, spinets were small and had only one string per note. It is tempting to assume that spinets were a kind of "poor man's harpsichord," but their prevalence among the British gentry and musical elite, including the celebrated composer Henry Purcell, proves otherwise, especially in the first half century of the spinet's history. They stayed fairly well in tune; were stylish, affordable, and compact; and possessed a sweet tone suitable for domestic music making.

Key number 54 is dated 1700 and initialed by Edward Blunt, who was in the final year of his apprenticeship with Keene. Later, they would become business partners.

Stephen Keene's long career began in 1662, following his apprenticeship in London under Gabriel Townsend. Keene bridged the transition from the virginal, such as his 1668 example below, to the fashionable new spinet. Before being restored to the Crown, Charles II of England had spent much time in France. He brought back to England French fashion, including what in France was known as the *espinette* and in England and America as the spinet or spinnet.[1] The earlier English virginal and the French *espinette*, both illustrated below, form the immediate antecedents of English spinets. Keene was among the first and most influential spinet makers, and his apprentices included several who would distinguish themselves in the trade. The opposite page shows a few of the details that illustrate the transition from seventeenth- to eighteenth-century keyboard design.

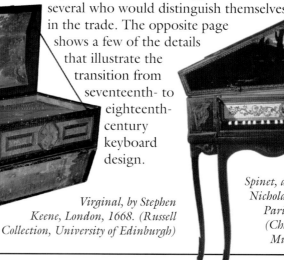

Virginal, by Stephen Keene, London, 1668. (Russell Collection, University of Edinburgh)

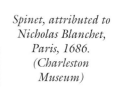

Spinet, attributed to Nicholas Blanchet, Paris, 1686. (Charleston Museum)

A Closer Look

Stephen Keene and other early English spinet makers employed design details imported from the Continent. The light-wood interior (1) is a vestige of a tradition that originated in central Europe and then flourished in Italy. Thin-walled instruments of light wood were placed in protective, more substantially built outer cases. The Keene spinet simulates this inner-outer construction with light cedar interior veneer in an otherwise darker walnut instrument.

Another design detail that may have come from the old inner-outer construction scheme is the use of carved scrolls (2) that flank the ends of the keyboard. When light inner instruments were housed in separate outer cases, these scrolls served as aids in pulling the instrument out of its separate outer case. Keene created the white-black-white lines by sandwiching five layers, using three types, of wood. Each part was laid out without the aid of templates, accounting for the layout lines scribed with a compass and just visible on the side of the scroll.

A short-octave keyboard (3) extends the usable range of a keyboard by three scale steps just by adding one key. This trick is accomplished by tuning the bottom B down to G. The rarely needed C-sharp and B-flat keys are then tuned to A and B respectively, resulting in the most important keys down to G. This keyboard has split sharps to fill out the short octave. The front halves of the two split sharps play the normal pitches (C-sharp and E-flat), and the back halves play the special short-octave pitches (A and B). This keyboard compass would soon become obsolete as the five-octave standard took hold. By 1726, when the Aston spinet was made (entry no. 3), a five-octave compass was common.

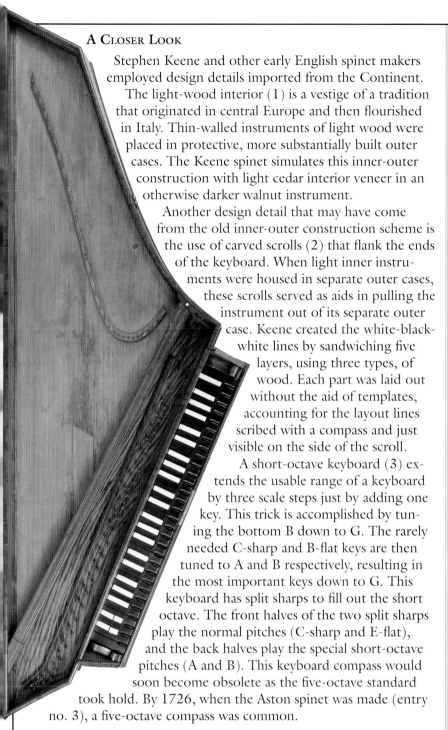

An intricate floral marquetry picture decorates the central panel on the nameboard. This decorative device was common in English spinets from the 1680s to the 1710s. It is less symmetrical than it appears at first.

Black Naturally

The fashion up to around 1700 was for reversed keyboards: naturals of ebony and sharps of ivory. This was true in Germany as well as England and France, as the two seventeenth-century examples on the bottom of the opposite page show. This style was about to change in England.

The keys are further decorated with scribe lines and rounded natural heads. The fronts of the natural keys are decorated with trefoil-embossed paper.

Changes over Time

Replaced elements include the lock escutcheon, vertical portions of the case molding, the left jack rail bracket, the keyboard cloth, the plectra, the hinges, and at least part of the stand. There are repairs, some due to insect damage, to the otherwise original soundboard and lid.

2 | Spinet

Thomas Hitchcock
London ca. 1715

The members of the Hitchcock family were the preeminent spinet makers of eighteenth-century London. Forty-two spinets survive from the Hitchcock workshop. Three members of the family, all named Thomas, have confused scholars as to who started the business. Two of the Thomases, presumed to be related, though not father and son, were in partnership around the time this spinet was made. Recent scholarship has identified the Thomas Hitchcock who completed his training in 1701 as the likely founder of the Hitchcock business.[3] A lineage of craftsmen can be traced from Stephen Keene, maker of the previous entry, through his apprentice Edward Blunt to Thomas Hitchcock, who founded the house of Hitchcock after serving as a journeyman for Blunt.

The serial number 471 appears in four places, including the front of the tuning pin block.

The earliest surviving spinet by London's noted Hitchcock family of spinet makers has been in Virginia since the early eighteenth century. Serial number 471, applied to the instrument in four places by the maker, is the lowest number on the surviving spinets from that influential workshop.

The importance of the spinet as Hitchcock's earliest surviving work is magnified for historians of Virginia furniture by the stand, made of American black walnut. On the basis of workmanship and stylistic details, the stand has been attributed to Peter Scott, a prominent cabinetmaker in early eighteenth-century Williamsburg.[1]

The John Crawford family owned the spinet when they moved from York County, adjacent to Williamsburg, to what is now Botetourt County in western Virginia around 1740.[2] Little else is known of the spinet's history. A key lever is inscribed on the top "N° 1 Iuly + 12th 1760" and on the side, "Wm A[?]hor[?]." These may indicate an episode of renewal at a time when the spinet would have been about forty-five years old and ready for repair. The spinet is on loan to Colonial Williamsburg from the Botetourt County Historical Society and Museum.

The nameboard has a prominent calligraphic inscription. The key fronts are black-painted moldings. The engraved lock plate is the only brass hardware remaining from the original construction.

A Closer Look

This Hitchcock spinet was made midway between the dates of the Stephen Keene and Cawton Aston instruments in entry numbers 1 and 3. Together the three spinets illustrate a continual progression of style during the first quarter of the eighteenth century. Like the earlier Keene spinet, the Hitchcock spinet has light veneer on the interior and scroll-sawn brackets at the ends of the keyboard. New since Keene's spinet, however, is the appearance of white natural keys that were to characterize most English keyboards up to the present day. Hitchcock's sharps are sandwiches of ebony and ivory, a decorative touch that also appears on entry numbers 3 and 12.

Hitchcock curved the nut on just some spinets until at least the 1750s. Compared to spinets with straight nuts, this design shifted the plucking closer to the center of the string, causing a less nasal and more flutelike tone. Hitchcock's use of brass tuning pins in this example is very unusual.

Restorative Conservation

Due primarily to moisture exposure long ago, this spinet was in poor condition prior to conservation treatment at Colonial Williamsburg: Several keys were missing entirely, and several of the ivory key tops had been replaced long ago with bare wood. The case finish showed signs of water damage. The nameboard was badly distorted, making it impossible to reassemble the instrument.

Conventional restoration could have returned the instrument nearly to its appearance when new, but such an approach would have stripped the instrument of most of its historical evidence and significance. Colonial Williamsburg conservators designed their treatments to improve the spinet's external appearance without affecting surface evidence. Special procedures were used to straighten the distorted nameboard without affecting Hitchcock's inscription and serial number. A mouse hole and other damage still visible in the soundboard betray years when the spinet was home to rodents. Replacing the soundboard, however, would sacrifice critically important historical evidence and was never considered. Old degraded finishes were left alone, with only removable tinted wax added to improve appearance. A reproduction lid replaced a crude earlier substitute. Mechanical parts, string fragments, and the soundboard were lightly cleaned and otherwise preserved unchanged.

(above) Top view of spinet with jacks removed. The jack rail does not survive.

(right) Some of the jacks. Fragments of bird quills remain in the tongues.

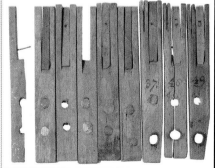

Left end of the spinet before treatment in the Colonial Williamsburg conservation labs.

Changes over Time

Some materials in this spinet exist only in trace amounts, such as bits of wire still stuck to some tuning pins and fragments of cloth and leather in the action. The fact that the instrument was not restored to playing condition in modern times helped to preserve a great deal of valuable historical evidence that would have been lost during conventional restoration. Although much affected by age, mice, and exposure to moisture, the instrument endures as a voluminous record of Hitchcock's earliest construction methods.

During an episode of inexpert renewal sometime around the late nineteenth century, the lid was replaced, two crude keys were added to replace missing ones, and cloth patches were used to cover splits in the soundboard and bottom.[4] Fortunately, this renewal did not erase important interior evidence.

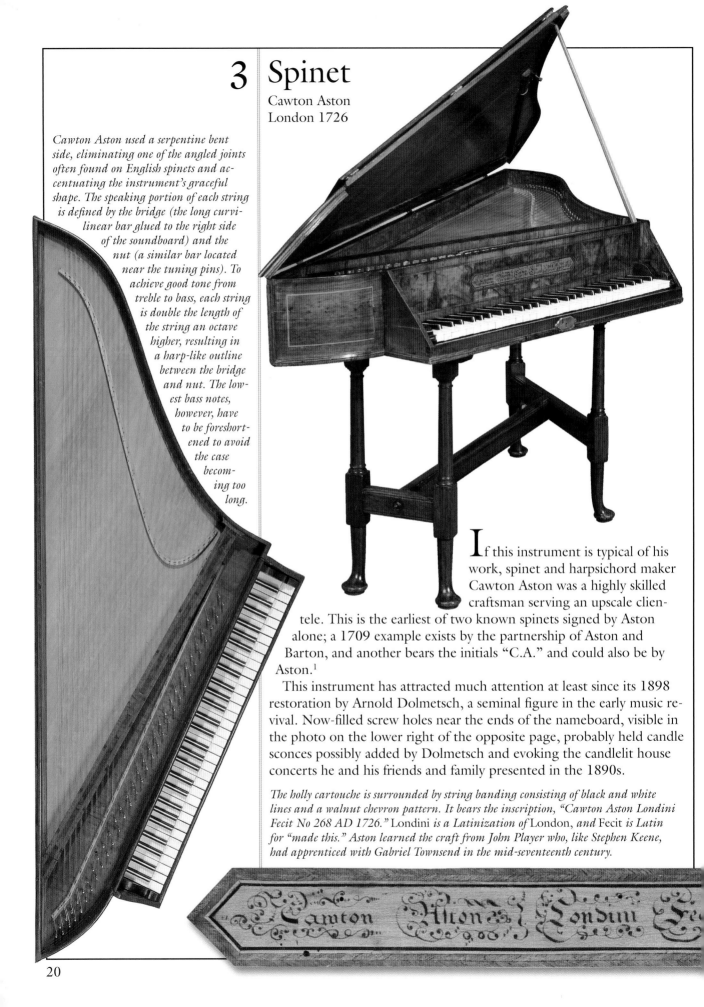

3 Spinet

Cawton Aston
London 1726

Cawton Aston used a serpentine bent side, eliminating one of the angled joints often found on English spinets and accentuating the instrument's graceful shape. The speaking portion of each string is defined by the bridge (the long curvilinear bar glued to the right side of the soundboard) and the nut (a similar bar located near the tuning pins). To achieve good tone from treble to bass, each string is double the length of the string an octave higher, resulting in a harp-like outline between the bridge and nut. The lowest bass notes, however, have to be foreshortened to avoid the case becoming too long.

If this instrument is typical of his work, spinet and harpsichord maker Cawton Aston was a highly skilled craftsman serving an upscale clientele. This is the earliest of two known spinets signed by Aston alone; a 1709 example exists by the partnership of Aston and Barton, and another bears the initials "C.A." and could also be by Aston.[1]

This instrument has attracted much attention at least since its 1898 restoration by Arnold Dolmetsch, a seminal figure in the early music revival. Now-filled screw holes near the ends of the nameboard, visible in the photo on the lower right of the opposite page, probably held candle sconces possibly added by Dolmetsch and evoking the candlelit house concerts he and his friends and family presented in the 1890s.

The holly cartouche is surrounded by string banding consisting of black and white lines and a walnut chevron pattern. It bears the inscription, "Cawton Aston Londini Fecit No 268 AD 1726." Londini is a Latinization of London, and Fecit is Latin for "made this." Aston learned the craft from John Player who, like Stephen Keene, had apprenticed with Gabriel Townsend in the mid-seventeenth century.

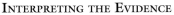

Interpreting the Evidence

The rail at the rear of the keyboard (1) originally acted to stop the key when it was fully depressed. Layers of cloth originally fastened to the underside cushioned the keys to silence the impact. The cloth was removed long ago when its function was replaced by a new front rail (7).

Vertical brass pins (2) form a rack for guiding the keys. The keys in later keyboards would be guided instead by pins in the front rail. Aston embedded rectangular lead weights (3) in the keys, positioning the weight individually to adjust the balance of the key levers. Most keyboards are still balanced this way today.

Pads on the tops of the keys (4) cushion the jacks that pluck the strings. Although worn and fragile, the leather appears to be original. A smaller layer of wool cloth under the leather makes the cushion softer. Many of the cloth pieces have been replaced, probably because of insect damage.

The balance rail (5) has vertical pins to position the key levers. Originally the balance rail had a single strip of wool cloth. Cut marks in the balance rail, not quite visible in this photo, reveal how the cloth had been cut away in the front or back of each balance pin to facilitate the rocking of the key levers.

The scroll-sawn end blocks (6) provide a grip for removing the key frame. They are a late vestige of the much older inner-outer style of construction as described on page 17.

The front rail (7) with its thick cloth layer is a later addition. Notice the lighter color of the front rail wood. The rest of the key frame had darkened from nearly three centuries of surface oxidation, but this wood is obviously newer.

The key covers (8) are ornamented with a sandwich of ebony and ivory sharps, three decorative lines scribed into the ivory naturals, and turned ivory arcades on the fronts of the keys.

This spinet is ordinary in its exterior decoration of simple light-wood string inlay. The inside, however, is far more highly decorated. The inner rim and nameboard are richly veneered in panels of stump walnut surrounded by chevron stringing and walnut crossbanding.

The keyboard (withdrawn from the spinet). The first few keys are removed revealing the key frame, which supports and guides the keys.

Changes over Time

The 1898 restoration by Arnold Dolmetsch probably accounts for the addition of a jack rail thumb latch (later removed) and replacement of the soundboard and soundboard moldings, parts of the lid, the bridge, the hinges, and the tuning pins (replaced again in 2010). Other restorative alterations over the years include an access hatch cut into the bottom, a front rail added to the key frame, and cleats added to stiffen the lid. Some jacks have also been replaced.

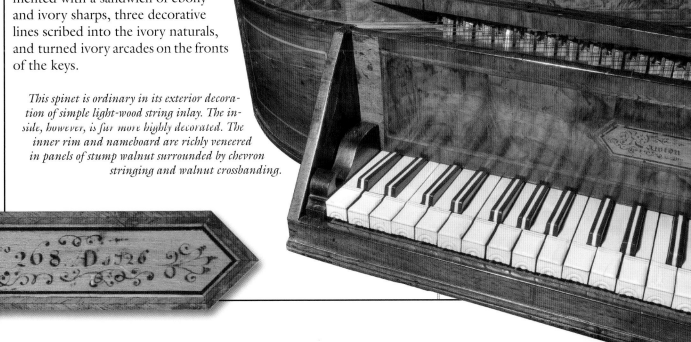

Gilt metal rose bearing the initials "INC."

4 Harpsichord

I. N. Cusseneers
Düsseldorf 1726

In Search of an Attribution

A replacement jack rail inscribed "CUSSENEERS DUSSELENSIS FECIT MDCCXXVI" is the basis for the attribution of this harpsichord. Presumably transcribed from older markings that are now lost, the inscription could be accurate since a made-up inscription would tend to be more fanciful. The initials "INC" cast into the rose are also consistent with the attribution.

Despite the inscription, scholars have speculated about the regional origins of the harpsichord. Some have considered England because of its oak case.[1] Antwerp is a candidate because of its rose, inner-rim papers, and painted soundboard and because CUSSENEERS is a likely mistranscription of Kusseneers, a surname concentrated in Antwerp and Belgium.[2] A theory was also advanced that the maker was one Cuisinier, an early eighteenth-century French maker about whom little is known.[3]

Although there are compelling arguments for each of these places of origin, the inscription on the early twentieth-century jack rail names Düsseldorf, Germany.[4] Lending credence to this provenance are the instrument's several Germanic characteristics, including the double curve of the bent side, the frame-and-panel construction of the lid, and the narrow, four-octave compass, which was retained in Germany after it had disappeared in England.

With its block-printed inner-rim papers, serpentine bent side, stand with curved stretcher, frame and panel lid, inner-rim molding, narrow compass, and registers that originally projected through the cheekpiece, this harpsichord bespeaks its German origins. Clearly, this was a keyboard design tradition that contrasted markedly with English norms. Considering that many of the keyboard makers in London and America had emigrated from Germany and vicinity in the eighteenth century, it may seem surprising that their work for the English market deviated so greatly from this native German style. Invariably, however, it was the local market and not the makers' training or habits that dictated style.

A mid-twentieth-century rebuilding left this harpsichord heavily altered. The changes, however, were mostly internal so its appearance is largely unchanged. In the context of the Colonial Williamsburg collection, the instrument visually represents the ancestral keyboard culture of about half of the English and American makers represented in the collection, including Albrecht, Astor, Ball, Beck, Buntebart, Dettmer, Garcka, Geib, Huber, Kirckman, Pether, Stodart, Zopfe, and Zumpe.

(left) John Challis poses in his workshop in the only known photo of the Cusseneers harpsichord before his 1949–1950 restoration.

(below) Challis's inscription front and center on the nameboard.

ON THE CUSP OF CHANGE

This harpsichord represents two historical events in almost equal measure: the time of its original construction, presumably in 1726, and the period of John Challis's 1949–1950 rebuilding. Ironically, the mid-twentieth-century work itself was largely delegated to Challis's apprentice, William Dowd, who with Frank Hubbard in the following decade initiated a sea change in attitudes about the importance of preserving period design in restoration and making reproduction instruments.[5] Challis's passion for dependability above all else had meant constant attention to workmanship while also freely discarding old designs and materials in favor of those he felt were more stable and reliable. Dowd inherited the same passion for dependability and workmanship, but—noting the superior tone of historic instruments—he and Hubbard chose to adhere much more closely to the materials and designs of period makers. The results of Dowd's new philosophy are represented in the Colonial Williamsburg collection by a harpsichord he made for the Foundation in 1968.[6]

ALTERATIONS OF 1949–1950

Challis replaced the tuning pin block twice. Remarkably, the original pin block and the initial replacement, along with the original veneer, survived under separate ownership. Now back with the harpsichord, they provide important evidence about the harpsichord's original configuration.[7] Challis also increased the scale from 307 to 333 millimeters and replaced the key levers, the jacks, the registers, all internal framing, and the soundboard bars. He also reduced the case height and added pedals and his trademark splines in the case joints.

SURVIVING A RESTORATION

The drastic changes wrought by the 1949–1950 rebuilding would not be acceptable by today's restorative conservation standards. Although the historical evidence is now fragmentary, the instrument remains rare and worthy of preservation. And much survives. Even though he replaced the key levers, Challis reused the original bone key tops. More importantly, the original soundboard and bridges survive, along with most of the nameboard and stand. Although Challis made a new action, it appears that he retained the original compass and disposition of one four-foot choir and one eight-foot choir plucked by three rows of jacks.[8]

5 Spinet

John Woolfinden
England 1725–1740

This spinet by John Woolfinden presents itself modestly on the outside. When opened, however, the spinet surprises the beholder with richly ornamented surfaces. The nameboard is covered with vertical-grained veneer similar to rosewood with light string inlay forming geometric shapes surrounding a simple inscription inlay. The jack rail and inner rim have dark vertical veneer and horizontal line stringing like the nameboard. Most striking, and highly unusual, is a large eight-pointed mariner's compass design ornamenting the underside of the lid. Light-wood string inlay surrounds the lid underside, as it also does the top. Several episodes of sometimes heavy-handed restoration have dimmed what must have been a superior spinet.

Consistent with the above-average decoration is the construction of the solid walnut case with hidden dovetails. Many features of the instrument recall the 1726 Cawton Aston spinet (entry no. 3) and argue for the earlier part of the date range. These include the interior that decoratively outshines the exterior; a removable nameboard with lozenge-ended inscription inlay; the double bent side; the curved left case piece; the five-octave, GG–g3 compass; and scroll-shaped keyboard end blocks. If the stand is original to the spinet, it argues for the latter part of the date range, or it could have been added later.

The elaborate eight-point mariner's compass motif inlaid under the lid is unusual.

Who Was John Woolfinden?

This spinet is the only known work of John Woolfinden. He might have been in the one-third of English spinet makers who were outside of the London mainstream. Although the decorative and structural design is ambitious, the almost rustic lettering of the nameboard inscription suggests the maker might have been provincial. An American origin is possible but statistically unlikely, and the antique dealer from whom the instrument was purchased in 1937 is known to have imported some of his stock from England.

Woolfinden first appears in the literature as a brief entry with the date "c. 1725" in Philip James's *Early Keyboard Instruments* (1930), presumably based on a sighting of this instrument before its move to Williamsburg.[1] Such an early date is consistent with the many features the instrument shares with the dated 1726 Cawton Aston spinet, although provincial makers were sometimes behind the times.

The walnut lid is decorated on top with light string inlay and a thumb molding around the perimeter. Decorative hinges are pierced brass.

Changes over Time

Hundreds of small holes in the stand suggest this spinet was ravaged by wood-boring insects at one time. This damage would account for the extensive restorations that have deprived the spinet of much original material.

In his 1962 assessment of the spinet, Hugh Gough, one of the spinet's restorers, stated that the spinet had been thoroughly "done over" around the turn of the twentieth century.[2] Pre-1962 alterations involved replacing the tuning pin strings, jack rail (although the end brackets are probably original), pin block, jacks, brass lock hasp, and soundboard and its molding. The inner-rim veneer was removed on all but the spine and not returned.

Gough made all new molded key fronts (reporting that no originals existed to copy), reclothed and "refitted" the key frame, bleached the keys, removed at least part of the bottom to repair ribs, and replaced some frame members.

The left bracket holding the jack rail (1) is normally made to look like a continuation of the removable jack rail (2). The restorer who replaced the jack rail made little effort to match the appearance of the end bracket, neglecting to copy the cross-grain dark veneer. The work is inexpert, but, from the viewpoint of the historian for whom the instrument is a historical document, workmanship becomes a way to distinguish restorations from original work.

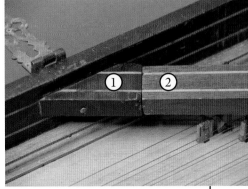

6 Chamber Organ

Unknown Builder
England ca. 1740

As a performer, George Frideric Handel was most noted for being an organist. His dominance of the music scene in eighteenth-century England contributed substantially to the popularity of chamber organs in the homes of the few who could afford them. The largest musical instrument in the Colonial Williamsburg collection is an organ originally built for Kimberley Hall, an imposing country house in the south of England.

Chamber organs were often left unsigned by their makers. This example was believed, for a time, to be the work of celebrated English organ builder John Snetzler. Though insufficient evidence supports this theory, the builder did share with Snetzler at least some German training.[1] A unique and curious detail deep in the wind-chest reveals the maker's cross-regional allegiances. His use of German-style sponsils and an English-style table board—both labeled in the exploded drawing on page 28—are redundant and are not known to coexist in any other organ.

Keyboard, stops, desk, and pedal.

A Fortuitous Installation

Dating to the 1690s, the Sir Christopher Wren Building of the College of William and Mary is the oldest college building in the United States. On loan to the university, the organ now stands in the chapel, which was added in 1732. Although a reference to an organ at the college appeared in 1806, nothing more is known of that instrument, and it would not be until 1970 that the Kimberley organ would find a perfect fit in the west gallery of the historic chapel.[2]

CHANGES OVER TIME

Like many complex artifacts, organs typically pass through a sequence of use and obsolescence followed by reevaluation. If not discarded, the organ goes through a change of role, often under new ownership and usually accompanied by substantial alteration, after which it begins the sequence again. Enough is known of the history of this organ to trace several repetitions of this sequence.[3]

The story of this organ begins in about 1740 when it was built for Kimberley Hall, albeit with some recycled parts. Most of the wind-chest and some of the pipes were taken from an earlier organ in which the keys were situated above the wind-chest, unlike the present configuration with keys below the chest. Two of the present ranks of pipes also appear to be from the earlier organ.[4]

In the 1770s, Kimberley Hall was sixty years old and ready for re-modeling. At that time, the organ's glazed doors were removed, and the organ was painted white. An 1828 move from Kimberley's music room to a new alcove in a drawing room prompted the trimming of the cornice and alteration of the pumping mechanism where they conflicted with the alcove.[5] The white paint was removed from the case, and the present paper stop labels were added.

Kimberley Hall was remodeled again in 1951, and the organ was relegated to storage in the Kimberley stables, where it was when Noel Mander, a noted London organ builder, purchased the instrument. Presuming the organ to be the work of the celebrated organ builder John Snetzler, Mander replaced the badly corroded pipe feet and reversed the 1828 alterations of the cornice. He also discarded the hand-pumping mechanism and installed an electric blower. In 1954, Mander sold the organ to Colonial Williamsburg.[6]

(left) Rear view of the Sir Christopher Wren Building of the College of William and Mary. The chapel is the wing on the right.

(above) An interior view of the chapel.

LIFE IN WILLIAMSBURG

Colonial Williamsburg had purchased the organ for the ballroom of the Governor's Palace, but the instrument was deemed out of proportion. A second ill-fated installation came in 1963, in the lobby of a new conference center.[7] The only alteration at that time was replacement of the 1954 blower.

In 1970, Douglas Brown erected the organ in its current and most sympathetic home. Brown removed the redundant sponsils and replaced the table board, wisely saving all original parts with their important historical evidence. Brown maintained the organ's rare state of preservation by documenting his work. The Snetzler attribution, however, did not survive Brown's analysis.[8]

The organ was temporarily moved to the Colonial Williamsburg conservation labs in 2001, where museum conservators and organ specialists collaborated to reconstruct the lost hand pumping mechanism and the original fifth-comma tuning temperament. Minor cosmetic repairs, a new blower, and some leather patching completed the treatment.[9] Remarkably, the organ retains its circa 1740 bellows, pipework, and key work.

Kimberley Hall, Norfolk, England.

A Look Inside

Ever since their emergence in early Roman times, pipe organs have been among the high-tech marvels of their time. As the diagram on the right shows, five component assemblies constitute an organ.

The wind-chest serves as a switching station directing air from the bellows into the desired pipes. The organist begins by selecting and pulling stop knobs. The stop knobs move sliders, which activate one or more ranks of pipes, each rank having its own characteristic sound quality. This organ has five-and-a-half ranks of pipes.

When the organist depresses a key, the other end of the key lever pushes upward on a wooden tracker. The tracker pushes another lever that pulls a sticker, finally opening a pallet in the wind-chest.

Meanwhile, the bellows have built up some air pressure in the pallet box. When the pallet opens, air rushes upward past the pallet into a channel in the bar frame that intersects with whatever sliders have been opened. The sliders then allow the air to escape upwards out of the wind-chest into the desired pipes.

Due to the orientation of the bellows, only their general location can be shown in this side-view cross section.

The reconstructed pumping handle. Note the telltail on the right. A small ivory weight is tethered by a string to the bellows inside the case. Its rise and fall shows the pumper how fast to work.

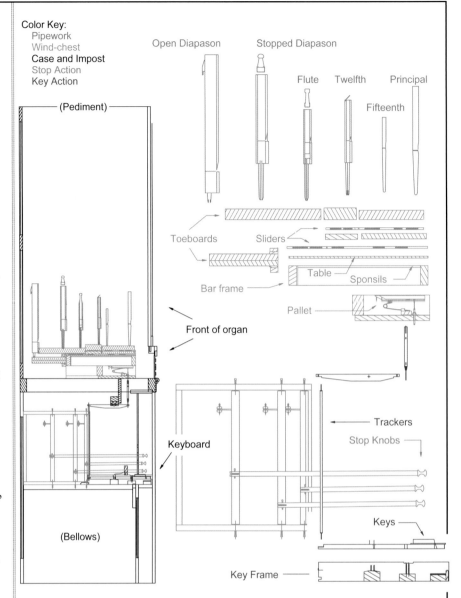

Cross-sectional diagram of the organ. The assembled organ is shown on the left. Major groupings of components are shown in exploded view and double the size on the right. The color key (upper left) distinguishes among pipework, wind-chest, case work, stop action, and key action.

Furniture on an Architectural Scale

With its imposing height, bold cornice and pediment, recessed key desk enclosed behind double doors, and ornamented pipework standing above like a second story, the organ is almost architectural in scale and style. The case belies the somewhat more modest instrument of five-and-a-half ranks inside. As if to complete the picture of an instrument meant by its first owners to impress, the wear on the keyboard was surprisingly minimal when the organ came into the collection, indicating it received little musical use in its first two centuries.

The conspicuous lack of pedals is typical of even the largest British chamber organs of the period and contributed to their interchangeability with harpsichords. Transcriptions of Handel's organ concertos were particularly popular on both instruments in the period.[10]

Spinet 7

John Zopfe
London 1745–1750

Adaptive and restorative changes tend to occur most frequently when an artifact changes hands. That might explain why the Zopfe spinet, which remained in the same family for two centuries—and indeed in the same house for most of that time—survived with so little change. Repairs made during the early period of use included shimming the tuning pins, repairing the bottom molding, and possibly replacing the bass hitch-pin rail. Several keys and jacks are now missing.

Recent conservation has included cleaning the soundboard and other minimal stabilization treatments.

An accurate reproduction now serves to fulfill the artifact's destiny as a *musical* instrument while also preserving the original from any further erosion of historical evidence. Through its 1989 clone, the Zopfe spinet is charming Williamsburg guests once again.

(left) Top view of the Zopfe spinet with the keys and jacks removed.

(below) Reproduction of the Zopfe spinet made by Marcus Hansen and Edward Wright using period woodworking tools and methods in Hay's Cabinetmaking Shop in Colonial Williamsburg's Historic Area.

Joanna Tyler took this spinet with her when she moved from Williamsburg to Charlotte County, Virginia, in 1775. She soon married Wood Bouldin, a Revolutionary soldier, and her spinet remained in the same family and at the same house for the next two centuries until it was returned to Williamsburg to be part of the collection in 1976.[1] According to family tradition as published by a descendant in 1888, Joanna Tyler Bouldin delighted a group of French soldiers with her spinet playing during the soldiers' encampment in Charlotte County in 1781.[2]

The spinet is likely to have been purchased by her parents since it was made in the late 1740s, shortly before her birth. The Tyler family had auspicious musical and political associations. John Tyler, Joanna's brother, was a governor of Virginia and thought to have played his cello at the Governor's Palace with Thomas Jefferson and Governor Fauquier during his college years. His son John was the tenth president of the United States.[3]

The maker of the spinet was John Zopfe, a London tradesman originally from Schwanden, Switzerland, where he was listed as a clavichord maker and where his wife's uncle, the much better-known harpsichord maker Burkat Shudi, also originated.[4]

This is the only surviving example of Zopfe's work, and it is somewhat eccentric. The balance points for natural and sharp keys are in a single line, so the naturals have a slightly lighter touch than the sharps. Three other details are more typical of harpsichords: the use of upper and lower jack registers, bottom-last case construction, and front guide pins for the keys.[5]

8 Harpsichord of Two Manuals

Jacob Kirckman
London 1758

A HARPSICHORD FOR MARTHA

The harpsichord maker best known in America was London-based Jacob Kirckman, whose work for a famous Virginian is well documented.

While in Paris as ambassador to France, Thomas Jefferson took the opportunity to purchase numerous pieces of French furniture for Monticello, his house in Charlottesville, Virginia. His daughter Martha accompanied him and took lessons in Paris from the well-known French harpsichordist and composer Claude Balbastre.[3] Although Paris was home to Pascal Taskin, France's leading harpsichord maker, Jefferson chose for Martha a double-manual instrument from Jacob Kirck-man of London. The instrument was delivered to Monticello.

Jefferson's harpsichord has not survived, but correspondence about the order offers a revealing glimpse into Jefferson's musical interests and the business of Britain's preeminent harpsichord maker Jacob Kirckman.[4]

Harpsichords were more common in parts of continental Europe than they were in England until the mid-eighteenth century. Until then, spinets were the keyboard instruments of choice in England for even the well-to-do, and, in the seventeenth century, virginals were the dominant plucking instruments (see p. 16).[1] Harpsichords continued their rise in popularity in England and America during the third quarter of the eighteenth century even as square pianos began to take over the spinet market.

Unlike the market for spinets, which had been produced by a large number of small workshops, the harpsichord market was heavily dominated by just two massive London workshops: that of Burkat Shudi and that of Jacob Kirckman.

Before starting their rival businesses, Shudi and Kirck-man both worked for the harpsichord maker Hermann Tabel. In their hands, English harpsichords reached the highest level of refinement. While traveling and reporting on the musical scene in France and Italy, musician and writer Charles Burney wrote in 1771, "To persons accustomed to English harpsichords, all the keyed instruments on the continent appear to great disadvantage."[2]

Kirckman adorned the soundboard of each of his harpsichords with a cast-brass rose, which served a purpose more decorative than acoustic. With its Gothic tracery surrounding a seated King David playing a harp, the rose evokes a biblical scene from the Psalms of David: "I will praise you with the harp for your faithfulness, O my God." Flanking the king are Kirckman's initials, the I representing J in the Latin alphabet.

Harpsichords and Their Expressive Resources

The expressive techniques available to players of all members of the harpsichord family, including virginals and spinets, involve methods of ornamentation and articulation (see p. 15). Unlike spinets and virginals, however, harpsichords also offer the ability to control registration through mechanical gadgetry that changes the quantity and quality of sound.

Harpsichords have two or three sets of strings, along with hand-stop levers and sometimes an additional keyboard, all of which allow the player to choose which sets of strings are sounding. These choirs of strings and their on-off levers are called *stops* and are similar in function to the many stops on an organ, where each stop controls a set of pipes. Selecting which stops are sounding gives the player control over volume and characteristics of tone. Also similar to organs, harpsichords sometimes have a set of strings sounding an octave higher than normal. Even the terms for these stops are taken from organs, in which the lowest C pipe is eight feet long for normal pitch and the same pipe on another stop tuned an octave higher is four feet long.

The harpsichord pictured on the facing page has two choirs of strings at eight-foot pitch and one at four-foot pitch. The second eight-foot stop adds volume to the first, and the four-foot stop adds brilliance and yet more volume to the tone. Each set of strings has its own row of jacks. The quills either pluck the strings or miss them depending on whether the stop is on or off.

A specialty of English harpsichords is the frequent addition of a lute stop. This solo stop consists of a separate row of jacks playable from the upper keyboard and plucks closer to the ends of the strings, producing a distinctive nasal tone.

Compared to Continental examples, English harpsichords were designed to maximize the contrast in volume and tone from one registration (selection of stops) to another. This characteristic of English harpsichords was important in part because of the popularity in England of playing transcriptions of ensemble music, such as Italian and light opera, Handel concertos, and music heard at coffee-house concerts. The harpsichord had to function as an orchestra.

These characteristics of English harpsichords owe much to the use of dogleg jacks for one of the eight-foot stops (see photo). This notched shape allows the jacks to rest on both manuals; when that stop is turned on, its set of strings plays from both manuals. In France, harpsichordists preferred the ability to play an upper eight-foot stop in one hand while playing a lower-manual eight-foot stop with the other hand as a duet or dialog between nearly equal voices. The dogleg jacks of English harpsichords made such a dialog impossible. More important to English taste, the dogleg jacks enabled stop combinations with greater contrast in volume between the manuals.[5]

A buff stop does not appear on any of the three Kirckman harpsichords in the Colonial Williamsburg collection, but it was not uncommon on English harpsichords. The buff stop consists of a sliding batten with leather pads that touch one of the eight-foot choirs giving it a harp-like sound. (The continuing search for expressiveness picks up in entry no. 9 with pedals, swells, and machine stops.)

Changes over Time

Sometime, probably in the last quarter of the eighteenth century, the tongues of this harpsichord's dogleg jacks were altered to accommodate leather plectra. The mellow and slightly more piano-like tone of leather plectra grew more popular in the last quarter of the century and was sometimes retrofitted on older harpsichords, as it was here. The other registers retain their bird-quill plectra.

An 1898 date on the key slip between the keyboards may indicate a restoration and may be when the key fronts were painted red over the original clear coating.

The instrument was owned and used by the British Broadcasting Corporation before coming to America, where it was restored again, this time by Lotta Van Buren.

Colonial Williamsburg acquired the harpsichord in 1983 and prepared it for use in the Governor's Palace. To reduce restorative alterations and other wear and tear from musical performances, the author made an accurate copy of the jacks, keys, and registers for use in the instrument. The original mechanical parts are stored for their preservation.

A full-size dogleg jack and its position on the upper and lower key levers. The plectrum protrudes horizontally from the jack tongue just below the red damper cloth. The plectrum is leather, an early replacement of crow quill. The limewood keys have leather-covered cloth pads to cushion the keys against the jacks.

9 | Harpsichord of Two Manuals

Jacob Kirckman
London 1762

STANDARD MODELS AND OPTIONS

Kirckman made single- and double-manual harpsichords in approximately equal numbers. The Colonial Williamsburg collection includes both models for the period around 1760. Because spinets were primarily the purview of specialist spinet makers, Kirckman rarely made them. His chief rival, Burkat Shudi, made no spinets at all.

The standard Kirckman double-manual harpsichord of that period (shown in this and the previous entry) had two eight-foot registers, one four-foot register, and a lute stop. Shudi doubles were substantially the same.

The lack of buff stops on the three Kirckman harpsichords in the collection is surprising since the buff stop was the easiest and least costly to make and provided an attractive musical effect.

PEDALS, SWELLS, AND MACHINES

The pedal, which was added later, turns off the four-foot stop, allowing an immediate echo effect. The pedal modification was an early indicator of a change in musical taste. Pedals became common so players could change volume by changing registration without waiting for a pause in the music. Some harpsichords had pedals that opened louvers or sections of the lid to control volume, or they controlled complex machine stops for changing multiple stops at once or in sequence.

The growing desire for dynamic control would find its ultimate voice in the pianoforte, which made its debut in Britain and America within the decade.

Jacob Kirckman immigrated to London from Alsace around 1730 and worked for Hermann Tabel. If Charles Burney's amusing story is true, Kirckman's brilliance for business was soon proven. Just one month after Tabel's 1738 death, Kirckman "married his master's widow, by which prudent measure he became possessed of all Tabel's seasoned wood, tools, and stock in trade."[1] Later, according to Burney, Kirckman's shrewd judgment was again revealed when a fad for the English guitar threatened the harpsichord's popularity. Allegedly he solved the problem by distributing a number of cheap guitars to girls of low social status. As guitars lost their snob appeal, harpsichords regained their former share of the market.[2]

It was the quality of Kirckman's harpsichords, however, that earned him the patronage of the royal family and a place of dominance in the harpsichord market throughout the English-speaking world. Kirckman shared with Burkat Shudi a near monopoly in the production of harpsichords in England during the final half century of the harpsichord's popularity. Unlike in France where harpsichords were limited to the aristocracy, England had a large and growing gentry class that could afford such luxuries, and Kirckman was the most capable to fill the need. About 170 Kirckman harpsichords survive to the present day—about triple the number of surviving Shudi harpsichords.[3]

Exploring a Double-Manual English Harpsichord

The upper eight-foot keyboard (1) of a two-manual English harpsichord plays the lute stop (2), which plucks close to the eight-foot nut (3), and it plays the dogleg eight-foot stop (4). The lower manual (5) also plays the dogleg eight-foot plus the four-foot stop (6) and the second eight-foot stop (7). The four-foot strings (8) are on a lower level a little beneath the eight-foot strings (9). Stops are turned on and off by means of the knobs (10), which are—from left to right on the plan view—the lute (11), the four-foot (12), and two eight-foot stops (13 and 14). Jack rails (15) limit the upward rise of the jacks.

The eight-foot strings are stretched from the tuning pins (16), over the nut (3) and bridge (17), to the hitch pins (18). The four-foot strings sound an octave higher and have their own nut (19) and bridge (20). The tuning pins are embedded in the pin block (21), a thick plank of solid oak. The soundboard (22) is of spruce and only one-eighth inch thick. A rose hole (23) holds a cast-brass decoration (pictured on p. 30). The casework consists of a spine (24), tail (25), bent side (26), and cheekpiece (27). The inner framework (28) braces the case against the string tension.

Changes over Time

The pedal was probably added later in the eighteenth century. The lower keyboard was also altered so the balance points were further back. Lotta Van Buren restored the instrument and sold it to Colonial Williamsburg in 1934. About six campaigns of re-pair, restoration, and conservation have taken place since then.

So many episodes of repair can mean much loss of historical integrity, but the lower keyboard balancing is the only significant design alteration. The case, the soundboard, and nearly all of the mechanical components are presumed to be original. Most of the action cloth and the bottom boards have been replaced.

The pedal has been rendered inoperable so the harpsichord can function in the original manner.

(left) A plan view shown without jacks, jack rail, or rose.

(below) A cross-section elevation view.

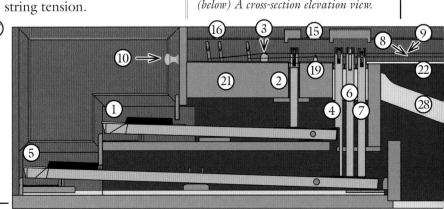

10 Harpsichord of One Manual

Jacob Kirckman
London 1762

Research by Reproduction

Reproducing historical instruments is first an act of conservation that allows the new instrument to take most of the wear and tear of use. The effort is equally valuable as historical research, revealing much about forgotten technologies. The makers of Kirckman's mechanical actions were decades ahead of their time in the precision of their workmanship yet without the benefit of machine tools. How did they do it? Answers came by studying sometimes microscopic tool marks and by doing workshop experimentation during the process of reproduction.

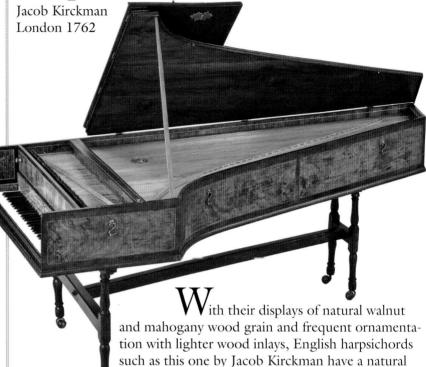

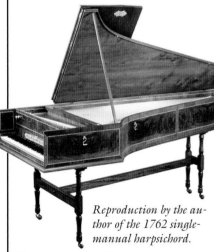

Reproduction by the author of the 1762 single-manual harpsichord.

Changes over Time

Of the three Kirckman harpsichords in the collection, this one has the fewest restorative alterations. Traces of what is probably the original wax finish are preserved under the hinges, and, thanks to minimal polishing over the years, the hinge screws still have some of the original gilding. Nevertheless, some parts are replaced, including most of the action cloth, the name batten, and the strings.

With their displays of natural walnut and mahogany wood grain and frequent ornamentation with lighter wood inlays, English harpsichords such as this one by Jacob Kirckman have a natural kinship with British and American case furniture.

Other characteristics, however, are peculiar to keyboard instruments. Some differences resulted from the need to construct keyboard cases out of straight-grained oak, selected for its strength and ease of bending.[1] Such a plain wood meant the instruments had to be clothed in decorative veneers. First walnut and later mahogany in often flamboyant grain patterns served the purpose. Inlaid lines of holly or similar light-colored wood and crossbanding at the perimeters formed repeating rectangles ornamenting the case exterior. The fanciest veneers and inlays were reserved for the keyboard surround, where this instrument has purpleheart rather than walnut crossbanding. As with most British and American keyboard instruments, the long side was left without veneer since the usual placement was against a wall.

This instrument's jewelry-like brass hardware is also typical of English harpsichords while being rare in other types of furniture. Included are oversize strap hinges for the lid, butterfly hinges for the lid flaps, decorative lid hooks for the sides, stop knobs above the keys, a cast rose in the center of the soundboard, and bolt covers for the stand. Some evidence suggests the brasses were originally covered with tinted coatings in imitation of gold.

Appearing decades after the fashion had moved to cabriole legs for most other furniture forms, this instrument's turned legs and horizontal trestles were still common on harpsichords. The straight legs supporting the 1758 example, however, would have been considered fashionable by furniture standards of the time (entry no. 8).[2]

One of three strap hinges on the lid.

Spinet 11

William Harris
London 1764

By the 1760s, spinets were past their heyday. More people could now afford harpsichords. With its multiple stops, the spinet's larger cousin had more musical resources that gave better control over tone and volume. The spinet, with its single set of strings and no stops, began to slip from an earlier position of importance, reduced to being a "poor man's harpsichord."

This spinet was made only two years before the advent of square pianos, which would hasten the spinet's obsolescence. Although multistop harpsichords remained musically viable for another quarter century, coexisting with pianos, spinets were a direct casualty of the square piano. Not only did pianos provide a way to continually change volume, but they also competed with the spinet's role as the cheaper alternative to harpsichords. The spinet was doomed.

Whoever owned this spinet nevertheless made an intriguing, but probably unsuccessful, attempt to add musical color. A buff stop similar to the type used in square pianos of the 1770s and 1780s was added sometime after the spinet was made. Eventually removed, the buff stop probably consisted of a leather- or cloth-covered batten that touched the strings when a pedal was depressed, creating a harp-like sound. It seems likely that the present leather plectra replaced earlier bird quills at the same time. Both alterations would have made the spinet sound mellower and more like a piano.

Furniture historians have puzzled for years over this anachronistic hybrid, half-cabriole stand that was sometimes used for keyboard instruments.[1] The horizontal trestle with Jacobean-style turnings above and more current cabriole legs below has been amusingly termed the "Jackendale" style, but there is no evidence that it was thought curious in its period.[2] Jacob Kirckman used a richly carved version on his finest harpsichords.

The keyboard withdrawn from the spinet. Metal pins at the rear of the key levers guide the keys, and a padded overrail limits their motion.

The inscription inlay on the name batten is lettered in ink; William is Latinized: "Gulielmus Harris Londini Fecit 1764."

The Makers

This is the earliest known spinet by William Harris, one of several spinet makers with that surname working in London.

The bottom key is signed "Fricker 1764." Nothing is known of Fricker except that his signature also appears on a 1750 spinet. He should not be confused with a slightly later grand piano maker in London named William Frecker.[3]

Another key is marked "S[l or t]ep[c or i]ons No. 6." The identity of that workman is not known.

Fricker's signature on the lowest key.

Changes over Time

A century or more after the addition of the buff stop and conversion to leather plectra, the spinet was restored in London by G. W. Goss.[4] Goss or others removed the buff stop, veneered the spine, replaced the action cloth, and did several other repairs.

12 | Bureau Organ

Abraham Adcock and John Pether
London ca. 1760

CHAMBER ORGANS IN THE COLONIAL SOUTH

Musical instrument merchants from Baltimore, Norfolk, Williamsburg, and Charleston advertised organs in several types. Period references most commonly mention barrel organs, sometimes called "hand organs" to distinguish them from "finger organs," which are played with the fingers. Pianos were said to be "organized" when they were equipped with organ pipes playable from the piano keyboard.

Robert Carter in the house next door to the Governor's Palace also owned a chamber organ. After unsuccessfully attempting to purchase Carter's organ, Thomas Jefferson considered ordering one in 1786 from organ builder Samuel Green of London.[4]

A 1780s portrait possibly by Daniel Badger of Charleston, South Carolina. The unknown sitter signals his skill and interest by posing with a chamber organ.

In 1775 tensions rose in Williamsburg as Revolutionary sentiments grew. John Murray, Earl of Dunmore and royal governor of Virginia, hastily retreated from the Governor's Palace in Williamsburg, leaving behind three organs, a harpsichord, a pianoforte, and other musical instruments.[1] One of the organs was probably a chamber organ similar to this one, which is exhibited in the ballroom of the reconstructed Governor's Palace. Another of the three organs was a small crank-driven serinette for teaching tunes to birds, ordered by the governor in 1773.[2] The third organ was likely a barrel organ, such as the one that was advertised in 1767 in the *Virginia Gazette* in Williamsburg.[3]

The keyboard of this chamber organ folds up, the pumping pedal detaches, and the machine stop pedal retracts, leaving the external appearance without anything to suggest it is anything other than a large desk. Keyboard instruments were also occasionally disguised to look like sewing cabinets, sideboards, or tables.

A Look Inside

The organ has 265 pipes and a compass of C–e3 (four octaves and four notes). To fit it within the bureau form, the makers had to fit four stops comprising five ranks of pipes into a small space. The four stops include an eight-foot diapason and four-foot principal flute, both of wooden pipes; a metal two foot; and a two-rank quint mixture in metal. The last stop sounds two pipes for each note, so, for example, playing a C sounds C and G.

The metal quint mixture and two-foot stops add brilliance to the otherwise mellow tone of the wooden pipework. A small foot lever—visible in the photo below on the right half of the organ's base—is a machine stop (called a *shifting movement* in Britain), which is used to turn off the mixture and two-foot stops to produce quick echo effects.

The opening below the keyboard reveals (top to bottom) the metal mixture pipes, the mechanical key action, and the wind-chest. A rod attached to the bellows rises and falls to indicate when more air is needed.

(left and above) Close-ups of the hand stops flanking the keyboard with their turned and engraved ivory knobs.

Provenance

The early history of this organ is not known. It is contemporaneous with the small organ that Abraham Adcock loaned to the church of St. John, Wolverhampton, England, in 1760. His resulting acquaintance with Sir Samuel Hellier resulted in orders for two new organs.[5]

The organ was purchased for Colonial Williamsburg's collection in 1958 from British organist Geraint Jones, who recorded on the instrument and took it on tour through England, Germany, and France. The interior bears witness to the organ's European peregrinations with the red rubber stamping of a French customs agent.

The organ with pipework, wind-chest, and mechanical action exposed.

ADAPTABLE AND PORTABLE

Besides changing stops or using the machine stop, the organist can elicit more volume by propping open the lid and slant front or opening the vents on either side of the case (see photo below). Pedals for pumping either on the front or the side allow the organist to play with or without an assistant to work the bellows.

Brass handles on either side of the case are for moving the organ. The pipes, mechanical action, and wind-chest lift off the lower bellows section independently, the two sections separating at the seam just above the lower handle.

The bureau organ with side sound vent open, top propped open, and side bellows pedal in place.

THE MAKERS

According to the *Biographical History of England* published in 1806, Abraham Adcock was not only an organ builder but also "one of the best performers on the trumpet in the kingdom; and played the first trumpet in Handel's oratorios for several years."[6] As a musician playing primarily trumpet, but also bassoon, horn, and violin, Adcock participated in several of Handel's Foundling Hospital concerts, the Three Choirs Festivals, and the Theatre Royal, Drury Lane.[7]

It was not unusual for professional musicians to supplement their incomes with various other types of employment, and, although Adcock was celebrated as a trumpet player, this instrument is a credit to his skill also as an organ builder. The Adcock and Pether partnership produced one other surviving and very similar bureau organ. Adcock's work is further preserved in the surviving case, keyboard, and nameboard from an organ he built in 1759 for an Anglican church in the village of Church Langton.[8]

John Pether, Adcock's junior partner, was one of five Pethers making keyboard instruments in London in the last half of the eighteenth century. George Pether had worked for Kirckman and left several surviving square pianos. William Pether and a son by the same name were organ, harpsichord, and piano makers. One 1775 harpsichord bears the name of a William Pether. Finally, an organ builder named Eaton Pether signed one of the pipes in an organized Longman & Broderip square piano now at the Metropolitan Museum of Art.[9] Perhaps not coincidentally, Eaton Pether apprenticed with Abraham Adcock in 1752.

CHANGES OVER TIME

The organ has escaped major alterations. The bellows weights were replaced with springs in 1958, but the original weights had been retained and were reinstalled in the organ in 2001.

Sometime prior to the mid-twentieth century, the pitch was raised and the original cone-tuned metal pipes were fitted with tuning slides. During restorative conservation in 2001, the tuning slides were removed and the pipes lengthened for cone tuning, and the damaged and partially missing shifting movement was also reconstructed.

Part Two

Sea Change
The Transition from Harpsichord to Piano
1765–1800

Baroque music was well served by the harpsichord and organ, both of which could be made louder or softer by turning their stops on or off, usually between movements. The last third of the eighteenth century, however, saw a dramatic shift towards a new musical aesthetic that demanded a different type of expressiveness. Players now required the capacity to shape musical phrases by frequent, sudden, or gradual changes of volume. Harpsichord makers began providing pedals for changing sound more frequently. Complex machine stops and swell mechanisms were sometimes added that could affect a gradual increase or decrease in volume with the press of a pedal.

It was the pianoforte with hammers rather than quill plectra to excite its strings, however, that gave musicians control of dynamic nuance by how sharply they pressed the keys. John Zumpe's introduction of the square piano in 1766 launched an industry that completely supplanted the harpsichord in England and America by the end of the century.

Although America declared its independence from British rule in 1776, its independence from London as its primary source for musical instruments would not come until the following century.

13 | Square Piano

John Zumpe
London 1766

A GERMAN INFLUENCE

During the eighteenth century, many German instrument makers chose to relocate to London. The economy in England was more promising, the environment ideal for industry, and a rising middle class and the global British Empire were in the market for musical instruments. In 1761, the young King George III married Charlotte, a musically refined princess from the north of Germany. Around the same time, an influx of Germans would be particularly important to the great success of the new pianoforte. Among them were instrument maker John Christoph Zumpe and composer Johann Christian Bach, son of the celebrated Johann Sebastian Bach. The cast of characters was in place to start a musical revolution.

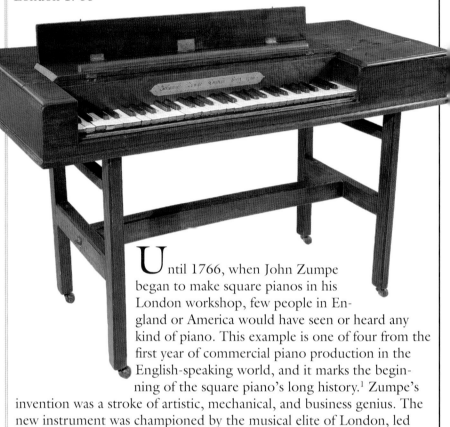

Top view of the Zumpe square piano with the lid removed. By any standard, the soundboard (covering the right third of the photo) is tiny and the keyboard range slightly smaller than that of harpsichords of the period. Both were very soon enlarged as the English piano continued through a period of rapid evolution.

Until 1766, when John Zumpe began to make square pianos in his London workshop, few people in England or America would have seen or heard any kind of piano. This example is one of four from the first year of commercial piano production in the English-speaking world, and it marks the beginning of the square piano's long history.[1] Zumpe's invention was a stroke of artistic, mechanical, and business genius. The new instrument was championed by the musical elite of London, led by Johann Christian Bach.[2] Over the following twenty-five years, the production of square pianos would surpass that of all other piano types.

The first pianos made in England were small, rectangular, decoratively and mechanically simple, and, compared to the harpsichord, cheap. Yet their economy belied a new kind of expressiveness that took the music world by storm. People called the new instruments by the terms *piano, fortepiano, pianoforte,* and *square piano*. To distinguish the square piano from the much larger and less common grand piano, it was often simply called *small piano forte*.

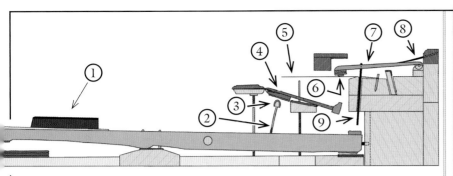

THE ACTION

Zumpe invented a remarkably simple mechanism. When the key (1) is depressed, a wire post (2) with a wooden head covered in leather (3) bumps against the hammer (4), which pivots on a hinge of thin leather to strike the string (5). A damper pad (6) is on the end of the horizontal damper lever (7), which is hinged by a continuous pivot wire near the back wall of the case. The damper is pressed down against the string by a baleen (whalebone) spring (8) protruding from the case rim. A baleen sticker (9) hanging from the damper lever transfers the upward movement of the key to the damper lever.

Piano mechanisms necessarily allow each hammer to bounce away from its string, leaving the string free to vibrate. More complex designs include an escapement, whereby the piece that lifts the hammer towards the string drops back before the hammer actually reaches the string. Zumpe's action, later called the *English single action*, lacks an escapement. The front of the key hits bottom before the hammer reaches the string, leaving it free to fly up against the string on its own.

The earliest English square pianos had no pedals. To raise the dampers, Zumpe provided a hand lever. The undamped sound continued until a hand was free to move the lever again. This was not just a crude version of today's damper pedal. Rather, it was meant to change the character of the piano's sound, more like that of a music box or hammered dulcimer. When this piano was new, the resulting sound might have been compared to the keyed pantalon, a type of dulcimer with a keyboard. In fact, when Zumpe invented the square piano, he may have been basing the new instrument more on the pantalon than on the harpsichord.

The four surviving pianos made by Zumpe in 1766 show clues of an inventive mind still working out a plan. Was the lowest sharp key really needed? Zumpe first thought so, gluing a sharp to the lowest natural key lever (left) and then numbering the uncut key panel with separate numbers for these two lowest keys. It appears, however, that Zumpe later changed his mind because the first two keys were never cut apart. Note the numbering on the top of the first four key levers (below left) and the renumbering on the bottom of the opposite ends of the same keys (below right). Indecision about whether to include the low F-sharp is also reflected in the installation of two hammers for the bottom key lever, one of which never functioned.

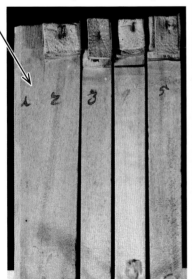

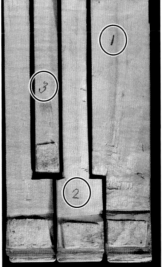

CHANGES OVER TIME

Two design corrections were made very early, perhaps in the Zumpe workshop: the part of the rear case rim that held the damper springs was made to be detachable; and the lockboard, originally hinged to the front of the case, was rehinged to the lid flap to create a music desk. The spring rail and a rail over the tops of the damper levers were both eventually lost. An additional layer of leather was added to the hammers perhaps within a decade or two, leaving the original, single layer in place.

After arriving from Germany in 1761 and working for harpsichord maker Burkat Shudi, John Zumpe opened his own shop on Princes Street where he made English guitars. When he returned to keyboard instruments in 1766, it was not harpsichords but pianos that he made. This piano was one of his first. The inscription plaque (above) uses the original German form of his first name and the Latin phrase Londini Fecit, meaning "made this." The inscription includes Zumpe's address on Princes Street, Hanover Square. After the 1760s, Zumpe abandoned his habit of spelling the street name "Princess."

An old unrestored instrument like this one gives clear evidence that it was truly cherished as a musical instrument and not just held up as a silent monument to the wealth of its owner. Note the wear on these ivory key tops. Even the decorative scribe lines have worn away in places.

It is a little-known fact that there is one key on the keyboard that tends to get more wear than any of the others. It appears below in the center of the photo. It is the D an octave above middle C. A key signature of at least four sharps or four flats is needed before the D key gets relief from the sharp or flat key above and below it.

A CLOSER LOOK

Deep inside the piano is interesting evidence of a long history from original design to early and later use and repairs.

The original single layer of dark-brown hammer leather can still be seen under a layer of white leather, which was probably added before 1800.

The extra layer of leather might have been a modernization rather than a repair. It would have given the piano a more mellow and less harpsichord-like sound in keeping with changing ideals of piano tone.

The key levers are made of limewood. The familiar exposed parts covered with ebony and ivory are at the other end.

These leather pads cushion the baleen sticker that transfers motion up to the damper lever.

The hammers are made of mahogany with a tiny head of light wood glued to the end. A slip of vellum serves as a hinge inserted in the other end of the hammer (not visible).

Guide pins for the hammers. Within a decade, piano makers realized they were simply unnecessary.

The light vertical grooves in this key were left behind during an old repair. The color is light because the more recently exposed wood has not had as much time to oxidize.

The lowest notes of a square piano are so much shorter than their mathematical ideals that the piano maker must compensate by adding some extra bulk to the strings. In order to preserve the flexibility of the string, bulking is done by wrapping a thinner copper wire over the brass core wire. The technique was not needed in harpsichords, but John Zumpe would have used the technique in his guitars, and he would have seen it in clavichords.

Cloth was and continues to be used in all piano actions to cushion between moving parts. This green napped wool was called baize.

Small slips of baleen (whalebone) were used by Zumpe to guide the keys in a slot in a rack at the rear of the case. Many are damaged by insects.

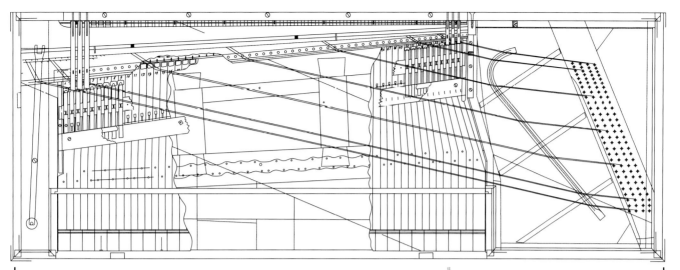

To Restore or to Replicate?

The 1766 Zumpe piano narrowly escaped restoration in the late 1960s. At that time, most museums considered restoration to be the best means of preservation. After learning how to interpret material evidence in old surfaces, we now recognize that restoration can be a threat to valuable historical evidence in old artifacts. This is not just a piano; it is a voluminous document of the earliest methods, materials, and designs of England's first commercial piano maker.

The best form of preservation, then, was to interpret all that evidence to make an accurate reproduction, shown on the left. Future generations will still be able to interpret for themselves the still-undisturbed evidence in the original instrument. Old instruments are the primary documents of greatest use to today's makers of instruments for early music.

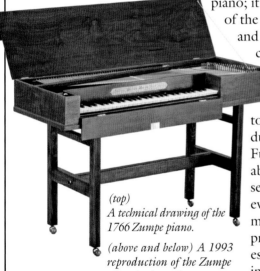

*(top)
A technical drawing of the 1766 Zumpe piano.*

(above and below) A 1993 reproduction of the Zumpe piano by the author.

Collecting, Recording, and Testing the Evidence

The survival of nearly all of its original parts, including cloth, leather, and strings, allowed the Zumpe piano to reveal a great deal of detailed information about its construction and the maker's methods. The author made detailed notes and drawings (see above and top of p. 41) describing the instrument and interpreting the evidence. Reexaminations of the original revealed greater levels of detail as new questions arose during the reproduction process. Understanding about period construction methods also improved with testing in the workshop. This process brought Zumpe's workshop into better focus and resulted in an instrument he would have recognized.

14 Harpsichord

John Kirshaw
Manchester 1769

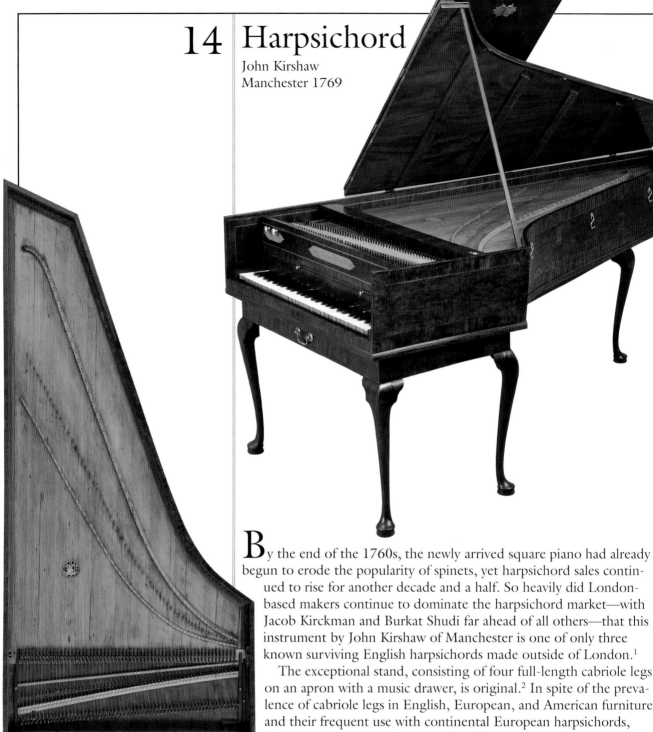

Top view showing the layout of the hand stops, registers, rose, and four-foot and eight-foot bridges and their nuts, tuning pins, and hitch pins.

By the end of the 1760s, the newly arrived square piano had already begun to erode the popularity of spinets, yet harpsichord sales continued to rise for another decade and a half. So heavily did London-based makers continue to dominate the harpsichord market—with Jacob Kirckman and Burkat Shudi far ahead of all others—that this instrument by John Kirshaw of Manchester is one of only three known surviving English harpsichords made outside of London.[1]

The exceptional stand, consisting of four full-length cabriole legs on an apron with a music drawer, is original.[2] In spite of the prevalence of cabriole legs in English, European, and American furniture and their frequent use with continental European harpsichords, inexplicably no other surviving English harpsichord has them.[3] Trestle stands were the norm, with legs that were turned, straight and untapered, or half-turned and half-cabriole in a style unique to keyboard instruments, as in entry number 11.

This harpsichord also differs from mainstream English harpsichords with its rear rather than front pins to guide the key levers, four-foot strings that do not pass through holes in the eight-foot nut, and jacks with rectangular mortises instead of slots for the dampers. Several other technical details are precisely in line with Kirckman's practice however, including the string scale, the length of the natural heads, and the lateral dimensions of the keyboard.

Cast-
brass
roses used by
Kirshaw (left)
and Kirckman (right).

A ROSE IS NOT A ROSE

Comparing the rose from this harpsichord with that of the 1758 Kirckman harpsichord in entry number 8 strongly suggests that Kirshaw intentionally blurred the line between his work and that of the much more successful Jacob Kirckman. Lacking a significant acoustical function, a rose was used as a trademark by the Kirckman firm, which changed designs only three times over its history. Not only did Kirshaw deign to copy Kirckman's overall design with its seated figure of King David playing a harp, but Kirshaw also took advantage of the coincidence of their initials, J.K., the Latin *I* representing *J*.[4]

If Kirshaw was seeking a marketing advantage by causing some to confuse him with Kirckman, he was not the only harpsichord maker to do so. Two years after this instrument was made, Kirckman took another maker, Robert Falkener, to court for selling fake Kirckman harpsichords. A period newspaper advertisement implies the counterfeiting problem was enough to boast, "Harpsichords to be sold cheap, among which is a real Kirkman's."[5]

Kirshaw's unusually stylish cabriole stand and his choice of elaborate veneers speak well of his work, but the cast rose, with its aspirations for equality with Kirckman, falls short of the more finely rendered rose of his rival.

CHANGES OVER TIME

A pedal was added some time in the eighteenth century, apparently for turning off the four-foot and back eight-foot choirs. The pedal survives but not the associated hardware.

A 1961 restoration involved refinishing, veneer repairs, the addition of lid cleats, and the replacement of cloth but minimal replacement of other parts.

Except for a few of the lid flap hinges, which appear old and possibly original to the instrument, the exterior brasses are modern.

NAMING STOPS

Unlike organs with their greater number of stops, harpsichords rarely had stop labels. Musicians could be expected to remember the functions of three or four stops. Kirshaw's addition of stop labels on this harpsichord offers an unusual opportunity to see what terms were used in eighteenth-century England. The eight-foot stops are labeled "1 Unison" for the front row of jacks and "2 Unison" for the back row. The four-foot stop is labeled "Octave." It is sometimes thought that *buff stop* is a modern term, but the label clearly marks it as such.[6]

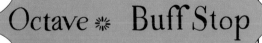

Octave ❋ Buff Stop

(above) A traced drawing of the faded label under the left pair of stop knobs.

*(left) Front view of the keywell and soundboard. The faded cartouche has the penned inscription "John Kirshaw Manchester 1769." The right pair of stop knobs is labeled "2 Unison * 1 Unison." These control, respectively, the back and front rows of the eight-foot jacks.*

15 | Square Piano

John Zumpe and Gabriel Buntebart
London 1770

GABRIEL BUNTEBART

A prestigious maker in his own right, Gabriel Buntebart was part of an influential group responsible for the early popularization of the piano. Emigrating at the same time and from the same small town in northern Germany from where the young Queen Charlotte had come, he likely had business connections with the musical queen. He was a close friend and business partner with an equally effective trendsetter, Johann Christian Bach. Buntebart went into partnership with John Zumpe for the decade beginning 1768. For part of the year that this piano was made, Buntebart carried on the business while Zumpe journeyed to Paris and Germany.

Similar in design to John Zumpe's 1766 example (entry no. 13), and made not long after, this piano is most interesting because of several campaigns of rebuilding. The most radical change came perhaps in the late 1780s. Within twenty years of its construction, it had already fallen behind in its technology and musical resources. By comparison to newer instruments of the time, the keyboard range was narrow, it had inconvenient hand stops instead of pedals, and the damper mechanism was difficult to maintain. But the late 1780s had not been too late to bring the instrument somewhat up-to-date. Had the owners waited much later, technological advances would have rendered the instrument too far out-of-date to be capable of catching up.

Time was not to leave this piano alone, however, even after it became too old to modernize. Eventually, it changed roles from being an ordinary piano with more or less currency to being an "antique," prompting an entirely different kind of alteration. Instead of updating the piano, the effort went in the other direction. Restorers attempted to turn back the clock, paradoxically "returning" the piano to a state it never actually knew. The following pages examine the evidence of this piano's changes over time.

The inscription plaque reads "Johannes Zumpe / et Buntebart / Londini Fecit 1770, / Princes Street Hanover Square." The plaque is original, but the nameboard to which it is attached was replaced in the 1780s modernization. All but one of the seven other Zumpe and Buntebart pianos from 1770 use the more correct plural form fecerunt. *The piano is also marked "XXIIII" in several places. This number may indicate this piano's place within a batch and is not a serial number.*

CAMPAIGNS OF MODERNIZATION AND RESTORATION

This piano has been in at least five principal states since its construction: Originally it had three hand stops (bass dampers, treble dampers, and buff stop), no pedals, and a GG–f3 compass. The 1780s modernization increased the compass down to FF, fused the two halves of the damper lifter, and replaced the hand stops with two pedals. Sometime a bit later, the buff stop and its pedal were removed. When purchased by Colonial Williamsburg in 1980, the piano had lost its stand and pedals. In a 1982 restoration, a reproduction trestle stand was made based on the 1766 Zumpe piano (entry no. 13); the lost buff and its hand stop were reconstructed; and, based on a misinterpretation of the trapwork evidence, a knee lever was added for lifting the dampers. The hand stop and knee lever were subsequently removed.

The photos at right show some of the evidence for alterations, beginning with the damper system. (Some parts are identified with the same number in more than one photo.) In the present altered state, leather buttons (1) atop wood sticks (2) transfer motion from the far ends of the keys up to the damper levers (3). Pieces of cloth (4) damp the strings. The present red felt is a replacement for earlier woven wool or soft leather. Before the alterations, the stickers (2) were baleen, and they hung from pivot pins in rectangular mortises in the damper levers. The new arrangement improved serviceability and allowed the redundant mortise to be filled with lead (5), adding some weight to improve damping. The 1766 Zumpe piano (entry no. 13) retains the original design with pivoting baleen stickers. Finally, the system of damper levers was altered to pivot out of the way (as in the center photo), making it much easier to replace strings. An unused mortise in the left case rim (6) is a vestige of the original design in which the damper overrail (7) extended all the way to the case rim. The original baleen damper springs are missing, leaving only their holes (8).

The 1780s compass enlargement required a great deal of work: The original keyboard ended in the bass at GG with no GG-sharp, so two sharp keys and a natural key had to be added. Note the lengthening of the hammer rail (9), balance rail (10), and key slip (11); the moving of one balance pin (12); and the addition of three more balance pins (13). Rather than cut rack slots (14) for the new keys, front pins were added, only one of which remains (15). The massive block of wood (16) that fills the left end of the case had to be cut back and the cheek (17) moved to make room for the enlarged action. A later updating left the piano with rounded corners (18).

The support block (19) is all that is left of the hand stops. Past alterations left no room for them.

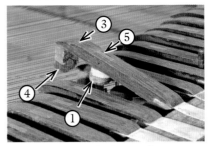

(above) Detail of the damper levers showing one of them raised as its key is depressed.

(below) Detail of the damper action with the keyboard and hammer action removed. The damper levers are shown pivoted up.

(bottom) Bass end of the piano with nameboard and nine keys removed.

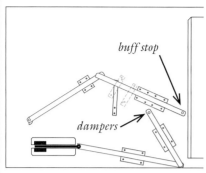

A drawing reconstructing the pedal trapwork (a system of rocking levers) that had been added in the 1780s but later removed. The pedals pulled at the points indicated, and the trapwork transferred the motion to the needed location.

(right) The present appearance of the bottom underside where evidence remains for the now-missing trapwork. The front of the instrument is at the top.

A COMPARATIVE STUDY

Comparison with other examples from the same workshop and even the same year is revealing. The Boston example shows the original design of the Williamsburg piano with enough room on the left for three hand stops, a compass ending at GG in the bass and with a dummy GG-sharp, and a soundboard with the grain parallel to the spine and passing through the tuning pins. The Boston damper system, though missing its overrail, also escaped the Williamsburg modernizations.

The Smithsonian example has the unaltered design for its dampers and hand stops, but it has original FF and FF-sharp keys, a larger soundboard, and longer bass strings.

Three pianos, all made by Zumpe and Buntebart in 1770. The center one is the Colonial Williamsburg example. The top one is in the collections of the Museum of Fine Arts, Boston, and the bottom the Smithsonian Institution. The photos are at the same scale and aligned to allow for comparison. Red reference lines indicate alignment along the left sides of keys AA and f3.

HISTORY IMPRINTED

Chapters in the history of this piano can be read in physical evidence on the underside of the bottom. Of particular interest are witness marks and empty screw holes (left half) where three pedals once existed.

The drawn reconstruction of the 1780s pedal trapwork (above left) indicates in blue the surviving evidence in the form of abandoned screw holes and shadows formed by uneven oxidation. Red lines on the drawing complete the layout of pedal trapwork.

The green dashed lines in the drawing indicate pivot blocks for a later damper pedal, which would have been the only pedal at that time. The 1982 restoration reused that most recent pivot location for a new knee lever to actuate the dampers. The 1982 knee lever is now removed.[1]

Photograph © 2012 Museum of Fine Arts. Boston

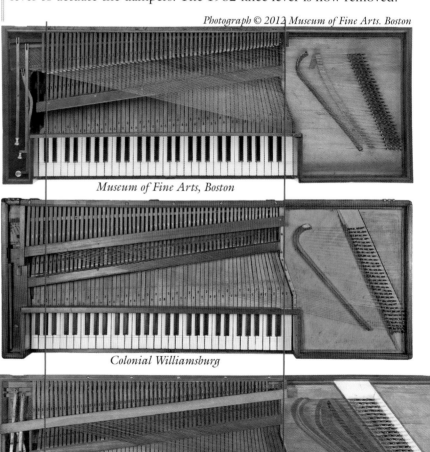

Museum of Fine Arts, Boston

Colonial Williamsburg

Smithsonian Institution

Chamber Organ 16

W. H.
England 1782

Chamber organs were popular in the late eighteenth century for the few who could afford them. Compared to stringed keyboard instruments, organs were more stable in their tuning. They added an ecclesiastical air to family prayers, and their versatility made them ideal for transcriptions of music written for various other instruments and ensembles.

With casework that closely relates to bookcases, chamber organs were an ideal canvas on which organ builders could exploit the fashionable designs of Chippendale, Ince and Mayhew, and Malton.[1] From its frame-and-panel lower half to its architectural broken pediment, dentil molding, and pierced tympanum, this imposing mahogany case proclaimed the wealth and taste of its owners.

Behind the gilded dummy pipes of the facade stand 156 wooden pipes in three ranks: an eight-foot stopped diapason; a four-foot flute; and a two-foot fifteenth, divided so the treble and bass could be turned on or off independently. A foot lever operates a machine stop that turns off the flute and the fifteenth for sudden echo effects (see photos, just to the left of the pumping lever). The divided two-foot stop and machine stop give the organist capabilities that are otherwise available only on a larger organ with additional keyboards and make such a small organ surprisingly versatile.

A later shortening of the pipes rendered the pitch to A-440. The temperament of quarter-comma meantone reflects the persistence of that primitive temperament in England long after it faded from use in other European countries.

Who Is W. H.?

The initials W. H. cut into the front of the wind-chest along with the stamped date 1782 may indicate William Holland, a minor London organ builder listed in Pigot's Directory forty years later. The 1782 inscription might indicate when the older wind-chest was adapted to a new organ incorporating the present case.

Changes over Time

A 1980 restoration by the firm of Taylor & Boody revealed that the wind-chest, with its primitive solid grid construction, had been recycled from an older, possibly seventeenth-century organ of forty-seven notes.[2] Other work in 1980 included releathering, reconstruction of twenty-two new two-foot pipes, and the removal of some late nineteenth- or early twentieth-century enlargements.

17 Square Piano

Frederick Beck
London 1785

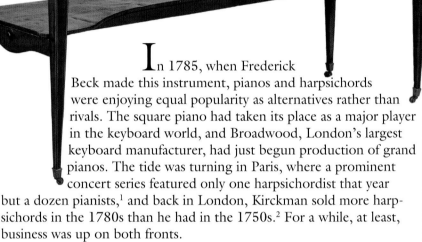

SQUARE PIANOS AND ENGLISH GUITARS

In eighteenth-century Anglo-American society, most musical instruments had developed strong gender associations. Pianos and English guitars, for example, were thought best suited to girls. So important were young women to the market for these products that they may have shaped the development of the English piano as much as composers and concert performers did.[4]

Frederick Beck and John Zumpe started their separate businesses as guitar makers in the 1760s. For both, the sudden popularity of the piano beginning in 1766 meant there was no time or economic incentive to make guitars after that.[5]

Jacob Kirckman saw the guitar as a threat to his business of selling harpsichords. Piano makers Zumpe, Beck, and Thomas Haxby instead saw guitars and pianos as two products for their core market: young women.

Portrait of Lucy Randolph Burwell of Virginia probably by Matthew Pratt.

In 1785, when Frederick Beck made this instrument, pianos and harpsichords were enjoying equal popularity as alternatives rather than rivals. The square piano had taken its place as a major player in the keyboard world, and Broadwood, London's largest keyboard manufacturer, had just begun production of grand pianos. The tide was turning in Paris, where a prominent concert series featured only one harpsichordist that year but a dozen pianists,[1] and back in London, Kirckman sold more harpsichords in the 1780s than he had in the 1750s.[2] For a while, at least, business was up on both fronts.

Frederick Beck followed in the footsteps of his fellow London piano maker John Zumpe, who initiated the square piano in England. Beck may have emigrated from Germany as Zumpe did, and his pianos share many similarities with those of Zumpe.[3] The mechanical action of this piano is based on the simple design invented by Zumpe. The solid mahogany case has straight black/white string inlay and a bead molding around the inner rim. An ogee molding embellishes the front and sides at the bottom. As usual in old keyboard instruments, the keywell has extra decoration, including a brown-stained curly sycamore panel and holly stringing surrounding the light-wood, oval-ended inscription cartouche.

The lack of a folding music desk behind the nameboard is consistent with period depictions of square pianos played with their lids down.

The oval-ended inscription inlay on the nameboard is marked in ink "Fredericus Beck Londini Fecit 1785 / No 10 Broad Street Soho."

Two hand stops control the dampers and the buff stop.

Detail of the buff stop mechanism.

A LOOK INSIDE

Beck used Zumpe's single-action design, which remained in common use for two more decades. The more sophisticated English double action, soon to be patented by John Geib, would begin to take over.

In 1785, hand-operated levers were still the preferred way to change stops in square pianos. Whether lifting the dampers or applying the muted sound of the buff stop, changes were applied to entire pieces or movements. Pedals would not come into widespread use for another decade.

The keyboard possesses the standard five-octave compass, FF–f3, but without the lowest sharp key.

A FRENCH CONNECTION

In the early years of piano production, America was not the only place outside of England relying on London for the popular instruments. The list of pianos confiscated from the aristocracy following the French Revolution included pianos by Beck, Zumpe, and several other London makers.[6] A 1777 ledger of the celebrated French harpsichord maker Pascal Taskin lists a debt owed to "Mr. Beck in London" that is enough for three or four square pianos. A piano by Beck also shows up in the 1789 inventory of Parisian harpsichord maker Jacques Goermans.[7] Some evidence suggests Beck might have moved to Paris and continued making instruments in his late years.[8]

Interior of the piano.

THE BUFF AND DAMPER STOPS

As the photo above shows, a buff stop consists of two sliding battens. As the hand stop thrusts the lower batten (1) to the left, the soft leather-topped upper batten (2) slides upward, partially muting the strings to produce a soft, pizzicato sound.

The Kirshaw harpsichord (entry no. 14) also has a buff stop. Buff stops first appeared in harpsichords at least by the seventeenth century.

CHANGES OVER TIME

The stand was updated when the piano was about fifteen years old. The amateur effort approximates the newer French frame design but without an apron (see p. 58).

Hugh Gough's 1962 restoration, marked with his card on the soundboard (see photo), included rehinging the hammers, replacing all key fronts, resecuring the bottom, replacing the pin block, and repairing the soundboard. The hammers and dampers are original but have many repairs.

51

18 | Grand Piano

Longman & Broderip
(Culliford & Co.)
London 1790

PEDALS: BACK TO BACKERS

In a tradition that extends to the present day, depressing this piano's right pedal lifts the dampers off the strings and depressing the left pedal shifts the keyboard so the hammers strike only one or two of the three strings, according to the position of a hand stop in the treble end block (photo below).

It was Americus Backers, the first to make grand pianos commercially for the English market (1771) and the one credited with developing the English grand action, who first included two pedals on his pianos.[4] Culliford attached the pedals to the two legs under the keyboard, and that idea too goes back to Backers.

A vertical-sliding hand stop in the treble end block determines whether the keyboard shift stops at the due corde position or (as shown here) the una corda position.

The back of the nameboard is inscribed in ink "Culliford & Co / Makers Jan. 7 / 1790." Culliford's serial number 166 is inscribed on the top of the yoke of the tuning pin block. The enameled Longman & Broderip inscription plaque is a reproduction.

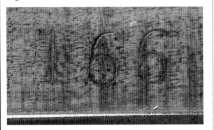

Longman & Broderip was London's largest merchant specializing in the full range of printed music, musical instruments, and accessories. Some of the keyboard instruments bearing the Longman & Broderip label were supplied to them through the so-called putting-out system, whereby the instrument makers were paid only for their labor, with all necessary materials and work space provided. Prior to his move to New York, John Geib (entry no. 32) made pianos for Longman & Broderip under the putting-out system. Culliford & Co., who completed this piano in 1790, was an independent maker but under exclusive contract to sell only through Longman & Broderip. The company rented adjacent shop space from Longman & Broderip but supplied their own materials and sold complete instruments to the dealer.[1]

Thomas Culliford's career bridged the transition from plucking to striking keyboard instruments. Although he was exceptionally prolific in his production of spinets, harpsichords, and square and grand pianos, he is relatively less well-known, as so much of his output was sold under the names of other makers and retailers. His business partners at the time this piano was made were William Rolfe and Charles Barrow. The company must have had many employees in order to keep up with its contractual obligation to supply Longman & Broderip with two to three hundred keyboard instruments per year.[2] While most makers would have subcontracted for hardware such as tuning pins and pedal trapwork, Culliford & Co. was a large enough operation to include its own blacksmith shop.[3]

A Look Backward and Forward

The three top-view photos below, shown at the same scale, place the Longman & Broderip/Culliford piano in context with its relatives from approximately a quarter century before and after. The first impression may be of little change over that half century, but the details tell a story of technological evolution. Not visible in the photos is the most radical change: from the harpsichord's plucking action to the piano's hammer action, signifying a major shift in musical aesthetics.

Twenty-eight years its elder, the Culliford piano shares with the Kirckman harpsichord the same five-octave compass, slender case outline, and continuous bridge and nut. Both have a gap for the jacks or hammers to reach the strings, but the Culliford required three iron arcs, just visible below the jack rail, to withstand the piano's greater string tension.

The Stodart piano, made twenty-six years after the Culliford example, includes John Broadwood's invention of the divided bridge. The compass had expanded in both directions to six octaves, and still-greater string tension required five iron arcs, each with metal plates to distribute their bearing on the tuning pin block.

To accommodate the hammer action, on both pianos the tuning pin block is thinner than that on the harpsichord, even though pin blocks on pianos must bear far more string tension. The wedge-shaped area on the keyboard side of the tuning pins on both pianos is a stiffening yoke.

Changes over Time

The piano was restored around the 1890s, at which time the lateral brass bar was added between the cheekpiece and spine and a metal plate and screws were added to secure the tail hitch-pin rail. Nearly half of the key fronts and many ivory natural tops were replaced, as were all the action cloth and one of the pedals. For unknown reasons, a lock was also added to the nameboard.

More recently the case exterior was refinished and the Longman & Broderip nameplate replaced.

Though much damaged over time, the hammers are original, unaltered, and nearly complete. The tuning pins and dampers are separated from the piano, but they survive.

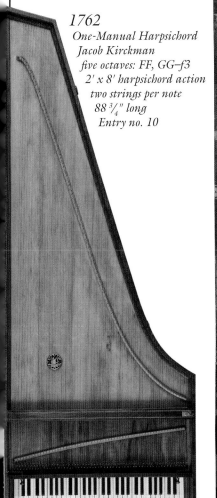

1762
One-Manual Harpsichord
Jacob Kirckman
five octaves: FF, GG–f3
2' x 8' harpsichord action
two strings per note
88 ¾" long
Entry no. 10

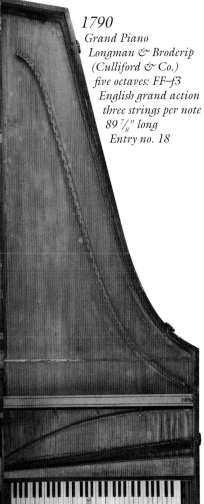

1790
Grand Piano
Longman & Broderip
(Culliford & Co.)
five octaves: FF–f3
English grand action
three strings per note
89 ⅞" long
Entry no. 18

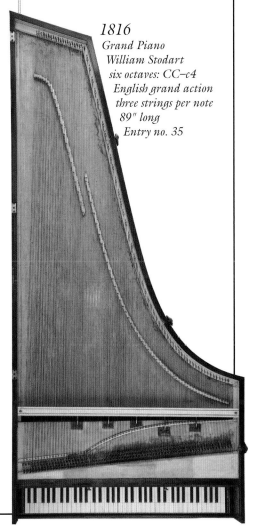

1816
Grand Piano
William Stodart
six octaves: CC–c4
English grand action
three strings per note
89" long
Entry no. 35

19 | Square Piano

Longman & Broderip
London 1788–1789

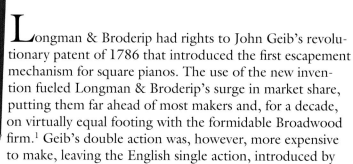

Makers, Music Engravers, Printers, Publishers, Etc.

Besides selling all sorts of musical instruments, parts, tuning tools, and other accessories, the firm of Longman & Broderip published or sold symphonic music in parts; concertos; chamber music; vocal and instrumental solos, usually with keyboard accompaniment; and popular music. Some of Europe's most important composers published through Longman & Broderip, including J.C. Bach, Haydn, Mozart, Pleyel, and Johann Schobert. With their extensive catalog and far-reaching sales, Longman & Broderip had considerable influence on the music being played throughout the English-speaking world.[4]

Enameled copper inscription plaque.

Changes over Time

A number of restoration attempts have left the piano without its original exterior finish, top portion of the pin block, action cloth, and spring rail. The stand is original but missing its music shelf. The casters and bolt covers are reproductions. The inscription cartouche is original but has some repairs.

Longman & Broderip had rights to John Geib's revolutionary patent of 1786 that introduced the first escapement mechanism for square pianos. The use of the new invention fueled Longman & Broderip's surge in market share, putting them far ahead of most makers and, for a decade, on virtually equal footing with the formidable Broadwood firm.[1] Geib's double action was, however, more expensive to make, leaving the English single action, introduced by John Zumpe in 1766, as a cheaper option. An advertisement in a 1794 Edinburgh paper offered "LONGMAN and BRODERIP'S PLAIN and PATENT PIANO FORTES."[2] This 1788–1789 example, with its single action, is the plain model. A statistical likelihood argues for its origins in Thomas Culliford's shop, and the piano has the same white-black-white string inlay as the 1790 grand piano by Culliford (entry no. 18), serving as corroborating evidence.

The piano has three hand stops, including two for the damper, which is divided between b and middle c. The third hand stop is for a buff stop (see p. 51). Although pedals had been used on square pianos as early as 1782 by Schoene & Co., pedals were not widely adopted on squares until the mid-1790s. Broadwood almost never provided hand stops and did not begin offering pedals until 1805.[3]

Top view showing lever overdampers, music desk, and hand stops.

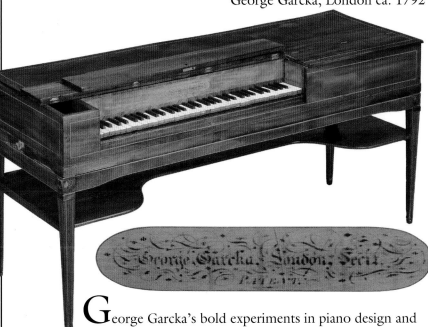

Square Piano 20

George Garcka, London ca. 1792

G eorge Garcka's bold experiments in piano design and his early use of the extended compass nevertheless failed to save him from a 1793 bankruptcy.[1] A patent awarded to Garcka just eleven months before closing his shop included two innovations. One of them, a continuation of the soundboard all the way to the left end of the instrument, was employed in this piano.[2] Although the feature is not mentioned in the patent, this soundboard is also doubled. The two layers are held about a quarter inch apart by a spacer around the perimeter. Only the lower layer of the soundboard is attached to the belly rail (the wall between the action and the area under the bridge).[3] John Broadwood had previously patented another type of double soundboard, but any hope that either method provided better quality or quantity of tone surely went unrealized.[4]

This piano also deserves special attention for its remarkably early use of the five-and-a-half-octave compass, at least a year before the additional keys appeared with any frequency on Broadwood pianos.[5] This compass was more challenging than simply making a few more keys since there was a space problem to be solved. The solution invented by William Southwell (see entry no. 23) did not become widely known until two years later.[6] Garcka simply crowded in the extra notes. He may have hoped the expansive soundboard would compensate for the tight squeeze between the crook of the bridge and the hammer opening.

J. BLAND, NO. 43 HOLBORN

Besides being a dealer in instruments, John Bland, who stamped his name and address on the soundboard of this piano, was also a publisher and seller of music. Bland convinced the Viennese composer Franz Joseph Haydn to visit London and to let Bland publish some of his music. Within months of this piano's sale, Haydn himself spent his first night at the same address in London.[7] If, indeed, the Garcka piano had been present during Haydn's visit, the distinguished guest would have been surprised to see a piano with a five-and-a-half-octave compass. Such a keyboard was rare in London and would not become common in Vienna for a dozen more years.

Stamping on the soundboard: "J.BLAND No43 / HOLBORN LONDON." The number 1335 may be Bland's ledger number.

CHANGES OVER TIME

Restorers have done very little to the piano beyond the addition of a reproduction music shelf in the stand and some external finish treatments. Nearly all internal elements, including strings, cloth, and leather, are original. The baleen damper springs were replaced with brass wire very early. Missing parts include the two pedals, dust board, buff batten, and bolt covers.

Top view showing full-length soundboard.

21 Square Piano

James Ball
London ca. 1791

(below) James Ball arrived in London by 1787 and remained at his address on Duke Street, Grosvenor Square, through the 1820s.

(bottom) Top view of the piano showing the interior. Note the candle shelves, one over each end of the keyboard.

James Ball was another of the several German emigrants making pianos in London in the late eighteenth century.[1] This five-octave square piano with its extra music desk speaks of the importance of keyboards as versatile accompaniment to singers and almost all other musical instruments.

Because part of this piano's lid serves as the second music desk, Ball divided the lid down its center rather than at the usual place along the nameboard.

Music desks were a particular interest of this piano maker. Ball submitted a patent in 1790 proposing, among other improvements, a new type of adjustable music desk.[2] This piano originally had the patented desk, although it was lost long ago. The present desk over the keyboard was added by a restorer to replace the much more elaborate original. For some years, it was a mystery why the nameboard had a wide notch cut out of its upper edge, but Ball's original patent drawings explain the evidence.

The drawing below, based on another Ball square piano, shows the patented music desk. Unlike most square piano desks, this design allows for adjusting the angle and sliding the desk forward. The top portion of the nameboard (the part now missing from this piano) is part of the sliding desk. Ball did not stop there to give musicians every advantage to see their music. He also provided a candle support for illumination on either side of the main desk.

CHANGES OVER TIME

Early owners of the piano made an attempt to delay its obsolescence by updating the stand: the straight legs were slightly tapered, a music shelf was added, and it may have been at that time that the brass casters were added. A complete restoration in the 1990s, prior to its acquisition by Colonial Williamsburg, put the piano in good playing condition but, as a historical document, left the instrument as virtually a reproduction of itself.

Drawing of Ball's patented adjustable music desk, shown with the right candle shelf folded back.

Grand Piano 22

James Ball
London 1794–1805

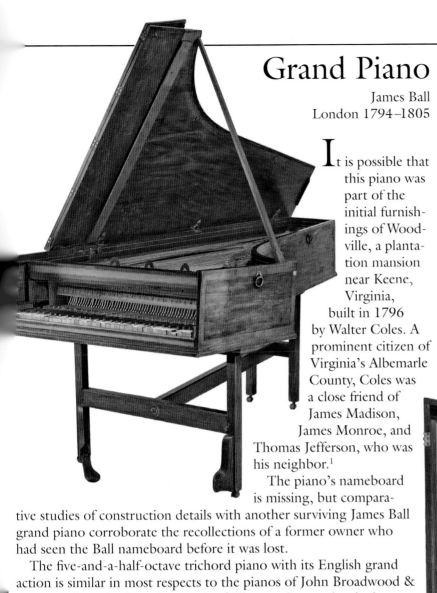

It is possible that this piano was part of the initial furnishings of Woodville, a plantation mansion near Keene, Virginia, built in 1796 by Walter Coles. A prominent citizen of Virginia's Albemarle County, Coles was a close friend of James Madison, James Monroe, and Thomas Jefferson, who was his neighbor.[1]

The piano's nameboard is missing, but comparative studies of construction details with another surviving James Ball grand piano corroborate the recollections of a former owner who had seen the Ball nameboard before it was lost.

The five-and-a-half-octave trichord piano with its English grand action is similar in most respects to the pianos of John Broadwood & Son, London's leading piano maker.[2] The two legs under the keyboard hold the pedals: the right for lifting the dampers and the left for shifting the keyboard. A hand stop in the right end block determines whether the hammers strike two strings per note (due corde) or just one string (una corda).

Every detail of an unaltered historical instrument gives another keyhole view of the past. The undersides of the ivory key tops, for example, show tool marks that indicate an unusually early use of some type of circular saw. The idea of such a machine had been patented by Samuel Miller in 1777 and was not yet in wide use.[3]

CHANGES OVER TIME

This piano's importance lies in its preservation of the type of historical evidence that is usually lost during restoration or rebuilding. At least fragments remain of presumably original strings, leather, and cloth. The rare survival of the original lid stick is partly due to its being hinged to the case. Its length indicates that lids were propped at a high angle compared to modern conventions. Besides the nameboard, some of the ivory key tops and the comb-shaped rack that guides the jacks are also lost.

The only repairs are from the early period of use and indicate that the piano received enough play to require renewal. Some of the keyboard balance pin mortises were shimmed, and a layer of leather was added to the hammers.

(below) The damper jacks retain their original leather and wool layers. The cloth was damaged by insects, but its survival leaves no doubt of Ball's original design.

(right) Top view of the piano showing divided bridge and nut, hinged lid stick, and four iron braces between the tuning pin block and the soundboard. Tide lines and water spots on the soundboard indicate that it had been subjected to water.

23 | Square Piano

John and Archibald Watson
Edinburgh ca. 1797

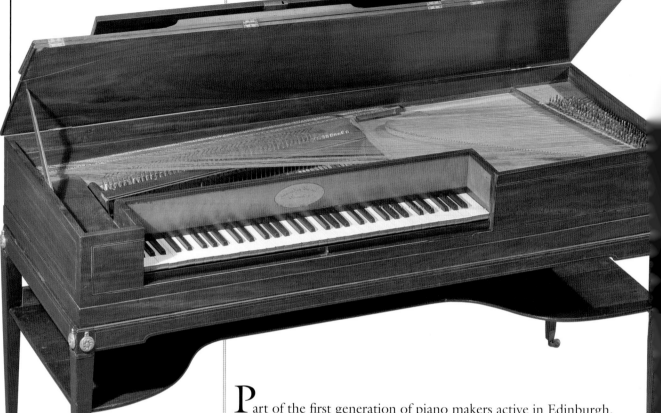

The "French Frame"

From about 1780, the most popular type of stand for British square pianos was what the Broadwood firm called a *French frame*. Its four square, tapered legs have brass casters and a narrow apron. A music shelf is usually included, though it is often lost, leaving only notches in the legs. Like the front of the apron, the shelf was cut back for leg room. French frames were stylish but rather underengineered, often resulting in damage at the joints. The style would be supplanted around 1806 when the fashion would favor six turned legs.

Part of the first generation of piano makers active in Edinburgh, the brothers John and Archibald Watson received their training in London.[1] They may have worked in the large manufactories of John Broadwood or Robert Stodart, both of whom were themselves from Scotland and might have had a preference for employing others from their home country.

In fact, a number of details on this piano beg comparisons with the early square pianos of John Broadwood and Son. Like Broadwood, the Watson brothers chose an understated, no-frills design lacking fancy veneers and musical extras such as pedals and stops; they appeared more interested in musical quality than visual or mechanical ornament. The solid mahogany case is decorated only with a white-black-white line inlay forming a border around the front and sides. An oval cartouche with an inscription against a light-wood background and a purpleheart border graces the keywell.

The makers adopted the new compass of FF–c4 adding a half octave above the long-accepted standard of five octaves. Only two of the dozen surviving pianos by John and Archibald Watson had this newer compass. Their method of fitting the additional keys had been patented by William Southwell in 1794 and involved placing the top ten keys on a separate key frame in a compartment under the soundboard. Another popular innovation from Southwell, fret-sawn vents in the nameboard, was not adopted here, perhaps in keeping with the Watsons' preference for decorative simplicity.

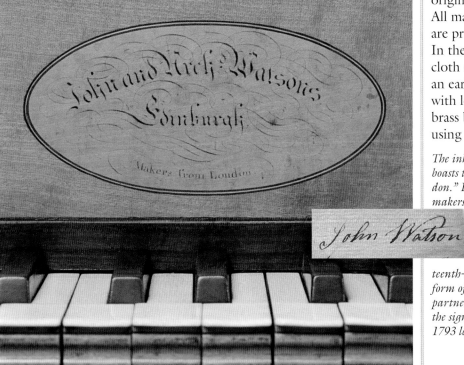

The keyboard, hammer, and damper mechanisms removed from the piano. The hammers are hidden behind the horizontal hammer rail to which the hammers are hinged. The brass levers showing above and below the hammer rail are dampers. Note the small pieces of red damper cloth on the damper levers (at the top of the photo). The hammers are bumped toward the strings by the stiff wire jacks each topped with a leather-covered block. The block also lifts the tail of the damper, pivoting the damper pad away from the string allowing the string to vibrate until the key is released.

SELECTING FROM THE INNOVATIONS OF OTHERS

The makers employed the English single action, as invented by John Zumpe thirty years before. This extremely simple mechanism remained in use by other British and Continental makers for fifty years, appearing only in less expensive pianos in its final years. In 1800, John Geib's patent for an escapement action would expire, freeing other piano makers to adopt the popular new mechanism (see pp. 72 and 99).

The idea of cast-brass underdampers, if not possibly the metal hardware itself, are from Broadwood, whose 1783 patent expired about the time this piano was made. This damper design was an improvement over Zumpe's original overdampers, which required a baleen (whalebone) spring to press down on each damper resulting in an undesirable resistance at the key.

The 1783 Broadwood patent that introduced brass underdampers also marked the beginning of Broadwood's enduring preference for placing the tuning pins at the left ends of the strings. The Watsons, however, preferred to keep the tuning pins on the right.

CHANGES OVER TIME

Early repairs and updates were minimal and included the addition of lead weights on the tops of the key levers near the wire jacks (see photo above). A metal bracket had also been added to one corner to stabilize the stand.

Restorative conservation in 1982 involved replacement of original strings and some cloth. All materials removed at that time are preserved in museum storage. In the same restoration, green cloth on the hammer heads from an earlier restoration was replaced with leather, and the four missing brass bolt covers were replaced using conjectural designs.

The ink inscription on the nameboard boasts that the makers were "from London." Extra cachet was due instrument makers in Edinburgh, New York, and Philadelphia who could claim to be from the principal center of culture and piano making. It was common practice in eighteenth-century Scotland to use the plural form of the family name when business partners were brothers. The inset shows the signature of one of the makers from a 1793 legal document.

24 | Square Piano

George Dettmer, London mid-1790s

AN UNJUST SCALE

According to a principle known by all instrument makers, each string in a musical instrument should be double the length of the string an octave above. This is known as *just scale*. The result for stringed keyboard instruments is that the string band (the area occupied by the sounding portion of the strings) takes

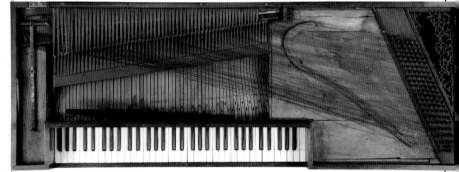

Typical

This entry

on a harp-like shape, as seen in the blue outline traced from the 1804 Kirckman piano (entry no. 27).

Strictly followed, just scale results in string lengths increasing exponentially toward the bass. Instrument makers follow just scale as far as possible, but, to avoid instruments being too long, they foreshorten the bass strings.

The less tightly curved bridge in this piano seems insignificant at first, but a mathematical analysis of all the string lengths reveals something truly radical. Dettmer's idea was to spread the foreshortening evenly over most of the string band so almost none of the scale is just.[2] With the tonal benefits of just scale gone, however, consequences surely outweighed the benefits, and Dettmer soon dropped the idea.

George Dettmer made pianos for resale under the names of various other makers and many more in partnership with William Dettmer, his son. The only two known pianos inscribed with his name alone, though spelled two different ways, are in the Colonial Williamsburg collection (see also entry no. 31).[1] This piano is well preserved, except for the loss of the music shelf and bolt covers from the stand and fragments of veneer and fretwork.

HOW TO ADD "ADDITIONAL KEYS"

Adding another half octave above the long-standard five was still a new idea in the mid-1790s, and the adventurous piano makers who first tried the new compass had to solve the space problem (see, for example, George Garcka, entry no. 20). William Southwell's patent for putting the additional keys on a separate key frame operating under the soundboard in its own compartment was still in effect when this instrument was made, and the method used by Dettmer pushes the limits of patent infringement. The additional keys are, as Southwell proposed, on their own key frame, but Dettmer's soundboard cantilevers over a single belly rail, so there is not a walled compartment for the additional keys.

Keywell showing decorative inlay and the inscription boasting "Patent Action."

George Dettmer London
Patent Action Piano Forte Manufacturer

PART THREE

STRIKING DEVELOPMENTS
PIANOS AND THE TECHNOLOGY RACE
1800–1830

By the dawn of the nineteenth century, London's former harpsichord makers had turned to the piano and were in a race for technology. London's monopoly on musical instrument manufacturing was also about to change. America's nonimportation laws against Britain from 1807 through the War of 1812 fueled a burgeoning American piano industry.

A fusion of demographic, economic, and commercial changes that accompanied the Industrial Revolution had an early beginning in keyboard instruments. More than any other product of the time, keyboard instruments demanded high-precision workmanship and high-volume production to accurately make the many identical action parts of even a single instrument. Division of labor and the use of hand-powered protomachines and templates brought a new perfection to hand workmanship and made the instruments reliable, cheaper, and more widely available. The stage was set for the final sprint that would virtually complete the development of the modern piano within a quarter century after 1830. The harpsichord had slipped into a long slumber to emerge at the end of the nineteenth century with a duel repertoire of old and new music.

25 Square Piano

Charles Albrecht
Philadelphia 1800–1805

PENNSYLVANIA GERMANS

Well before the American Revolution, southeast Pennsylvania was an attractive destination for Germans seeking a new life in North America. As they had in London, some of them brought a talent and proclivity for keyboard instrument making. Indeed, the American piano industry that would lead the world in the nineteenth century had its first blossoming in Pennsylvania.[5]

By the 1790s, Philadelphia was the largest city in America and, for that decade, served as the nation's capital. It was there and in the rural southeast of Pennsylvania that the stage was set for an early burgeoning of musical culture and piano making, primarily due to a clever, resourceful, and music-loving population of German Americans.

Reaching a new American threshold of workmanship and design, Charles Albrecht is considered by some historians to be the first professional piano maker in the United States. Born in Germany and catering to a mixed market of Anglo-American and German-American customers, his pianos drew from English and German traditions. This particular piano is mechanically and decoratively within the London style.[1] Albrecht's other pianos variously employed the double action, Schoene's action, and the German action. He sometimes included hand stops, pedals, or knee levers. One example even provides knee lever–operated swell shutters over the soundboard.[2]

By 1800, Albrecht was the most prolific American maker of pianos, with about twenty of his pianos surviving today.[3] Philadelphia, also home to piano maker Charles Taws and several smaller workshops, was the leading center of manufacture in the country at the end of the eighteenth century, a distinction that would eventually be taken over by New York.

Albrecht employed Joshua Baker, who signed the instrument on the bottom under the action. Baker, whose signature also appears on two other Albrecht square pianos, was listed as a "piano forte maker," "instrumentmaker," and "piana forte maker" in Philadelphia directories between 1810 and 1816. He later joined in partnership with piano maker Thomas Loud Evenden.[4]

The piano has a five-octave compass and uses Zumpe's single action with lever overdampers and a hand stop to raise the dampers. The piano is very well preserved and received a minimally intrusive restoration before coming into Colonial Williamsburg's collection. The strings and the music shelf are replacements.

(above) The pointed oval cartouche bearing the maker's name is characteristic of Albrecht's work and that of other Pennsylvania makers. The inscription reads "Charles Albrecht / Maker / Philadelphia."

(right) Top view showing the hand stop for raising the dampers, lever overdampers, soundboard, tuning pins, and J-shaped bridge.

Square Piano | 26

John Huber, Harrisburg, Pa., 1805–1809

<D>esigning and building a piano involves a daunting array of skills and knowledge, including woodworking and metalworking; structural, mechanical, and acoustical engineering; and the fabrication of high-precision mechanisms in a wide range of materials. It is a surprise, therefore, to find such a craft being practiced in rural settings a hundred miles from the nearest urban center. Such was the case with several Pennsylvania German piano makers, including John Huber.

Although Charles Albrecht had achieved an almost pure English expression (see the previous entry), Huber's interpretation of the English style clearly reveals his German heritage. Unlike on any known British piano of the period, Huber constructed the lid with breadboard ends, meaning separate narrow boards are joined to the ends of the main panels, the grain running perpendicular to each other. The black-stained or painted bridge and ogee profile finishing the treble end of the hitch-pin rail, both visible on the photo below, are German in origin and cannot be found on any British piano. Wire gauges marked on the keys also follow German rather than British numbering conventions.

Other details, while not necessarily German in origin, illustrate Huber's creativity and independence from the norms of English square piano construction. Instead of the keys and hammers sliding out of the piano as a unit, Huber's hammers are hinged to a massive rail that is attached to the interior so the key frame slides out independent of the hammers. The upper flats of the tuning pins, normally forged on an anvil, are shaped only by filing. The guide pins for the hammers and lever dampers are of thin wire, as are the damper springs, which were more typically baleen. A tapered wood panel protecting the springs is also unusual.

MEET JOHN HUBER

The two earliest of Huber's four known instruments were made in Northampton (near Allentown), Pennsylvania, and are more overtly German in decorative and mechanical details. Both were made for German-speaking customers. The third example—English in style and almost identical to this piano—was made for an English-speaking customer. Huber made the two English-style pianos after his relocation to Harrisburg, Pennsylvania, sometime around 1800.[1]

The piano is the work of an ingenious craftsman who was apparently self-taught. Even when catering to the Anglo-American market, Huber's workmanship nevertheless spoke with a strong German accent. The piano truly embodies the spirit, ingenuity, and passion for music that gave birth to the American piano industry.[2]

(above) Huber's copperplate-printed paper label behind glass.

(left) Top view of the piano. Note the black-stained or painted bridge and the characteristic ogee profile on the hitch-pin rail extension, very near the treble end of the bridge.

27 Square Piano

Joseph Kirckman
London 1804

MAKING THE SWITCH

The old rival harpsichord workshops of Kirckman and Shudi-Broadwood both retooled for piano production during the last quarter of the eighteenth century and continued to thrive far into the piano era. Broadwood got a strong head start in making pianos, but by 1890 the Kirckman factory briefly regained the lead. In that year Kirckman sold 1,300 pianos and Broadwood about 1,000. The Kirckman firm was finally sold in 1896 to Collard & Collard company.[4]

Jacob Kirckman dropped the c in the Kirckman name from legal documents as early as 1755, but the firm retained it on formal keyboard inscriptions until 1806.

The Kirckman workshop began selling pianos in the early 1770s while continuing their dominance of the British harpsichord market.[1] During the last quarter of the eighteenth century, as pianos and harpsichords remained viable alternatives, the Kirckman firm catered to both markets. The latest surviving harpsichord by any maker was produced by Kirckman in 1800, just four years before this piano was made.[2] About two-thirds of the Kirckman output in the early nineteenth century were square pianos, and most of the rest were grands, plus a few vertical pianos.[3]

Joseph Kirckman took over the business in 1794 after the death of his father, Abraham Kirckman. Abraham was the nephew of Jacob Kirckman, who headed the firm when the three harpsichords in the Colonial Williamsburg collection were made (entry nos. 8, 9, and 10).

Never restored, this piano retains its original strings, cloth, and leather. The piano was an inexpensive model with the simplest of mechanical actions and minimal decoration. The relatively plain nameboard has curly maple veneer, an ink inscription, and no fretwork vents. The mahogany case with zigzag inlay stringing rests on a simple French frame stand. The pedal and music shelf are missing.

Top view with lid removed. Note the decorative soundboard vent, tuning pins on the right, and full five-and-a-half-octave compass and simple J-shaped bridge.

The keyboard and action removed from the piano.

ADDING KEYS, RESPECTING PATENTS

Piano makers had a problem to solve. How could they add another half octave of keys without relying on the clever method still under patent by William Southwell? The patent included a way to put the top half octave (the so-called additional keys) on a separate key frame under the soundboard and let the hammers strike through a slot in the soundboard (see entry no. 28).

Kirckman's solution was to condense five and a half octaves of hammers into the space formerly occupied by five, mostly by packing the treble hammers very close together. This method resulted in an extreme offset in the key levers, visible in the photo above.

By 1804, many piano makers passed over the old English single action invented by John Zumpe, preferring John Geib's English double action, the patent for which had run out by 1800. However, the single action remained easier to make and was common in cheaper pianos. Southwell's improved dampers were still under patent, so the Kirckman piano also retains the horizontal overdampers invented by Zumpe.

The bass end of the piano interior showing the damper and hammer actions. The piano lacks any pedals or hand stops.

DATES ON NAMEBOARDS

Joseph Kirckman included the year 1804 at the end of the formal inscription on the nameboard. It is a great convenience for keyboard historians that instrument makers often included a year in their inscriptions, taking all guesswork out of determining dates of production.

What accounts for this tradition and why was it abandoned not long after this piano was made? Perhaps the makers hoped to give the impression of a momentous construction, like the dated cornerstone of an important building or the inscription on a monument. Some customers probably appreciated the date when the purchase marked the occasion of a marriage or purchase of a house.

A more prosaic explanation is that a date was a type of built-in obsolescence in a society highly driven by changing fashions. Indeed, pianos were frequently updated when they became old-fashioned. It is not unusual to find dates altered by owners to make a piano seem newer. When a piano finally has the status of antique, altering dates to make them appear earlier has proven tempting for unscrupulous dealers.

Detail of a lid hook and zigzag string banding on the case. Lid hooks were decorative, but they also secured the lid when the instrument was turned sideways while being moved through a doorway.

28 | Square Piano

George Astor & Co.
London 1800–1810

SOUTHWELL'S 1794 PATENT

Patents ranged from the profoundly influential to the ludicrous. In piano history, the group of improvements patented by the Irish maker William Southwell in 1794 is an excellent example of the former. Within a few years of Southwell's invention, and often before they had legal rights to do so, piano makers enthusiastically adopted several elements of his plan. The patent included a way to add a half octave of additional keys without enlarging the case by cleverly arranging some keys under the soundboard. A new type of damper (see next page) was even more important in piano history. Decorative nameboard vents became almost universal on square pianos for a half century. They, too, were Southwell's idea.

"NEW PATENT"!

Soon after John Broadwood's 1783 patent, his firm began adding the word "Patent" to their nameboards. Later, after adopting Southwell's 1794 patent, the maker of the piano in this entry and other English and American makers began to proclaim "*New* Patent."[5] By the 1820s, most English and American nameboards boasted patents without a clear association with any particular improvement. It was simply the marketing equivalent of "new and improved."

Keyboard with "additional keys."

Who made this piano? By the opening of the nineteenth century, the London piano industry had become a vortex of interconnected entrepreneurs, including makers, dealers, and several, such as George Astor & Co., who were both. Business and innovation were driven and shaped by fierce competition while lawyers stayed busy processing bankruptcies, mergers, and patent infringements. A maker's inscription on the nameboard of a piano was only a hint of who actually made the instrument, as makers and dealers outsourced the manufacturing of pianos to be sold under their own names.

Astor was another German immigrant making and selling instruments in London. His famously successful brother, John Jacob Astor, had started out in the musical instrument business with George, but his venture to import and sell his brother's musical instruments in New York City quickly took second place to a more lucrative trade in furs.[1]

Back in London at the time this piano was made, George Astor was selling pianos under his own name and supplying pianos to be labeled and sold by Broderip & Wilkinson. That firm had taken over part of bankrupt Longman & Broderip.[2]

In this piano the maker used William Southwell's patented method of adding additional keys at a time when many makers were using Southwell's patent without the legal right to do so. Several of the makers represented in this book were involved in the resulting litigation, including Longman, Broderip, Wilkinson, Culliford, Astor, and one Ludewig Augustus Leukfeld, who makes his appearance now.[3]

It is likely that Leukfeld made this piano for Astor. This arrangement would have been legal until 1801, after which an exclusive contract with Broderip & Wilkinson explicitly forbade Leukfeld from making pianos with the Southwell patent for anyone else, including Astor. Subsequent court records reveal, however, that between 1804 and 1806 Leukfeld's largest customer was, indeed, George Astor, who received 143 pianos from Leukfeld, all having the Southwell patented design.[4] This may be one of those 143 unauthorized instruments.

The New Damper Is a Game Changer

Southwell's invention of a new type of damper—part of his 1794 patent—was so successful that grand pianos still use it today. The horizontal lever dampers of Zumpe's earlier English single action (see p. 99) relied on a baleen (whalebone) spring to press the lever against the string. An unwanted side effect resulted: the spring also made the key a little more difficult to depress, affecting the player's control.

The Southwell patent solved that problem. The new dampers were attached to the keys themselves by means of stiff wires and relied on the weight of the key levers to pull the dampers firmly against the strings. The new design damped the sound more efficiently with no spring required and was easier to adjust. There were only two disadvantages. During major repairs, the workman faced the painstaking job of reattaching each of the dampers when reinstalling the action. The second challenge came in designing a pedal that could raise all the dampers at the same time. This was still a new idea, and the maker of this piano tried the solution below.

Drawing of the Southwell damper in context.

Some Ideas Do Not Survive

Since the Southwell dampers were attached directly to the key levers, lifting the dampers would necessarily also raise the backs of the keys and slightly lower the fronts. Astor used an experimental method to lift the dampers that probably worked very poorly: depressing a pedal caused a sliding batten just behind the nameboard to press the fronts of the keys down, lifting the rears enough to raise all the dampers. That idea was soon superseded by the use of a damper underlever (see p. 99).

Only remnants remain of a mechanism that awkwardly raised the dampers by pressing down on the front half of the keys. Parts may have been removed because they worked poorly.

Top view of the piano's interior.

Changes over Time

Most of the condition problems, such as severe distortion from wood shrinkage, deteriorated leather components, and detachment of the tuning pin block, are the result of many years of string tension, aging of materials, and periods of excessive dryness.

Alterations from past repairs are minimal. They include a heavy clear coating on the soundboard, suggesting that the strings, though old, were replaced at the same time. The action cloth was replaced, but the hammer leather is original.

Past exterior alterations include replacement of the right nameboard fretwork and the cloth in both vents. The music shelf was replaced, and the lid rehinged with new hinges.

Lost parts include the soundboard vent and the damper pedal, along with some of its related components.

Detail from a piano bearing a Broderip & Wilkinson label shows the only other known example of the experimental damper-lifting mechanism. It retains the part now missing from the Astor piano. The piano's current location is unknown.

29 Grand Piano

John Broadwood & Son
London 1806

MEET THE PATRIARCH

Scotsman John Broadwood arrived in London in 1761 to serve as shop foreman for harpsichord maker Burkat Shudi. Following Broadwood's marriage to the master's daughter in 1769, the firm continued under the name Shudi and Broadwood. Two years later, Shudi signed the entire business over to Broadwood, who nevertheless retained Shudi's name on instrument inscriptions for some years.

John Broadwood's phenomenal success in business was largely due to his steady balance of conservatism and innovation. Even though square pianos were rapidly rising in popularity during the 1770s, the Broadwood firm did not begin making them until 1780. Although the firm's harpsichord sales reached their peak in 1784, revenue from piano sales already grew to equal that from harpsichords by the same year.[3]

John Broadwood retired in 1811 and died the next year. His firm survives to the present day.[4]

The serial number recorded on the bass end of the pin block is also found on several other places inside.

B roadwood pianos provide a key to understanding the history of pianos in Britain and America, thanks to the survival of instruments, company archives, and the firm's influence on its many smaller competitors. Serial numbers link actual pianos with ledger entries, sometimes recording shipping dates and first owners. Each instrument was made by hand, but, with production at high levels, Broadwood's pianos survive in great numbers. The combination of physical and documentary evidence allows scholars to determine the earliest appearance of each technological advance or decorative fashion, limited only by the survival rates of pianos.

The porter's book entry dated Saturday, November 22, 1806, records the departure of this very piano from the factory. "A G[rand] P[iano]F[orte] [with] add[itional keys extending a half octave above the old standard five octaves] 3 Pedals [serial] N[o] 3541 & Case." The entry credits George Smart for arranging the sale.[1] Taking delivery would be the wife of John Moseley of Great Glemham House, Tofts, Norfolk, where Moseley was serving as high sheriff.[2]

Entry in the Broadwood porter's book recording the departure on November 22 of grand piano forte serial number 3541 via Marsh & Co.'s wagon.

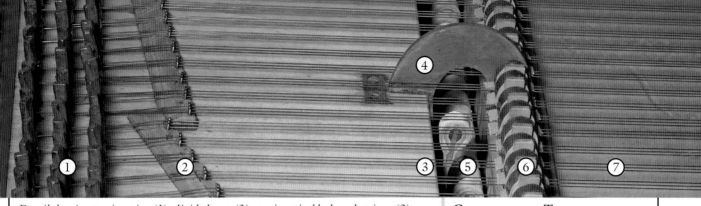

Detail showing tuning pins (1), divided nut (2), tuning pin block and strings (3), structural iron arc (4), hammers (5), dampers (6), and soundboard (7).

THE ENGLISH GRAND PIANO COMES OF AGE

The first commercially successful pianos in England were square pianos, introduced in 1766 by John Zumpe (see entry no. 13). Writing in the early nineteenth century, Charles Burney reported that grand pianos were being made in London even earlier, but that these were little more than experiments.[5] Grands did not begin to take hold commercially until 1771, when the harpsichord maker Americus Backers advertised pianos "the Size and Shape of a Harpsichord."[6] Backers invented the English grand action, which was adopted by all the English grand makers including Broadwood, who used it for nearly a century. It was John Broadwood's former coworker from the Shudi harpsichord shop, Robert Stodart, who continued the early development of the English grand and coined the term *grand piano-forte*.[7]

John Broadwood deserves credit for many of the advances that brought the grand piano to such a high level of sophistication by 1806. Chief among his improvements was to set the bass strings, which are made of brass, on a separate bridge. By compensating for the differences between brass and iron wire, the divided bridge reduced the abrupt change of tone between the lowest iron string and the beginning of the brass-strung section.[8]

Broadwood also changed the cross-section profile of the bridge to be almost rectangular. Further, a pattern of notches at the top of the bridge allowed all three strings of a note to have the same length and tension, potentially improving tuning stability.

Lacking patent protection, Broadwood's improvements were quickly copied by all other English makers and continue to be used by piano makers today.[9]

Top view showing the divided bridge. The four small iron reinforcement braces visible just below the damper would eventually evolve into a massive iron plate in modern pianos.

CHANGES OVER TIME

Although wear on the ivory key tops indicates the piano has had much use, the instrument is remarkably well preserved. Of the original five layers of leather covering the hammers, only the top layer had been replaced with cloth in an early episode of repair. That layer was replaced again with leather in 1985. Other work in 1985 included some cleaning and replacement of damaged cloth and leather. Removed materials were labeled and are preserved separately. Much of the old cloth and leather remains in place, including the dark blue listing cloth visible in the photo on the left parallel to the bridge.

The inner framing visible during the 1985 conservation. The profusion of wooden braces shows Broadwood's attempt to counteract six thousand pounds of string tension. The cases of pianos in this period nevertheless tended to distort.

30 | Square Piano

John Broadwood & Son
London ca. 1808

PERFECTION AT LAST

In his patented design, William Southwell placed the piano damper atop a wire, the other end of which screwed into the key lever (see p. 67). The final improvement in this piano, shown below, was to screw the damper wire into a separate lever instead, allowing the keyboard and hammer action to be removed separately. This basic design is still used in grand pianos today.

Wire-mounted dampers shown with keys and mechanical action removed.

A WHITE PINE RED HERRING

The piano's white pine soundboard is a potentially misleading piece of historical evidence. Because the timber was native to America and not widely used in the British furniture industry, the presence of American white pine in an artifact usually indicates construction in North America. Broadwood, however, discovered that the resonant American import was an ideal wood for making soundboards.

Top view showing Broadwood's placement of tuning pins on the left end of the strings along the back. John Broadwood adopted this arrangement in 1783. The hammers survive but are detached and do not appear in the photo.

On the first of January 1808, Thomas Broadwood became a partner with his father and stepbrother in what was by then the largest piano manufacturing firm in the world.[1] The addition of a second son to the business meant a name change to John Broadwood & Sons. With its "Broadwood & Son" nameboard inscription, this piano would seem to have been made in 1807 or earlier. It is marked, however, with the serial number 12589, indicating construction in early 1809. In fact, Broadwood square piano number 11854 (earlier by 735 pianos) is labeled "& Sons."[2] There are many possible explanations for such discrepancies in a high-volume operation such as Broadwood's. A few already-lettered nameboards, for example, may have been installed well after the time of a name change. Seemingly solid historical evidence can be misleading.[3]

The piano has a long history in Virginia, and, like every centuries-old artifact, it played a role in the lives and memories of generations of owners. Only occasionally do such memories live beyond the people who cherished them. In 1940 as this heirloom was being transferred from aunt to niece, the elder wrote that the piano was nearly sold out of the family at an estate auction in 1897. With heartwarming loyalty and an abiding sense of kinship, the daughter of one of the household's former slaves bought the piano and saw to its return to the family where it was eagerly welcomed home.

Square Piano 31

George Dettmer, London 1805–1810

<B>uilt at least a decade later than the piano of entry number 24, this example by the same George W. Dettmer was probably made shortly before William Dettmer, his son, was taken into partnership.[1] The piano is highly decorated with large-radius corners, inlaid marble ovals, complex inlaid string banding, floral painted nameboard, and unusual double-eagle nameboard and soundboard vents.[2] The plain key fronts, unusual in the period, are also found on the earlier Dettmer piano.

Keyboard instruments are inherently asymmetrical. To create a handsome symmetrical appearance similar to that of a sideboard, Dettmer designed the exterior so that, when closed up, the front was divided into thirds (photo lower right).[3]

For all its decorative sophistication, this piano is relatively simple as a musical instrument. Dettmer provided no pedal or hand stop to control the dampers. Pedals were not yet standard on square pianos and may not have been required for much of the popular music of the period.

CHANGES OVER TIME

It is ironic that the most beautiful artifacts often attract more frequent and well-intentioned—but often damaging—restorations. Among the original parts that have been replaced on this piano are the strings and tuning pins, the exterior finish, and the cloth in the action. The previously altered feet have been restored to their period appearance including reproduction casters.

Although the piano likely once had a music shelf resting on the lower stretcher, the considerable wear on the stretcher suggests either that no shelf existed or that it was discarded long ago.

The wire-mounted captive dampers are lost. This type of damper system is tedious to reinstall after removing the action for maintenance, making it particularly vulnerable to loss during unskilled restoration work.

(above) Top view of the piano showing the ornate soundboard vent and layout with deeply rounded corners. The tuning pins are modern replacements, and the captive wire-mounted dampers are missing.

(below) The richly decorated keywell with its unusual double-eagle fretwork vents.

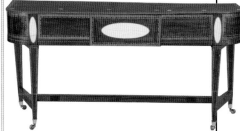

The large central inlay of white marble and the flanking ovals above the legs add to a striking presentation when the case is entirely closed. The design cleverly disguises the asymmetry of square pianos and gives the appearance of a sideboard.

32 | Square Piano

John Geib & Son, New York 1808–1809

THE BAFFLING INNER COVER

What was the purpose of the green painted panel of thin spruce in this piano? Although common in early square and some grand pianos, there is much debate about the device's original purpose and what to call it.[2] Was it for keeping dust out when the lid was open? Was it intended to suppress mechanical noise or add mellowness to the tone? If so, the effect is so subtle as to be hardly worth the effort.

The panel's typically colorful decoration and the frequent role of pianos in the education of girls may hint at another purpose: to serve as a kind of modesty panel protecting young students from the unsightly machinery inside. Whatever the cover's purpose, this example was apparently never completed, as a penciled instruction on the underside tells the painter it is "to be bordered with flowers."

CHANGES OVER TIME

The almost perfect preservation of the delicate nameboard decoration indicates the piano was always extraordinarily well cared for. A restoration around the middle of the twentieth century was so carefully done that it is difficult to distinguish restoration from period work. The pedals and soundboard vent are missing, and replaced parts include the strings, the tuning pins, some action cloth, and some screws. Two large bolts were added to the pin block.

An organ builder from Germany with his sights set on a new life in America, John Geib found himself honing his craft in London while waiting out the American Revolution. That is how he described himself in a 1783 letter of introduction to Benjamin Franklin, the American ambassador in Paris.[1] While in London, Geib secured his place in piano history with a 1786 patent for an escapement mechanism. Variously called the *Geib action* or the *English double action*, the invention was the first escapement mechanism to appear in English and American square pianos, becoming almost universal for more than a half century. For most of his time in London, Geib made pianos for Longman & Broderip through the putting-out system, whereby Longman & Broderip supplied all materials and paid Geib for his labor. After Longman & Broderip went out of business, Geib left with his family for New York in 1797. He and his three sons would be among America's most distinguished piano makers. John Jr. became a partner in 1803 to form John Geib & Son.

Top view. The bolts near the tuning pins are added, and the soundboard fretwork is lost.

New York Style

The New York piano industry in the early nineteenth century was beginning a rapid rise, and John Geib and his sons were among its leaders. Compared to Boston and Philadelphia, New York had a taste for the glitz and dazzle of contrasting carving, inlays, and painted ornament. This piano shares with the Dettmer example (entry no. 31) deeply rounded corners that give the instrument the appearance of a sideboard when closed. One of Geib's former partners in London, Ludewig Augustus Leukfeld, dubbed the type an "oval sideboard" pianoforte.[3] Other striking ornamentation includes mahogany veneer with contrasting maple banding and tombstone inlays, complex string banding, drawers with brass pulls, and a nameboard with delicate tassel-motif vents and painted flowers. Although an often-repeated story alleges that the well-known cabinetmaker Duncan Phyfe made these fancy cases for Geib, this claim is based on a false premise.[4]

A Look Inside

The interior view below shows the piano's key levers (1) and English double (Geib) action with the nameboard removed. An adjustable jack, or hopper, (2) transfers the motion of the key to an underlever (3), partly visible, which propels the hammer (not visible) to the string.

As the far end of a key lever (4) rises and the damper underlever (5) pivots upward with it, the damper (6), which is mounted on a wire between it and the underlever (5), lifts off the string. An unusual innovation of this design is the key lever's claw-shaped end (7), which not only raises the damper but also applies the weight of the key lever to pull the damper back down firmly against the string.

One of the piano's now-missing pedals operated a lid swell. The lid flap (8) over the soundboard is shown folded back. When the pedal was depressed, a knob (9) opened the lid for more volume. A cloth layer (10) on the lid acts as a cushion.

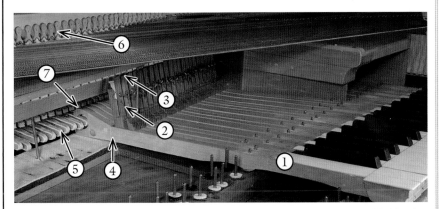

Left half of the nameboard showing the vent with delicate scrollwork and gilded leather backing and Geib's painted inscription. The back includes penciled instructions for the decorator "to have roses."

33 Vertical Piano

Robert Wornum Jr., London 1813–1820

A LITTLE SOMETHING FOR THE DRAWING ROOM

With its lavish decoration and a small footprint, Robert Wornum's upright pianoforte offered a new kind of musical furniture for the drawing room. Like the two other examples from the 1810s (entry nos. 34 and 35), this piano has highlights of brass inlay. Anthemion and scroll motifs decorate the lower panel, and brass stringing with ornamented corners outline panels on all sides. A pierced brass gallery around the carved gadroon–bordered top, cast egg-and-dart moldings, and other brass highlights dazzle against rich rosewood and pleated green silk. Rounded cheeks and a sycamore-veneered keyboard surround with sliding candle shelves—all supported on two turned, reeded, and acanthus-carved legs—draw attention to the ivory and ebony keys. This model was a showpiece for the drawing rooms of the affluent.

The back of the piano is enclosed and fully ornamented with veneer and stringing.

Through his innovative designs and patents, Robert Wornum Jr. of London finally established vertical pianos as a constant on the musical landscape. The idea of standing stringed keyboard instruments on end, however, began with harpsichords centuries before there were pianos. The earliest surviving upright piano was made in 1739 in Italy, where pianos were invented.[1] A few vertical pianos were also made in Germany at midcentury. A rare American example, made between 1745 and about 1760, remains in its original German Moravian home in Nazareth, Pennsylvania.[2] Around 1790, Robert Woffington of Dublin made a petite vertical piano of five octaves.[3] William Stodart, maker of the grand piano in entry number 35, patented the aptly named, eight-and-a-half-foot-tall "upright grand piano in the form of a bookcase" in 1795.[4] William Southwell also patented an upright version of the square piano in 1798, introducing the sticker action, which remained in use by other makers, including Wornum, long after the upright square was forgotten. Short-lived upright models by John Isaac Hawkins in Philadelphia and Matthias Müller in Vienna were independent efforts that coincidentally appeared in 1800. It was one of Hawkins's little uprights that Thomas Jefferson purchased in that year. After only two years, Jefferson returned it to the maker in hopes that the tuning could be made more stable. The piano was never returned.[5]

Over the course of the nineteenth century, square pianos evolved into massive objects that finally outgrew their domestic environment. Robert Wornum helped to put the upright piano on track to become the more practical instrument for the parlor.

Wornum the Upstanding

Robert Wornum Jr., son of a publisher and maker of stringed instruments, patented his "improved upright piano forte" in 1811 during his partnership with George Wilkinson.[6] Wornum began working on his own in 1813, making vertical, and, occasionally, grand pianos. The house of Wornum passed from father to son, lasting until the end of the nineteenth century.

With its strings running vertically from the floor to the top of the piano, this instrument is an early example of what Wornum termed a *harmonic piano-forte*. Restoration before the piano came into the Colonial Williamsburg collection left the instrument without its formal inscription, though an informal pencil inscription on the reverse side of the nameboard reads "harmonic" and the underside of the d1 key is signed, "Made by Rt Wornum Wigmore Street London." A near identical Wornum piano is marked on the nameboard, "New Harmonic Piano Forte / Robert Wornum Late Wilkinson & Wornum / No. 42 Wigmore Street Cavendish Square, & 3 Welbeck Street, London."[7] Wornum's concept was soon adopted by the firm Pleyel & Company in Paris, where the diminutive instruments were called *pianinos*.

Part of Wornum's success was his willingness to take risks with his designs. While his small vertical piano had lasting influence on the industry, his 1830s "Imperial Grand Horizontal Piano"—a large version of the so-called pocket piano with strings, soundboard, and framing in typical relationship to each other but mounted upside down over the lower case and action—never rose above the status of curiosity.[8]

Interior view showing treble third of keyboard, action, and tuning pins.

Front view of piano with cover panels and part of action removed showing the soundboard, bridge, nut, and tuning pins. Some bass tuning pin holes have been plugged and await replacement of the strings. The piano is bichord below C and trichord above.

A Look Inside

The interior view above shows the piano's adjustable hoppers (1), very much like the ones used in the double action on which this action is based. The use of stickers (2) to transfer the motion from the keys up to the hammers was an idea picked up from Southwell's earlier upright square design.

Wire extensions (3) pass between the hammers (4) to bear against the dampers (5), lifting them from the strings. A rod (6) transfers motion from the right pedal up to the damper system. As in grand pianos of the period, the left pedal shifts the keyboard and action so each hammer strikes only two or just one string, depending on the setting of a hand stop in the end block (7).

Wornum's well-known design improvements to the tape-check action came later and are to be seen in nearly all vertical pianos today.

34 | Grand Piano

John Broadwood & Sons
London 1816

A BROADWOOD FOR BEETHOVEN

During his travels in Europe in 1817, Thomas Broadwood paid a visit to the celebrated composer Ludwig van Beethoven in Vienna. On his return, Thomas quickly arranged for a Broadwood grand piano to be sent to Europe's most celebrated composer. Beethoven's Broadwood piano, now in the Hungarian National Museum, was made within a year of the one sent to Lady Skipwith, the two instruments matching in musical and mechanical aspects and in most details of their appearance.

Beethoven deeply appreciated the gift and pledged in his response to "look upon it as an altar upon which I shall place the most beautiful offerings of my spirit."[3] Historians disagree about the significance of Beethoven's endorsement of the Broadwood piano. Skeptics point to Beethoven's advancing hearing loss. Opinion tends to divide according to personal orientation, either to the London tradition of piano design and playing or to the Viennese tradition.[4]

Broadwood grand piano serial number 6942 was dispatched from the factory in London on July 17, 1816. It was one of four grands that were addressed to George Balls, an agent in Norfolk, Virginia.[1] The piano's final destination was Prestwould, a plantation house still standing and well preserved in Mecklenburg County, Virginia. It was there that Lady Jean Skipwith, already sixty-eight years old, received the piano. Her hand-copied book of music remains at Prestwould.

Pianos did not necessarily leave the Broadwood factory in the order in which they were completed. Of the four pianos headed for Virginia on that day in 1816, the highest and lowest serial numbers were over 108 grand pianos apart.

A Skipwith descendant gave the piano to the College of William and Mary in 1946.[2] It is on loan to the Colonial Williamsburg Foundation following extensive conservation there in 2003.

(left) Keyboard view.

(right) Lady Jean Skipwith's music book open to a page labeled "Favourite March in the Opera 'Ines de Castro' by Sig.ʳ Bianchi." The book remains at Prestwould.

A Half-Century Milestone

Since its commercial beginnings in 1766, the British piano industry had fifty years of growth behind it when this piano was made. Square pianos were well established in the market before Broadwood began to produce grand pianos in 1785.[5] While grands became the preferred type for the most serious concert use, square pianos continued their dominance in domestic situations.

Representing the state of the art at the half-century mark, this grand piano is adorned with quilted mahogany veneer and cast-brass moldings on vertical corners and around the bottom. The legs have black-stained rings, brass ferrules, and a cast floral ornament above each.

A Closer Look

As can be seen in the photo below, original iron screws with gilded heads (1) pass through the soundboard into the stiffening ribs beneath. Broadwood did not often use screws for soundboard ribs, but they appear on pianos with American histories. The screws were apparently intended to help hold together the instruments being exported to the steamy climate of the American South.[6]

This piano has three strings per note all the way to the bass end. It was made shortly before Broadwood began to use overspun strings for the lowest bass notes. When thickened by that means, there was room only for two strings per note or just one in the lowest bass.[7] The dampers (2) were made intentionally less effective in a section near the top (3). There are no dampers at all for the top nine notes (4), where empty damper jacks maintain a consistent weight on the keys. Three of the piano's five structural iron arcs (5) are visible, as are two of the lid hooks (6). The lid hooks, which catch brass loops on the lid, are operated using the decorative cast-brass rings on the exterior.

Two alterations are visible from past restorations. Reproduction tuning pins (7) from 2003 replace another set of pins from an early twentieth-century restoration at the Chickering factory in Boston. A metal reinforcement bar added by Chickering was replaced in 1976 and again in 2003, with Chickering's bolt (8) remaining in use in each episode.[8]

Detail of the treble section of the interior.

How Many Pedals?

Similar to the Broadwood grand piano of a decade earlier (entry no. 29), this piano has three pedals. Unlike the 1806 example, however, this piano has the separate treble and bass damper pedals together on the right, where they appear as a single split pedal. This is not so much a disguise as it is a convenience for more easily pressing the two damper pedals simultaneously. The ability to lift treble and bass dampers independently had first appeared in 1769, and by 1816 its popularity was fading.[9]

The left pedal shifts the keyboard for una corda or due corde, depending on the position of a hand stop in the treble end block. The left pedal has a black stripe down the center to create an illusion of symmetry with the divided damper pedal.

35 Grand Piano

William Stodart
London 1816

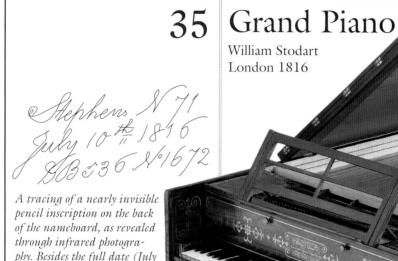

A tracing of a nearly invisible pencil inscription on the back of the nameboard, as revealed through infrared photography. Besides the full date (July 10, 1816) and Stodart's serial number (1672), two workmen added their own production numbers.

Detail of nameboard inlay.

A PASSION FOR INLAY

Metal inlay was surging in popularity when this piano was made. Stodart and other piano makers bought precast brass inlays from trade catalogs.[1] After drilling shallow holes in the rosewood veneer for chip clearance, sharp punches with perimeters matching the inlay were used to chop out the voids for the insertion of the brass pieces.[2]

Similar inlays can be seen in entry numbers 33 and 34.

Every historic instrument is superlative in some way if enough can be learned about it, but this 1816 grand piano by William Stodart is a true benchmark. Of the twenty-one surviving grand pianos signed by William Stodart alone, this one has the lowest reported serial number and is the only one with a known year of construction. It represents the fully developed grand piano on the cusp of the most radical change of all—the introduction of iron framing to the casework. Once the limitations of the all-wood case were out of the way, strings would become thicker, the compass larger, and hammers and mechanical mechanisms heavier, all in pursuit of more volume and tuning stability. The overall weight of the largest grand pianos would balloon from three hundred pounds for this 1816 example to over one thousand pounds today. Another component of the modern piano was just around the corner: Sébastien Erard's 1821 repetition action.

The Stodart piano takes pride of place in the Colonial Williamsburg collection also because of its well-documented provenance in a Virginia family with particular local significance. Originally purchased in Richmond by Thomas Rutherford for his daughter Jane, the piano passed through four generations before the family gave it to the Colonial Williamsburg Foundation in 2000. It was the Reverend William A. Rutherfoord Goodwin of the same family whose vision in the early twentieth century led directly to the restoration of Williamsburg and the establishment of the Colonial Williamsburg Foundation.

Cast-brass rings that control lid hooks on the inner rim include the face of the guardian Medusa, with her unblinking gaze, and rustic Pan, with his musical and erotic associations. Broadwood used a different cast rendering of the design in entry number 34.

The gold nameboard inscription displaying Stodart's royal warrant is in excellent condition. The piano has never been refinished.

A Look Inside

The photo below shows the action well with the keyboard and mechanical action removed. The underside of the tuning pin block (1) is overhead and the inside of the cheekpiece (2) is on the far right.

The damper jacks (3) are suspended from the strings out of sight above and are partly guided by a lower guide (4). The end of the metal trapwork for the damper pedal (5) is just visible where it thrusts a shelf (6) upward to raise the dampers. The lower parts of the structural iron arcs (7) are visible. The arcs hold open the gap between the pin block (1) and the belly rail (8) on which the soundboard is glued. A stop rail (9) is only long enough to affect the few keys that do not have dampers or a damper rail to stop the rise of the keys. Angled brackets (10) hold the action down if the piano is turned on its side. A powerful leaf spring (11) shoves the action leftward when the pianist releases the una corda pedal.

Meet the Stodarts

Robert Stodart, whose nephew made this piano, was a truly seminal figure in the history of the English grand piano. Soon after Americus Backers's invention of the English grand action, Robert Stodart left his employment with fellow Scotsman John Broadwood to further perfect the mechanism, adding to the commercial success of this larger sibling of the already-popular square piano. Stodart's 1777 patent for a combination harpsichord and piano details several refinements to Backers's grand action and is widely cited as the first use of the term *grand piano*.[3]

William and Matthew Stodart, Robert's nephews, continued and greatly enlarged the business.[4] In 1795, William patented an upright grand piano in the form of a bookcase. Forty-three grand pianos by William (with or without Matthew's name on the inscription) are known to survive, of which nine are the monumental vertical type.

A Stodart relative in Richmond, Virginia, likely imported this 1816 grand. An otherwise obscure firm named W. Stodart & Co. was listed as a Richmond retailer of music published by W. Dubois of New York in 1820.[5] It might have been Adam Stodart who ran W. Stodart & Co., for it is probably no coincidence that Adam Stodart began a partnership with Dubois in New York in 1822, selling music and manufacturing pianos.[6] Another brief encounter with the Virginia Stodart appears in 1820 when Thomas Jefferson asked his Richmond agent for help finding a set of harpsichord strings to repair daughter Maria's 1798 Kirckman harpsichord. Jefferson's agent turned to "Mr. Stoddart" a "celebrated Piano maker recently from Europe" for advice.[7]

The action well, shown with the keys removed.

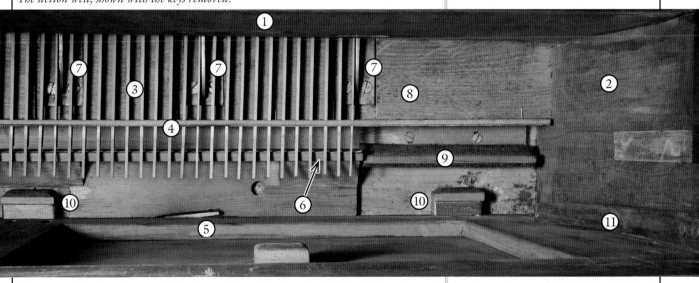

36 | Square Piano

Alpheus Babcock
Boston 1828

What's in a Nameplate?

Most of the pianos made by Alpheus Babcock before and after the period 1827–1828 give prominent credit to one of Babcock's financial backers, usually a member of the Mackay family. This is the only Babcock piano naming Norfolk, Virginia, music dealer C. Hall on the nameplate, and it was made during the period Babcock normally included only his own name. Presumably this example was prepaid by the Norfolk dealer.

Christopher Hall opened his book and music store in Norfolk in 1818. Advertising musical instruments and five hundred pieces of music in 1826, he claimed the largest stock of music in Virginia. Frequent advertising in the *American Beacon and Norfolk & Portsmouth Daily Advertiser* during this period indicates, however, that Hall must have had considerable competition.[5]

Hall's 1828 connection to Babcock may have contributed to Hall's eventually becoming an agent for Jonas Chickering in 1831, by which time Babcock was employed by Chickering.[6]

Alpheus Babcock was the principal piano maker in the newly important piano-making center of Boston during the 1820s when he produced most of the pianos bearing his name. His remarkable workmanship may account for so many surviving examples— about one hundred square pianos—many of which have been durable enough to escape restorative alterations.

Babcock received top honors in the 1824 and 1825 Franklin Institute exhibitions devoted to progress in the mechanical arts.[1] He is best remembered, however, for being the first to patent the one-piece iron frame.[2]

Six-leg models were on the wane by 1828, yet this instrument celebrates the piano as furniture, and, with its complex veneer scheme, reeded legs, inlays and moldings of brass, and apron drawers, it is elaborate by Boston standards.[3]

The piano is informally signed in four places on the interior by "W. Clark," who included the date July 8, 1828. Although Clark's name appears in at least seven other Babcock pianos, he does not appear as a piano maker in the city directories, and little is known about him. One of the other pianos with Clark's signature (serial number 158) bears a date four months later, hinting at a production rate of slightly better than one piano per week.[4]

The brass nameplate gives prominent credit to the Norfolk dealer Christopher Hall. While many of Babcock's pianos list a financial backer or dealer's name, Hall is the only one south of Philadelphia.

Detail of the action showing the patented lead-weighted hammer heads.

THE DRIVE FOR VOLUME AND TONE COLOR

The desire for more volume led to many piano innovations. A few months after this piano was made, John Mackay patented the method already employed here: the use of lead weights in the hammer heads to deliver more energy to the strings.[7] The Mackay family earned its wealth in the shipping industry and supported the piano makers Babcock and later Chickering as business partners. That the patent was filed in John Mackay's name rather than Babcock's is surprising, and it is not known what it means that this occurred during a period after Babcock no longer featured Mackay's name on piano nameplates.

Babcock was the only American maker to regularly employ the harmonic swell.[8] Patented in 1821 by William Frederick Collard in London, the mechanism provided players with more control over how quickly the sound stops after releasing the keys. The haze of sound that lingers after damping was appreciated in English and American circles, perhaps not unlike the echo of cathedral acoustics.[9]

The right end of the piano with the lid removed. The pedal-operated harmonic swell is the diagonal batten with layers of cloth on the underside to stop the sympathetic vibrations of the strings in the region between the bridge and hitch pins.

A close-up view of the iron bass strings with their wrapping of flat wire. The vertical pins are bridge pins.

BASS STRINGS CLOSE-UP

Babcock employed two innovations in his stringing of the bass notes. The first was his choice of iron rather than brass for the core wire. Iron helped to stabilize the tuning because all of the strings react to temperature changes at the same rate. Several subsequent American makers continued the practice, but it was rarely followed in England.

His second innovation was the use of flat iron wire to wrap the bass strings.[10] Nearly all pianos have wrapping on the bass strings to bulk the strings without adding stiffness. Babcock's innovative wrapping with flat wire meant more surface area for a good grip on the core, smoother sliding on the bridge and bridge pins during tuning, and less overall diameter for fitting into tuning pin holes and reducing chances of buzzing against adjacent notes.

CHANGES OVER TIME

This piano is very well preserved, with most of its original strings, leather, and cloth. The harmonic swell is original except for the batten itself, which is a reproduction.

37 | Square Piano

Joseph Newman, Baltimore 1831

A CONTINENTAL APPROACH

The tradition of piano making and playing that was centered in Vienna was radically different from the London-centered tradition that dominated America. Comparing this piano's layout in the top-view photo below to that of most British or American square pianos reveals a world of difference. The treble (shortest) strings and all tuning pins are close to the pianist. The soundboard is full width, and the bridge has plenty of room. The problems of soundboard and bridge spacing with which English makers struggled

whenever they extended the compass were solved here with generous space around the bridge.

Newman's Viennese design, however, had a structural weakness. The plank with the tuning pins could not be braced against the pull of the strings and could sag toward the soundboard, especially since its width greatly tapers in the treble.

Baltimore was the country's second largest city when this piano was made there. With the city's considerable population of citizens of German heritage, it was profitable for Joseph Newman and at least two of his Baltimore competitors to work in this Viennese style.[1] That pianos in a continental European style could be so popular in any American city is remarkable considering the nation's continuing orientation toward British culture and because immigrant piano makers generally adapted to local taste.[2]

In its ornamentation and musical and mechanical design, the piano is as cosmopolitan as Baltimore itself. The neoclassical Greek lyre with gilded eagles reflects nationalist taste and sentiment in Federal America. The transfer prints decorating the nameboard are of London architecture, and the rich carving and metallic-powder stenciling of the lyre and corner pendants are traits of the finest Baltimore furniture.[3]

(left) The Viennese, or German, action operates on a geometry unlike typical English actions. A hinged escapement catches the beak of the hammer, which is hinged to the key lever, flipping it towards the string.

(below) A top-view photo.

PICTURE THIS

The piano includes print transfers created by an unusual technique. Newman adhered recently published engraved images facedown on a clear coating, possibly while the coating was in a tacky state. He then removed the paper, perhaps by wetting and abrading it, leaving the ink stuck to the surface. Another clear coating completed the process.

The architectural scenes were engraved by Thomas Barber, whose caption under each image is backwards as a consequence of the transfer process. Newman's label in the central panel would have been printed backwards so the transfer process would leave it readable.

A LOOK INSIDE

Newman's tuning pins (1) are a late example of unbored pins, in which the string doubles over itself and relies on friction with the pin to hold. The three lowest notes are single strung, so the fatter over-spun strings (2) do not buzz against one another. This is the only square piano in the Colonial Williamsburg collection that is strung like all modern pianos: trichord in the treble, bichord in the tenor, and unichord in the bass. The lever overdampers (3) are hinged to a rail (4) that pivots upward when the damper pedal is pressed. The end of the bassoon batten (5) retains only fragments of the aged yellow paper arching over it. The gilded and patterned moderator rail (6) has leather tabs that intervene between the hammers and strings when the pedal is depressed. The cover block (7) protects the linkage from the pedal to the moderator.

Detail of the interior viewed from the left (bass) end of the case.

A TASTE FOR PEDALS

The four pedals are another example of Continental influence rarely seen in English or American pianos. The first pedal (beginning on the left) is used to imitate a bassoon. Depressing it raises a paper arch that touches the lowest three octaves of strings creating a buzz. Pedal two has the ordinary task of lifting the dampers. Pedal three is used to actuate the moderator stop, which interjects tabs of leather between the hammers and the strings, greatly softening the tone.[4]

The fourth pedal provides the sounds of Janissary, or Turkish, music. Depressing it rings a bell and strikes a drum. A fad for all things Turkish found expression in many aspects of fashion in late eighteenth- and early nineteenth-century Europe, not the least in music and musical instruments. Several composers published Turkish marches and battle pieces that gained effect with occasional imitations of cannon fire. The gimmick was not universally respected by serious composers, and the English rarely used Janissary stops.[5]

The six-octave keyboard in its rounded keywell with central inscription, architectural engravings, burl veneers, and rosewood crossbanding.

38 | Harpsichord

Chickering & Sons
under the direction of
Arnold Dolmetsch
Boston 1907–1908

FROM THIS SEED

Knowing it could not rely on antique instruments for all of its musical programming, Colonial Williamsburg ordered its first new harpsichord in 1949. The maker of that instrument was America's best-known harpsichord maker at the time, John Challis, whose love of harpsichords ironically came with a strong mistrust of historical technology. With its mix of modern and ancient, that instrument fully embodied the philosophy of its maker and the mid-twentieth century.

Four years later, the Chickering-Dolmetsch harpsichord featured in this entry was given to the collection, and, although not as extreme as the Challis harpsichord

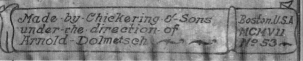

Inscription on the pin block dated 1907.

in its reliance on modern materials, the instrument was a hybrid of historical and modern design.

By 1971 when Colonial Williamsburg tradesman George Wilson copied a 1765 Kirckman harpsichord for the Foundation, the objective had shifted towards historical accuracy. Thereafter, each reproduction made for use at Colonial Williamsburg reflected the current state of historical research. Arnold Dolmetsch would be pleased to see the past coming into sharper focus.

Keyboard instruments and their music continued to blossom in America at an accelerating pace for the remainder of the nineteenth century. This final entry serves as a postscript to highlight the rediscovery of eighteenth-century keyboard music and the rebirth of its instruments after a century of obsolescence.

"This music of the olden time must in our day have an apostle," gushed a circa 1909 extended advertisement describing the work and mission of Arnold Dolmetsch.[1] The French-English musician, scholar, teacher, collector, and maker of historic instruments had recently moved to Boston to head a new department of early musical instruments at the piano manufacturing firm of Chickering & Sons. The instrument in this entry was the fifth out of thirteen double-manual harpsichords that Dolmetsch and his team made during his time at Chickering between 1905 and 1911. Most of the other instruments made by Chickering under Dolmetsch's supervision were clavichords, virginals, and spinets, totaling about eighty instruments.

Dolmetsch was one of a handful of musical pioneers who rediscovered a world of forgotten musical repertoire and the instruments that brought it to life. Their insight was remarkable for a time when the idea of re-creating historical types of music on old instruments was as unlikely as reenacting historical methods of surgery. The musical revivalists had to demonstrate that music of the past was even more worthy when expressed in the manner and on the instruments for which it was written. Dolmetsch's remarkable intelligence, charisma, musicianship, craft skills, and enthusiasm helped to launch a movement that has become a major part of the musical mainstream in our own time.[2]

Keyboard view with inscription dated 1908.

Detail of the pin block and action. Challis added the jack adjustment screws and dedicated damper jacks (second row from back) in 1953. A rank of peau de buffle (buffalo leather plectra) removed at that time is preserved in museum storage.

THE MUSICAL HIGH LIFE IN NEW YORK

This harpsichord, serial number 53 in the Dolmetsch-Chickering series, was made for Archer Gibson. In a letter to John D. Rockefeller Jr., Gibson described how he came to own the instrument. "[Chickering] financed a curious little gnome of a man, Arnold Dolmetsch, well under five feet tall, with a full beard, who lived and worked as though he were in the seventeenth century, making and playing the musical instruments of the period. I myself have taken part in performances with Dolmetsch at the Harpsichord. . . . I finally became the owner of a Master piece of Dolmetsch's efforts."[3]

A friend described Archer Gibson as "an organist who arranged concerts for all the old, wealthy families in New York—Fricks, Vanderbilt, Carnegie etc. . . . he always had many stories to tell about the young artists he booked in the wealthy homes—many who were just newly arrived from Europe: Heifetz, Kreisler, Elman, etc."[4]

Gibson also arranged house concerts for Alta Rockefeller Prentice, sister of Williamsburg benefactor John D. Rockefeller Jr. Gibson eventually left the harpsichord to Prentice, who gave it to Colonial Williamsburg in 1953.

(left) Top view of the harpsichord with the lid and jack rail removed.

(right) The underside of the harpsichord showing exposed framing and the metal trapwork for the pedal system. The internal framing and some construction details were probably influenced by Chickering engineers.

THE ART AND CRAFT

Arnold Dolmetsch was a product of the arts and crafts movement, one of the principal founders of which was his personal friend William Morris.[5] The movement sought to recapture decorative sensibilities that had been lost during nineteenth-century industrialization, and a revival of early music and instruments was an apt medium.

In his instruments, Dolmetsch combined decorative, musical, and mechanical details from many historical periods and regional styles. The registration (two eight-foot choirs, a four-foot choir, and a *peau de buffle* stop arranged for two manuals) followed an eighteenth-century French pattern. He took decorative details from French, German, and English traditions and from his own imagination. The profusion of stop-changing pedals was of his own era and characterized modern harpsichords until the 1970s.

CHANGES OVER TIME

John Challis was employed to prepare the harpsichord when it arrived in the Colonial Williamsburg collection. He replaced the leather plectra, replaced the *peau de buffle* stop with a rank of dampers, swapped register positions, and added adjustment screws to the jacks.[6]

Endnotes

Introduction (pages 2–7)

1. See Laurence Libin, "Progress, Adaptation, and the Evolution of Musical Instruments," *Journal of the American Musical Instrument Society (JAMIS)* 26 (2000): 187–213.
2. John Randolph Barden, "'Innocent and Necessary': Music and Dancing in the Life of Robert Carter of Nomony Hall, 1728–1804" (master's thesis, College of William and Mary, 1983), 24.
3. Robert Carter Letter Book, vol. 1, 1772–1774, 190–193, mss. div., Duke University Library, Durham, NC. Listed on a March 28, 1774, invoice for goods for Carter was "1 best plate for drawing steel harpsichord Wire." In his daybook for November 26, 1774, Carter noted that he "stretched a Wire," which "produced a tone, wch was in unison with D- in alt, of my Forte Piano—that Instrument being then in Concert Pitch" (vol. 13, 1773–1776, 55, mss. div., Duke University Library, Durham, NC). For more detail about that experiment, see Barden, "'Innocent and Necessary,'" 86.
4. Barden, "'Innocent and Necessary,'" 22, 87. Carter owned a copy of Dr. Robert Smith's *Harmonics, or the Philosophy of Musical Sounds* by 1771.
5. Ibid., 86–87. One of the makers most likely to have made Carter's piano was John Zumpe (see entry nos. 13 and 15). Zumpe's surviving 1766 piano at Württembergisches Landesmuseum in Stuttgart, Germany, is made with such an enharmonic keyboard.
6. William G. Perry to Allston Boyer, 4 November 1938, Colonial Williamsburg Foundation (CWF) archives.
7. Thomas Jefferson to Giovanni Fabbroni, 8 June 1778, in *The Papers of Thomas Jefferson Digital Edition*, ed. Barbara B. Oberg and J. Jefferson Looney (Charlottesville: University of Virginia Press, Rotunda, 2008), accessed Nov. 16, 2012, http://rotunda.upress.virginia.edu/founders /TSJN-01-02-02-0066. Interestingly, these musical concerns occupied Jefferson just as George Washington's army was emerging from its horrific winter at Valley Forge.
8. For more about the development of this archive, see John Ingram, "From Handel's *Acis and Galatea* to *American Harmony*: Going to the Source for the Music of Eighteenth-Century Williamsburg," *Colonial Williamsburg* 22, no. 1 (Spring 2000): 24–29.

Keyboard Musical Instruments in British and Anglo-American Society (pages 8–14)

1. John Locke, *Some Thoughts Concerning Education*, 7th ed. (London, 1712), 302.
2. See Richard Leppert, *Music and Image: Domesticity, Ideology and Socio-Cultural Formation in Eighteenth-Century England* (Cambridge: Cambridge University Press, 1988), especially chap. 2.
3. *Newbery's Familiar Letter Writer; Containing a Variety of Useful Letters, Calculated for the Most Common Occurrences, and Adapted to the Capacities of Young People, from an Early Age to the Time of Their Engaging in the Most Material Concerns of Life* (London, 1788), 79.
4. Arthur Loesser, *Men, Women and Pianos: A Social History* (New York: Simon and Schuster, 1954), 214–215.
5. Jenny Nex, "Longman & Broderip," in *The Music Trade in Georgian England*, ed. Michael Kassler (Burlington, VT: Ashgate, 2011), 26.
6. See Michael Cole, "Transition from Harpsichord to Pianoforte: The Important Role of Women," in *Geschichte und Bauweise des Tafelklaviers* (Michaelsteiner conference proceedings, vol. 68), ed. Boje E. Hans Schmuhl (Augsburg, GER: Wißner-Verlag, 2006), 54.
7. See Leppert, *Music and Image*, 167, about the basis for the guitar's feminine associations: "Given the history of its use it was an ideal emblem for the representation of the perfect woman, acquiescent and deferential." Chief among the socially acceptable instruments for men and boys were bowed strings and woodwinds.
8. Ibid., chaps. 3, 7, and 8.
9. See Cole, "Transition from Harpsichord to Pianoforte," 51, 56.
10. The poem is entitled "On Miss Anne Geddy Singing, and Playing on the Spinet," Purdie and Dixon's *Virginia Gazette* (Williamsburg), December 22, 1768.
11. See Leppert, *Music and Image*, 61–63.
12. Custis to Elizabeth Bordley Gibson, 4 July 1817, in *George Washington's Beautiful Nelly: The Letters of Eleanor Parke Custis Lewis to Elizabeth Bordley Gibson, 1794–1851*, ed. Patricia Brady (Columbia: University of South Carolina Press, 1991), 82.
13. For transcriptions of Hopkinson's papers, see appendix 14 of Raymond Russell, *The Harpsichord and Clavichord: An Introductory Study*, 2nd ed. (New York: W. W. Norton, 1973).
14. Burney to Thomas Jefferson, 20 January 1787, in *Papers of Thomas Jefferson Digital Edition*, accessed Nov. 16, 2012, http://rotunda.upress.virginia.edu/founders /TSJN-01-11-02-0061.
15. Robert Carter Day Book, November 26, 1774, vol. 13, 1773–1776, 55, mss. div., Duke University Library, Durham, NC.
16. Robert Carter owned the 1759 second edition of Robert Smith's treatise *Harmonics, or the Philosophy of Musical Sounds* (Barden "Innocent and Necessary,'" 22). See Barden also for a summary of Pelham's specifications for Carter's organ (15–20).
17. *The Diary of Colonel Landon Carter of Sabine Hall, 1752–1778*, ed. Jack P. Greene, vol. 2 (Charlottesville: University Press of Virginia for Virginia Historical Society, 1965), 618.
18. See Lisa E. Fischer, "Douglass-Hallam Theater: Excavation of an Eighteenth-Century Playhouse," CWF, accessed Nov. 19, 2012, http://research.history.org/Archaeo logical_Research/Research_Articles/ThemeVirginia /Hallam.cfm.
19. O. G. Sonneck, *Early Concert-Life in America (1731–1800)* (Leipzig: Breitkopf & Härtel, 1907), 265.
20. John W. Molnar, "A Collection of Music in Colonial Virginia: The Ogle Inventory," *Musical Quarterly* 49, no. 2 (April 1963): 150–162.
21. *The Vestry Book of the Upper Parish, Nansemond County, Virginia, 1743–1793*, ed. Wilmer L. Hall (Richmond: Library Board of Virginia, 1949), 201.
22. For a full summary of Pelham's life, see *The Peter Pelham Manuscript of 1744: An Early American Keyboard Tutor*, ed. H. Joseph Butler (Colfax, NC: Wayne Leupold Editions, 2005).
23. See Thomas Jefferson to Francis Hopkinson, 23 December 1786, in *Papers of Thomas Jefferson Digital Edition*, accessed Nov. 19, 2012, http://rotunda.upress.virginia.edu /founders/TSJN-01-10-02-0479.
24. John W. Molnar, "Art Music in Colonial Virginia," in *Art and Music in the South: Institute of Southern Culture Lectures at Longwood College, 1960*, ed. Francis B. Simkins (Farmville, VA: Longwood College, 1961), 69.
25. Otto Erich Deutsch, *Handel: A Documentary Biography* (London: Adam and Charles Black, 1955), 752–753.
26. See "Schedule of Losses Sustained by the Earl of

Dunmore, His Majesty's Late Governor of the Colony of Virginia, 25 February 1784," Public Record Office, London, Audit Office 13, bundle 28, no. 550, as transcribed in Graham Hood, *The Governor's Palace in Williamsburg: A Cultural Study* (Williamsburg, VA: Colonial Williamsburg Foundation, 1991), appendix 3. The losses sustained by the governor when he fled Williamsburg ahead of the Revolution included these three keyboard instruments plus two other organs. One of the organs was a serinette—a small crank-operated organ for teaching birds to sing—and a third was probably a barrel organ.

27. Jefferson to Hopkinson, 23 December 1786. The instrument was a separate pedal piano for use under a conventional square piano.

28. Jefferson to Thomas Adams, 20 February 1771, in *Papers of Thomas Jefferson Digital Edition*, accessed Nov. 19, 2012, http://rotunda.upress.virginia.edu/founders/TSJN-01-01-02-0040; Derek Adlam, "Clavichords in Georgian England: Handel, Mary Delany and the Granville Family," in *De Clavicordio VIII: The Clavichord on the Iberian Peninsula; Proceedings of the VIII International Clavichord Symposium, Magnano, 5–8 September 2007 = Atti dell'VIII Congresso Internazionale sul clavicordo*, ed. Bernard Brauchli, Alberto Galazzo, and Judith Wardmann (Magnano, Italy: International Centre for Clavichord Studies, 2008); Jefferson to Adams, 1 June 1771, in *Papers of Thomas Jefferson Digital Edition*, accessed Nov. 19, 2012, http://rotunda.upress.virginia.edu/founders/TSJN-01-01-02-0050; *Oxford English Dictionary*, 2nd ed., s.v. "forte-piano," updated September 2012, http://www.oed.com/view/Entry/73647.

29. Helen Cripe, *Thomas Jefferson and Music*, rev. ed. (Charlottesville, VA: Thomas Jefferson Foundation, 2009), 21, 46, 54; Barden, "'Innocent and Necessary,'" 62; Hopkinson to Bremner, 28 November 1783, and Hopkinson to Jefferson, 31 March 1784, in *Papers of Thomas Jefferson Digital Edition*, accessed Nov. 19, 2012, http://rotunda.upress.virginia.edu/founders/TSJN-01-06-02-0285 and http://rotunda.upress.virginia.edu/founders/TSJN-01-07-02-0056.

30. Cripe, *Thomas Jefferson and Music*, 47.

31. Kirckman objected to the celestina stop on account of its being unreliable and its tendency to leave deposits of resin on the strings, destroying the tone. Correspondence about the order and the added celestina stop involving Jefferson's friend John Paradise, who was then living in London (and later in Williamsburg), and Charles Burney, who acted as liaison with Kirckman, is published as appendix 15 in Russell, *Harpsichord and Clavichord*.

32. Jefferson to Burney, 10 July 1786, and Burney to Jefferson, 20 January 1787, in *Papers of Thomas Jefferson Digital Edition*, accessed Nov. 19, 2012, http://rotunda.upress.virginia.edu/founders/TSJN-01-10-02-0048 and http://rotunda.upress.virginia.edu/founders/TSJN-01-11-02-0061; Cripe, *Thomas Jefferson and Music*, 58, 61–62; *Mercury and New-England Palladium* (Boston), June 18, 1802.

33. Cripe, *Thomas Jefferson and Music*, 63–66.

34. Ibid., 43; *Philip Vickers Fithian: Journal and Letters, 1767–1774: Student at Princeton College 1770–72, Tutor at Nomini Hall in Virginia 1773–74*, ed. John Rogers Williams (Princeton, NJ: University Library, 1900), 43; Robert Carter Letter Book, vol. 1, 1772–1774, 190–193.

35. *Virginia Argus* (Richmond), December 1, 1804. I thank Carol Aiken for bringing this music master and miniaturist to my attention and for supplying details of their travels from her database.

36. *Virginia Gazette, &c. Extraordinary* (Richmond), October 17, 1792. The extended advertisement is quoted in full in *Music in Colonial Massachusetts, 1630–1820*. Vol. 2, *Music in Homes and in Churches*, ed. Barbara Lambert (Boston: Colonial Society of Massachusetts, 1985), 1092–1093.

37. An invoice written by Juhan to Williamsburg resident William Tazewell reads, "To one month's attendance ye

16th March." It is signed "James Juhan / Williamsburg le 2nd April 1787." The invoice is pictured on Ancestry.com, accessed Sept. 24, 2012.

38. See Michael D. Friesen, "Christian and John Veltenair, Musical Instrument Makers," *Early Keyboard Journal* (forthcoming).

39. Purdie & Dixon's *Virginia Gazette* (Williamsburg), January 8, 1767, and October 10, 1771.

40. This exceptionally rare and highly important organized upright grand piano came into the Colonial Williamsburg collection as this book went to press. It will be fully described in a future publication.

41. The spinets include examples by Johannes Gottlob Clemm (1739), John Harris (1769 and 1771), and Samuel Blythe (1789). The harpsichord is by Charles Trute with his partner Wiedberg (1794).

42. Statistics of surviving instruments are from "Clinkscale Online: A Comprehensive Database of Early Pianos, 1700–1860," accessed Nov. 19, 2012, www.EarlyPianos.org.

43. John-Paul Williams, *The Piano* (New York: Billboard Books, 2002), 30.

1. Spinet, Keene, 1700 (pages 16–17)

1. The most thorough history of the early English spinet is Peter Geoffrey Mole's "The English Spinet with Particular Reference to the Schools of Keene and Hitchcock" (PhD diss., University of Edinburgh, 2009), available online at http://hdl.handle.net/1842/3274, accessed Nov. 19, 2012.

2. Spinet, Hitchcock, ca. 1715 (pages 18–19)

1. Ronald L. Hurst, "Peter Scott, Cabinetmaker of Williamsburg: A Reappraisal," in *American Furniture 2006*, ed. Luke Beckerdite (Milwaukee, WI: Chipstone Foundation, 2006), 48–49.

2. Anne McClenny, "An 18th Century Spinet," *Journal of the Roanoke Historical Society* 6, no. 2 (Winter 1970): 42–44.

3. For a full study of the Hitchcocks and their instruments, see Mole, "English Spinet."

4. The work may have been part of the revival of all things colonial following the nation's centennial in 1876. The repairs are consistent with the instrument being set up as a prop representing the eighteenth century. None of the repairs would have served musical purposes.

3. Spinet, Aston, 1726 (pages 20–21)

1. See Donald H. Boalch, *Makers of the Harpsichord and Clavichord, 1440–1840*, 3rd ed., ed. Charles Mould (Oxford: Clarendon Press, 1995), 224–225.

4. Harpsichord, Cusseneers, 1726 (pages 22–23)

1. See Donald H. Boalch, *Makers of the Harpsichord and Clavichord 1440–1840*, 2nd ed. (Oxford: Clarendon Press, 1974), 22.

2. Donald H. Boalch proposed the theory that an otherwise unknown member of the Couchet family of Antwerp made the harpsichord (*Makers of the Harpsichord and Clavichord 1440 to 1840* [London: George Ronald, 1956], 19). Challis's choice not to repeat the Cusseneers inscription on the new jack rail he made for the instrument reflects his agreement with this attribution.

3. The French maker Cuisinier is listed in all three editions of Boalch, *Makers of the Harpsichord and Clavichord*, 21, 31, and 41, and is also mentioned in Russell, *Harpsichord and Clavichord*, 57.

4. "Dusselensis" appears to be an improvised Latinization. Besides Düsseldorf, it could refer to Düssel, a small town now incorporated into the city of Wülfrath. I thank Jan Großbach for this theory. E-mail to author, April 21, 2009.

5. Thomas Wolf (William Dowd's associate), personal communication with author, December 4, 1997. Challis had assigned Dowd the restoration project in 1949 near the end of Dowd's apprenticeship.

6. The 1968 Dowd harpsichord (accession number 2006-34, R) is a two-manual French model but with English-style veneer.

7. The original pin block, the first replacement pin block bearing the original pin block veneer, and the ca. early twentieth-century jack rail bearing the Cusseneer inscription had gotten disassociated with the harpsichord by 1976. Recognizing their potential importance, Tom and Barbara Wolf purchased the parts in that year and donated them to the Foundation, greatly adding to the historical record of this instrument.

8. During his examination of this instrument in 2009, John Koster noted several period harpsichords from central Europe with 1 x 8-foot, 1 x 4-foot, and three sets of jacks, two of which pluck the 8-foot choir at two distances from the nut. Switching between the two 8-foot ranks of jacks would result in a change of tone.

5. Spinet, Woolfinden, 1725–1740 (page 24–25)

1. Philip James, *Early Keyboard Instruments: From Their Beginnings to the Year 1820* (London: Holland Press, 1967; first published 1930), 79.

2. Hugh Gough to Mrs. A. Willard Duncan, 30 April 1962, CWF archives.

6. Chamber Organ, Unknown, ca. 1740 (pages 26–28)

1. Most of the technical data and analysis in this chapter is based on Dominic Gwynn's 1999 report "The Kimberley Hall Organ in the Wren Chapel of the College of William and Mary at Colonial Williamsburg" in the CWF object file, 1954-432.

2. The reference is in the accounts of Williamsburg cabinetmaker John Hockaday, who notes "Repairs to College organ" on July 19, 1806. As transcribed in Linda A. Hildreth, "The Fate of the Cabinetmaking Trade in Williamsburg, Virginia in the Post-Revolutionary Period" (master's thesis, College of William and Mary, 1988), appendix L, 139.

3. For more about the revolving life cycle of historic instruments illustrated with the Wren Chapel organ, see John R. Watson, *Artifacts in Use: The Paradox of Restoration and the Conservation of Organs* (Richmond, VA: OHS Press in association with the Colonial Williamsburg Foundation, 2010).

4. Technical description and analysis of the organ's alterations are detailed in Gwynn, "Kimberley Hall Organ."

5. Records of the Wodehouse family of Kimberley, Norfolk Record Office, Norfolk, England. Archive set KIM 8 Kimberley Hall includes account books and letters relating to work done on Kimberley Hall from 1835–1838. In "A Declaration of the Works Done at Kimberley Hall with a General Statement of the Accounts, by James Watson, March, 1838," there is an entry for "a recess made for the organ in the drawing room." I thank David Blanchfield for conducting this archival research in England.

6. CWF object file, 1954-432.

7. While in the conference center, the organ was photographed for Michael Wilson, *The English Chamber Organ: History and Development, 1650–1850* (Columbia: University of South Carolina Press, 1968), plate 12.

8. Brown's full report is in the CWF object file, 1954-432.

9. This conservation project was featured in Watson, *Artifacts in Use*, and John R. Watson, "Conservation of Six Historic Organs at Colonial Williamsburg," *The Tracker: Journal of the Organ Historical Society* 46, no. 3 (July 2002): 22–34.

10. Note, for example, the 1738 publication of Handel's first six concertos, op. 4 published by John Walsh. With Handel's consent, the set was titled "Six Concertos for the Harpsichord or Organ Compos'd by Mr. Handel."

7. Spinet, Zopfe, ca. 1745–1750 (page 29)

1. Joanna Tyler's life and family are detailed in her obituary, first published in the *Richmond (VA) Enquirer,* February 13, 1845, and subsequently reprinted in the *William and Mary College Quarterly Historical Magazine* 12 (1903–1904): 183–185; reprinted by Kraus, New York, in 1966.

2. See Powhatan Bouldin, *The Old Trunk, or Sketches of Colonial Days* (Richmond, VA: Andrews, Baptist & Clemmitt, 1888), 39.

3. Cripe, *Thomas Jefferson and Music,* 18.

4. See William Dale, *Tschudi: The Harpsichord Maker* (London: Constable, 1913), 31, 52, and James, *Early Keyboard Instruments,* 41n5, 79.

5. Zopfe's eccentric design is surprising considering he was not outside of the circle of instrument makers. He had a family relationship with Burkat Shudi, and organ builder John Snetzler served as a witness for Zopfe's will. All three were Swiss expatriates.

8. Harpsichord 2M, Kirckman, 1758 (pages 30–31)

1. Only one surviving English harpsichord predates 1700, and only five more are from the first quarter of the eighteenth century. See Darryl Martin, "The Native Tradition in Transition: English Harpsichords circa 1680–1725," in *The Historical Harpsichord*, vol. 5, *Aspects of Harpsichord Making in the British Isles,* ed. John Koster (Hillsdale, NY: Pendragon, 2009), 1.

2. Charles Burney, *The Present State of Music in France and Italy: or, The Journal of a Tour through Those Countries, Undertaken to Collect Materials for a General History of Music* (London, 1771), 288.

3. Cripe, *Thomas Jefferson and Music,* 35.

4. See Russell, *Harpsichord and Clavichord,* 177–182.

5. For more about the difference in musical resources between English and Continental harpsichords, see Mimi S. Waitzman, *Early Keyboard Instruments* (London: National Trust, 2003), 24–27, and John Barnes, "Two Rival Harpsichord Specifications," *Galpin Society Journal* 19 (April 1966): 49–56.

9. Harpsichord 2M, Kirckman, 1762 (pages 32–33)

1. Abraham Rees, *The Cyclopaedia; or, Universal Dictionary of Arts, Sciences, and Literature,* vol. 20 (London, 1819), s.v. "Kirckman, Jacob."

2. Abraham Rees, *The Cyclopaedia; or, Universal Dictionary of Arts, Sciences, and Literature,* vol. 17, 1st American ed. (Philadelphia: Samuel F. Bradford and Murray, Fairman and Co., [1805?–1822?]), s.v. "guitarra."

3. See Boalch, *Makers of the Harpsichord and Clavichord* (1995), 422–460.

10. Harpsichord 1M, Kirckman, 1762 (page 34)

1. This is why, when Thomas Jefferson asked via his agent John Paradise that Kirckman make his harpsichord of mahogany, "solid not vineered," Kirckman had to refuse. Jefferson to John Paradise, 25 May 1786, in *Papers of Thomas Jefferson Digital Edition,* accessed Nov. 19, 2012, http://rotunda.upress.virginia.edu/founders/TSJN-01-09-02-0473; and see Russell, *Harpsichord and Clavichord,* 179.

2. Reflecting the leading edge of furniture fashions of the time, Thomas Chippendale's *The Gentleman and Cabinet-Maker's Director* illustrates Chinese-inspired square-sectioned Marlborough legs on tables and chairs. See, for example, plates 28 and 56. 3rd ed. (London, 1762; repr. New York: Dover, 1966).

11. Spinet, Harris, 1764 (page 35)

1. The anachronisms of English harpsichord stands were first observed by R. S. Clouston, "Keyboard Instruments, and Their Relation to Furniture," *Burlington Magazine for Connoisseurs* 8, no. 32 (November 1905): 110–119.

2. Sheridan Germann, "Harpsichord Decoration," in *The Historical Harpsichord,* vol. 4, ed. Howard Schott (Hillsdale, NY: Pendragon, 2002), 86. There is some evidence that this stand may not be original; however, the 1765 William Harris spinet at the St. Louis Museum of Art has an identical stand that is also old.

3. For more about the 1750 octave spinet signed by Fricker,

see Howard Schott, *Catalogue of Musical Instruments,* vol. 1, *Keyboard Instruments,* 2nd ed. (London: Victoria and Albert Museum, 1985). For a discussion about piano maker William Frecker and the distinction with Fricker, see Marie Kent, "William Frecker: Piano Maker *c*1761–*c*1834," *Galpin Society Journal* 65 (March 2012): 5–22.

4. Goss recorded his restoration on a paper label on the back of the name batten in 1898.

12. Bureau Organ, Adcock and Pether, ca. 1760

(pages 36–38)

1. "Schedule of Losses Sustained by the Earl of Dunmore," as transcribed in Hood, *Governor's Palace in Williamsburg,* appendix 3.

2. According to an invoice for their purchase in 1773, Lord Dunmore ordered from London "A Chamber Organ" and "a very Small Organ for teaching Birds." James Minzies to John Norton, 12 June 1773, in *John Norton and Sons: Merchants of London and Virginia: Being the Papers from Their Counting House for the Years 1750 to 1795,* ed. Frances Norton Mason (Richmond, VA: Dietz, 1937), 330.

3. "*Just imported from* LONDON, A VERY neat HAND ORGAN, in a mohogany case, with a gilt front, which plays sixteen tunes, on two barrels; it has four stops, and every thing is in the best order. The first cost was 16 £ sterling, and the Lady being dead it came in for, any person inclining to purchase it may have it on very reasonable terms. Inquire at the Post Office, *Williamsburg.*" Purdie and Dixon's *Virginia Gazette* (Williamsburg), September 17, 1767.

4. Cripe, *Thomas Jefferson and Music,* 45. Jefferson's desire for a chamber organ for Monticello went unfulfilled.

5. See Catherine Frew and Arnold Myers, "Sir Samuel Hellier's 'Musicall Instruments,'" *Galpin Society Journal* 66 (June 2003): 6–26, and M. J. Holman, "Abraham Adcock: Musician and Organ Builder," revised April 2011, www.AbrahamAdcock.com.

6. Mark Noble and James Granger, *A Biographical History of England, from the Revolution to the End of George I's Reign; Being a Continuation of the Rev. J. Granger's Work: Consisting of Characters Disposed in Different Classes, and Adapted to a Methodical Catalogue of Engraved British Heads; Interspersed with a Variety of Anecdotes, and Memoirs of a Great Number of Persons, Not to Be Found in Any Other Biographical Work,* vol. 2 (London, 1806), 364.

7. See Christopher Kent, "A Further Note on Abraham Adcock," *Preserve Harmony* (newsletter of the Worshipful Company of Musicians), issue 33 (Autumn 2006): 2–3.

8. Ibid., 2. The other bureau organ was sold at Sotheby's (July 4, 1983, lot no. 161) and is illustrated in the auction catalog.

9. The 1775 William Pether harpsichord is owned by the author. The Longman & Broderip organized square piano is in the collection of the Metropolitan Museum of Art, accession no. 89.4.2803.

13. Square Piano, Zumpe, 1766 (pages 40–43)

1. The other 1766 Zumpe pianos are located at Emmanuel College, University of Cambridge, England; the National Music Centre in Calgary, Alberta, Canada; and Württembergisches Landesmuseum in Stuttgart, Germany.

2. For a full account of the advent of the square piano in London, see Michael Cole, *The Pianoforte in the Classical Era* (Oxford: Clarendon, 1998), 47–48.

14. Harpsichord, Kirshaw, 1769 (pages 44–45)

1. The only other surviving English harpsichords made outside of London and listed by Boalch are by Thomas Haxby of York and dated 1775 and 1777. Boalch also lists a second Kirshaw harpsichord (undated), but its location and survival are unknown. *Makers of the Harpsichord and Clavichord* (1995), 381–382, 460. One 1794 American-made harpsichord by the partnership of Trute and Wiedberg of Philadelphia also survives.

2. The conclusion that the stand is original is based on characteristic witness marks and wear on the understand of the harpsichord and on the stand itself, which shows normal signs of age and a purpose-built design with legs and apron correctly shaped for the harpsichord's outline and not adapted from a table. A Kirshaw spinet at Fairfax House in York, England, has a stand in the identical style, indicating the maker's preference for this design.

3. See Germann, "Harpsichord Decoration," 85.

4. Since Manchester city directories listed many more citizens spelling their name *Kershaw* than *Kirshaw,* it seems possible Kirshaw chose to spell his name with an *i* to further encourage confusion.

5. See James, *Early Keyboard Instruments,* 43n2. For more about Falkener, see Boalch, *Makers of the Harpsichord and Clavichord* (1995), 57, and Edward L. Kottick, *A History of the Harpsichord* (Bloomington, IN: Indiana University Press, 2003), 366.

6. See, for example, *The Harpsichord and Clavichord: An Encyclopedia,* ed. Igor Kipnis (New York: Routledge, 2007), s.v. "harp stop."

15. Square Piano, Zumpe and Buntebart, 1770
(pages 46–48)

Illustrated Boston example by Zumpe and Buntebart, London, 1770; mahogany; length 1266, width 471, case height 164, height with stand 759. Museum of Fine Arts, Boston; Leslie Lindsey Mason Collection, 17.1798.

1. Restoration of this piano to any coherent past state would be too intrusive and conjectural. Evidence of all past states is of interest and is best preserved with only stabilization rather than restorative conservation.

16. Chamber Organ, W. H., 1782 (page 49)

1. See Michael I. Wilson, *The Chamber Organ in Britain, 1600–1830* (Aldershot, ENG: Ashgate, 2001), 44–47. The pattern books by Thomas Chippendale (*The Gentleman and Cabinet-Maker's Director,* London, 1762), William Ince and John Mahew (*The Universal System of Household Furniture,* 1759–1763), and Thomas Malton (*A Compleat Treatise on Perspective, in Theory and Practice . . . ,* London, 1775) included designs for organ cases, but their designs for bookcases were equally adaptable.

2. According to the 1990 Taylor & Boody restoration report (CWF object file, 1980-187), the wind-chest originally supported only two ranks of pipes and a narrower compass, possibly C, D, E–c3. A grid carved from solid wood constitutes a very early type of wind-chest construction that held on in England longer than on the Continent. Evidence on the possibly original pallets suggests the wind-chest was originally part of a tracker rather than sticker action. This organ is #5 on the Taylor & Boody opus list.

17. Square Piano, Beck, 1785 (pages 50–51)

1. The series was the Concert Spirituel. See Howard Schott, "From Harpsichord to Pianoforte: A Chronology and Commentary," *Early Music* 13, no. 1 (February 1985): 33.

2. Michael Cole, *Broadwood Square Pianos: Their Historical Context, and Technical Development* (Cheltenham, ENG: Tatchley Books, 2005), 22.

3. In a biographical summary in Grove Music Online (accessed Nov. 19, 2012), Margaret Cranmer reports of Frederick Beck, "b ?Württemberg, bap. 30 May 1738," but Cole says there is no evidence of Beck's German origins (*Pianoforte in the Classical Era,* 80). On the similarity of Beck's pianos to those of Zumpe, Cole goes so far as to call Beck a "maker of exact Zumpe replicas" (70).

4. Cole analyzed several types of evidence and concluded that "about 80 per cent of players must have been female." "Transition from Harpsichord to Pianoforte," 51.

5. See Panagiotis Poulopoulos, "A Comparison of Two Surviving Guittars by Zumpe and New Details Concerning the Involvement of Square Piano Makers in the Guittar Trade," *Galpin Society Journal* 64 (March 2011): 49–59.

6. Albert G. Hess, "The Transition from Harpsichord to Piano," *Galpin Society Journal* 6 (July 1953): 88–90.

7. The Taskin account and Goermans's inventory are transcribed in Frank Hubbard, *Three Centuries of Harpsichord Making* (Cambridge, MA: Harvard University Press, 1967), 295, 310. The estimate that the debt owed Beck would cover three or four pianos is by Cole, *Pianoforte in the Classical Era*, 81.

8. According to "Clinkscale Online," two early nineteenth-century pianos made in Paris bear the name "Beck." The examples are in the collections of the Musée des Beaux-Arts in Tours, France, and the Musée de la Musique in Paris. According to Adélaïde de Place, a maker named Beck was in Paris in 1819–1822 (*Le Piano-forte à Paris entre 1760 et 1822* [Paris: Aux Amateurs de Livres, 1986], 180). It has not been verified whether these makers were the same maker or whether the maker(s) was a relation of the London Frederick Beck.

18. Grand Piano, Longman & Broderip, 1790 (pages 52–53)

1. For more about Culliford, see Jenny Nex, "Culliford and Company: Keyboard Instrument Makers in Georgian London," *Early Keyboard Journal* 22 (2004): 7–48.

2. See George S. Bozarth and Margaret Debenham, "Piano Wars: The Legal Machinations of London Pianoforte Makers, 1795–1806," *Royal Musical Association Research Chronicle* 42 (2009): 50–51. The 1786 contract between Culliford & Co. and Longman & Broderip specified Culliford would provide at least £5,000 worth of instruments each year.

3. Lance Whitehead and Jenny Nex, "Keyboard Instrument Building in London and the Sun Insurance Records, 1775–87," *Early Music* 30, no. 1 (February 2002): 11.

4. The historical record about whether Backers had help in developing the English grand action was corrupted for many years by an unsubstantiated claim by a Broadwood descendant that the invention grew from a collaboration among Backers, Robert Stodart, and John Broadwood. Backers's sole responsibility for the development of the English grand action has been clarified by Cole, *Pianoforte in the Classical Era*, 127.

19. Square Piano, Longman & Broderip, 1788–1789 (page 54)

1. Cole, *Pianoforte in the Classical Era*, 103.

2. *Caledonian Mercury* (Edinburgh), December 6, 1794. I thank Graham Gadd for drawing this advertisement to my attention.

3. Cole, *Pianoforte in the Classical Era*, 78, 108.

4. Peter Ward Jones, Peter Williams, and Charles Mould, "Longman & Broderip," Grove Music Online, accessed Nov. 19, 2012. For an analysis of the Longman & Broderip music offerings of 1789, see Loesser, *Men, Women and Pianos*, 229–231.

20. Square Piano, Garcka, ca. 1792 (page 55)

1. The bankruptcy and the transfer of Garcka's business to Bates and Co. are documented in *The World* (London), January 30, 1793.

2. *Patents for Inventions. Abridgments of Specifications Related to Music and Musical Instruments. A.D. 1694–1866*, 2nd ed. (London, 1871; facsimile, London: Tony Bingham, 1984), 26. Garcka's patent is no. 1849, dated February 4, 1792.

3. This double soundboard design is nearly identical to one in a very early George Astor square piano now at the Schenectady County Historical Society. Many other similarities between the two instruments raise the possibility that both were made either by Garcka or by Astor.

4. *Patents for Inventions*, 13. Broadwood's patent is no. 1379, dated July 17, 1783. As a rule, successful experiments were repeated and adopted and copied by competitors. This is

the only known Garcka piano with a double soundboard. The only known example of Broadwood's patented double soundboard is his no. 200 in the Colt Clavier Collection. As described in the patent, its design is very different, having an upper soundboard of conventional size and not extending to the left end of the case. Broadwood's proposed lower soundboard was to be about an inch above the bottom with a sound post (similar to that of a violin) to transfer the vibrations from the main soundboard. I thank David Hackett for information about Broadwood no. 200 (e-mail to author, June 21, 2012).

5. A. J. Hipkins reported on a now-lost letter from John Broadwood to Charleston correspondent Thomas Bradford in which Broadwood said his firm started extending the keyboard up to c4 in 1791. This often-quoted detail was reported by David Wainwright, *Broadwood by Appointment: A History* (London: Quiller Press, 1982), 75.

6. Southwell's 1794 patent with its scheme for adding additional keys is discussed in entry nos. 23, 27, and 28.

7. Frank Kidson, William C. Smith, and Peter Ward Jones, "Bland, John," Grove Music Online, accessed Nov. 19, 2012.

21. Square Piano, Ball, ca. 1791 (page 56)

1. According to Cole, Ball's German origins are specified on his application for British citizenship. *Pianoforte in the Classical Era*, 80.

2. Patent no. 1784, November 16, 1790.

22. Grand Piano, Ball, ca. 1794–1805 (page 57)

1. The connection to the Coles family is based on an oral report from the piano's former owner who purchased the instrument at a 1963 estate sale at Woodville. The connection may be tenuous since the house changed hands in and out of the Coles family several times. The coincidence of the piano's date with the construction of Woodville and of Walter Coles's marriage, however, favors a Coles association. Details of Walter Coles and his connection to Jefferson, Madison, and Monroe come from his 1854 obituary. See William B. Coles, *The Coles Family of Virginia* (New York: 1931; repr., Baltimore, MD: Gateway Press, 1989), 86–88.

2. The five-and-a-half-octave compass had just become standard for Broadwood in 1793, according to John Broadwood's letter to Thomas Bradford, a Charleston, SC, customer. See Wainwright, *Broadwood by Appointment*, 75.

3. According to the patent specification by Samuel Miller, his "Sawing Machine," patent no. 1152, dated 1777, was "An Intirely new Machine for the more Expeditiously Sawing of all Kinds of Wood, Stone, and Ivory." As quoted in Norman Ball, "Circular Saws and the History of Technology," *Bulletin of the Association for Preservation Technology* 7, no. 3 (1975): 87.

23. Square Piano, Watson, ca. 1797 (pages 58–59)

1. For more about the Watsons and the early piano industry in Edinburgh, see John Leonard Cranmer, "Concert Life and the Music Trade in Edinburgh c. 1780–c. 1830" (PhD diss., University of Edinburgh, 1991).

24. Square Piano, Dettmer, mid-1790s (page 60)

1. The piano in this entry is formally signed "Dettmar." Being earlier than any of the pianos signed with the spelling "Dettmer" may suggest this piano is by a George Dettmar distinct from the George Dettmer of entry no. 31. The unusual lack of molded key fronts on both instruments, however, offers physical evidence for the author's conclusion that the two inscriptions have variant spellings of the same maker's name.

2. If the string lengths are plotted on a graph that converts each string to its just-scale c2 equivalent, most keyboard instruments show a horizontal line with the foreshortening represented by a dip on the bass end. The graph for

this piano is one continuous downward arch from treble to bass.

25. Square Piano, Albrecht, 1800–1805 (page 62)

1. Michael Cole suggests that Charles Albrecht could have been exposed to Broadwood's designs via Alexander Reinagle who imported multiple pianos into Philadelphia from Broadwood (*Broadwood Square Pianos*, 59).
2. That instrument is in the Historical Musical Instrument Collection of the Vassar College Department of Music.
3. Analysis based on the "Clinkscale Online" database of early pianos.
4. The two other Albrecht pianos bearing Baker's signature are in the Smithsonian Institution collection (Smithsonian no. 288,399 and no. 315,681). The "Clinkscale Online" database of early pianos lists no surviving instruments by Baker but points out his later association with Thomas Loud Evenden.
5. For a summary of these beginnings in Pennsylvania, see Laurence Libin, "Pennsylvania, Cradle of American Piano Making," in *The Square Piano in Rural Pennsylvania, 1760–1830,* ed. Paul Larson and Carol Traupman-Carr (Bethlehem, PA: Payne Gallery of Moravian College, 2001), 3.

26. Square Piano, Huber, 1805–1809 (page 63)

1. For a thorough study of John Huber and the other three examples of his piano making, see Laurence Libin, "John Huber's Pianos in Context," *JAMIS* 19 (1993): 5–37, and Libin, "John Huber Revisited," *JAMIS* 20 (1994): 73–83.
2. See Libin, "Pennsylvania, Cradle of American Piano Making," 2–11.

27. Square Piano, Kirckman, 1804 (pages 64–65)

1. Cole suggests that Kirckman subcontracted the pianos they sold in the 1770s from others, including Christopher Ganer and Adam Beyer. *Broadwood Square Pianos*, 25n22.
2. However, a final harpsichord was said to have been made by Kirckman in 1809. See Boalch, *Makers of the Harpsichord and Clavichord* (1995), 106. Shudi and Broadwood had abandoned harpsichords by 1793.
3. These estimates are based on the surviving instruments. At the time of writing, the "Clinkscale Online" database lists twelve grand pianos by the Kirckman firm, nineteen square pianos, and four vertical pianos.
4. Cyril Ehrlich, *The Piano: A History,* rev. ed. (Oxford: Clarendon, 1990), 144.

28. Square Piano, Astor, 1800–1810 (pages 66–67)

1. John Jacob Astor did not stop importing musical instruments to his New York store, nor did he deal only in his brother's pianos. In 1796, he purchased six square pianos from John Broadwood for sale in America. Wainwright, *Broadwood by Appointment*, 78.
2. See Michael Kassler, "Broderip & Wilkinson," in *Music Trade in Georgian England,* ed. Kassler, 103.
3. Bozarth and Debenham, "Piano Wars," 45–108.
4. Ibid., 100.
5. See entry no. 23 for more about Broadwood's 1783 patent. After Longman & Broderip bought rights to John Geib's 1786 patent (described in entry no. 32), Longman & Broderip advertised the innovation on nameboard inscriptions with the phrase "By Royal Patent." These generalizations about nameboard patent wording are based on data in the "Clinkscale Online" database of early pianos. I thank Tom Strange for helping to identify nameboard patent language during the 1780s and 1790s (e-mail to author, September 13, 2012).

29. Grand Piano, Broadwood, 1806 (pages 68–69)

1. The Broadwood archives are preserved at the Surrey History Centre, Woking, Surrey, England. Musician George Smart was already indebted to John Broadwood for the gift of a new grand piano and a financial loan. Later becoming an important figure in nineteenth-century English musical life, Sir George Smart became a founding conductor of the Royal Philharmonic Society, composer to the Chapel Royal, and teacher of well-known musicians of the next generation including composer Arthur Sullivan.
2. For information about the Moseleys, see "The Peerage," last updated Nov. 14, 2012, http://www.thepeerage.com/p41488.htm, and John Gage, *The History and Antiquities of Suffolk: Thingoe Hundred* (London, 1838), 244.
3. Cole, *Broadwood Square Pianos*, 20, 53.
4. The firm, now called John Broadwood and Sons Ltd., is much diminished in size but has continued in business almost without interruption since its beginnings in the eighteenth century.
5. See Rees, *Cyclopaedia*, vol. 18, American ed., s.v. "harpsichord": "all the harpsichord makers tried their mechanical powers at piano-fortes; but the first attempts were always on the large size."
6. As quoted in Cole, *Pianoforte in the Classical Era*, 116.
7. Ibid., 129. Robert Stodart's patent (no. 1172, November 21, 1777) for a combination piano and harpsichord called the instrument a "grand forte piano." *Patents for Inventions,* 12. For a photo of the patent drawing and further remarks about it, see Michael Latcham "Pianos and Harpsichords for Their Majesties," *Early Music* 36, no. 3 (August 2008): 363–364.
8. See John Koster, "The Divided Bridge, Due Tension, and Rational Striking Point in Early English Grand Pianos," *JAMIS* 23 (1997): 5–55.
9. This observation and a fuller analysis of Broadwood's improvements can be found in Cole, *Pianoforte in the Classical Era*, 135–140.

30. Square Piano, Broadwood, ca. 1808 (page 70)

1. Wainwright, *Broadwood by Appointment*, 103.
2. See the "Clinkscale Online" database. The piano is number 671 in the database and is part of the Finchcocks collection.
3. It is not unusual for multiple, slightly different serial numbers to be marked on the same instrument. This piano is marked "12,598" on the tuning pin block and on the back of the nameboard and marked "12533" on the bottom of the dust board.

31. Square Piano, Dettmer, 1805–1810 (page 71)

1. William Dettmer, George's son, was a thirty-four-year-old widower when he married Phillis Harper in 1809. It is possible that that occasion also marks the commencement of the Dettmer & Son partnership.
2. Large-radius corners on square pianos were probably an added expense and appeared on a minority of generally high-end square pianos during the first two decades of the nineteenth century. Ludewig Augustus Leukfeld's piano forte shop is pictured on his trade card. The list of wares over the door includes "OVAL SIDEBOARD," and the illustration shows rounded square pianos being loaded onto a cart for delivery (see Kassler, "Broderip & Wilkinson, 107). Period references also use the terms *circular corner* and *rounded end*. I thank Thomas Strange (e-mail to author, June 25, 2012) and Colm O'Leary (e-mail to author, June 29, 2012) for bringing these sources to my attention.
3. This scheme to create a symmetrical appearance when closed was not necessarily Dettmer's idea. It was used by others, including William Stodart and, as the next entry shows, John Geib. Other methods were tried, such as the one used by Newman (entry no. 37) and later makers whereby the lockboard extends over the sound box to both front corners.

32. Square Piano, Geib, 1808–1809 (pages 72–73)

1. Geib's letter to Franklin is transcribed in Thomas Strange and Jenny Nex, "John Geib: Beyond the Footnote," *Eighteenth-Century Music* 7, no. 1 (March 2010): 84. This

article is the definitive source for information about John Geib and his family prior to their move to New York.

2. For a full discussion about the various points of view about inner covers, see Michael Cole, "Adam Beyer, Pianoforte Maker," *Galpin Society Journal* 48 (March 1995): 105–107, or the update on his website www.squarepianos.com /adam_beyer.htm, last updated April 2012.

3. See note 2 in entry no. 31.

4. See Michael Kevin Brown, "Duncan Phyfe" (master's thesis, University of Delaware, 1978), 55–56n61. "Since there are no indications of any arrangement between Phyfe and Geib, the most logical explanation [for the alleged collaboration] is that the information was probably mis-interpreted from a statement which appeared in Esther Singleton's *The Furniture of Our Forefathers*, (New York: Doubleday, Page and Company, 1900), p. 526."

33. Vertical Piano, Wornum, 1813–1820

(pages 74–75)

1. The piano by Italian Domenico del Mela is in the Conservatory of Music Luigi Cherubini in Florence. It is illustrated in Franz Josef Hirt, *Stringed Keyboard Instruments, 1440–1880* (Boston: Boston Book and Art Shop, 1968), 383.

2. The American origin of the Pennsylvania example, which is at the Whitefield House in Nazareth, is detailed in John Koster, "Woods in Early American Keyboard Instruments as Evidence of Origins," in *Postprints of the Wooden Artifacts Group*, June 1995 (St. Paul, MN: Wooden Artifacts Group, American Institute for Conservation, 1995), 13–21.

3. Darcy Kuronen, "The Earliest Upright Piano? An Instrument by Robert Woffington of Dublin," *Newsletter of the American Musical Instrument Society* 37, no. 3 (Fall 2008): 11–12.

4. *Patents for Inventions*, 29.

5. See Cripe, *Thomas Jefferson and Music*, 61–62.

6. *Patents for Inventions*, 66.

7. Kenneth Mobbs photographed the piano in August 1976 at the Finchcocks collection in England.

8. The term *imperial grand horizontal piano* is from the inscription of an 1838 example as quoted in Rosamond E. M. Harding, *The Piano-forte: Its History Traced to the Great Exhibition of 1851*, 2nd ed. (London: Heckscher, 1978), plate 1 (facing p. 176). The same instrument is further described and illustrated in C. F. Colt, *The Early Piano* (London: Stainer & Bell, 1981), 116–119.

34. Grand Piano, Broadwood, 1816 (pages 76–77)

1. Porter's book entry, July 17, 1816, Broadwood Archives, Surrey History Centre, Woking, Surrey, England. See also C. F. Colt to J. Wilfred Lambert, 18 and 22 February 1977, Earl Gregg Swem Library, College of William and Mary, Williamsburg, VA. Colt further reported that George Balls was apparently an important agent, ordering multiple pianos from Broadwood on several occasions.

2. The donors were Dr. and Mrs. John W. Price.

3. Beethoven to Thomas Broadwood, 7 February 1818, as translated in Wainwright, *Broadwood by Appointment*, 114. See also Broadwood's account of his visit to Beethoven (Broadwood to V. Novello as quoted in ibid.).

4. For a dramatic juxtaposition of these two points of view, see the reviews written by Kenneth Mobbs and Michael Latcham of concerts on Beethoven's restored piano in *Early Music* 20, no. 3 (August 1992): 527.

5. Cole, *Pianoforte in the Classical Era*, 132.

6. Two square pianos—an 1818 and a ca. 1808 example—also have original soundboard screws. Both have provenance in the Middle Atlantic region of the United States and both are privately owned in Virginia.

7. By 1820, Broadwood began overspinning the strings of the lowest two notes, which necessitated the use of only two strings because three strings in such proximity were likely to buzz.

8. The Chickering attribution is based on Peter Redstone who reported removing an iron brace from the bottom of the piano during his 1975–1976 restoration. It was marked "Chickering," and he estimated it to be early twentieth century. Personal communication with author, 1983. The new tuning pins and the bottom reinforcement bar were replaced in the 2003 conservation.

9. According to "Clinkscale Online," four examples appeared in 1769, including one by Zumpe and Buntebart and three by John Pohlmann.

35. Grand Piano, Stodart, 1816 (pages 78–79)

1. See, for example, James Barron's *Modern and Elegant Designs of Cabinet and Upholstery Furniture* (London, [1814]). The texture on the reverse side of the Stodart inlays indicates that they were sand-cast.

2. Each step of this procedure was revealed through examination of the physical evidence under two inlays that were lifted.

3. Strictly speaking, the 1777 patent refers to the instrument as a "grand forte piano" according to *Patents for Inventions*, 12.

4. Unpublished genealogical research by Juleigh Clark indicates that William and Matthew could have been brothers or cousins. They were not sons of Robert Stodart.

5. See Richard J. Wolfe, *Secular Music in America, 1801–1825: A Bibliography*, vol. 2 (New York: New York Public Library, 1964), 594, 598.

6. Nancy Groce, *Musical Instrument Makers of New York: A Directory of Eighteenth- and Nineteenth-Century Urban Craftsmen* (Stuyvesant, NY: Pendragon, 1991), 151–152.

7. As quoted in Cripe, *Thomas Jefferson and Music*, 60. The incident is interesting not only for the mention of a Stodart in Richmond but for the fact that Thomas Jefferson was attempting to refurbish a harpsichord so far into the nineteenth century.

36. Square Piano, Babcock, 1828 (pages 80–81)

1. Daniel Spillane, *History of the American Pianoforte; Its Technical Development, and the Trade* (New York: D. Spillane, 1890), 85–86. Among Babcock's competition for best horizontal piano were William Geib of New York and Loud & Brothers of Philadelphia.

2. The patent for an iron frame is dated December 17, 1825. Only two out of Babcock's many surviving pianos have the patented iron frame. The innovation nevertheless paved the way for the high-tension pianos of today.

3. Although Babcock had made four-legged models at least by 1824, the great majority of his surviving pre-1830 pianos have six legs. In London, Broadwood changed in 1828 from six to four legs for its square pianos.

4. Darcy Kuronen provided information about the Clark inscriptions in the other Babcock pianos (e-mail to author, April 19, 2006). Serial numbers and known dates are based on his unpublished list of surviving Babcock pianos.

5. James R. Hines, "Musical Activity in Norfolk, Virginia, 1680–1973" (PhD diss., University of North Carolina at Chapel Hill, 1974), 66–67.

6. Ibid.

7. See Spillane, *History of the American Pianoforte*, 86. The patent is dated August 14, 1828, which was a month after this piano was dated (July 8).

8. According to Darcy Kuronen, Chickering also used the harmonic swell though rarely. "An Organized Piano by Alpheus Babcock," in *Organ Restoration Reconsidered: Proceedings of a Colloquium*, ed. John R. Watson (Warren MI: Harmonie Park Press, 2005), 162.

9. What to some modern ears might sound like inefficient damping was described in glowing terms in an 1821 review of Collard's harmonic swell: "The prolonged vibration produces an extraordinary purity, power, and continuity of sound." "Mr. Collard's Patent," *Quarterly Musical Magazine and Review* 3, no. 11 (1821): 319. The patent and that review also involved a second bridge called the "bridge

of reverberation" to encourage even more after-ring, but it remains clear that after-ring was appreciated.

10. John Koster, *Keyboard Musical Instruments in the Museum of Fine Arts, Boston* (Boston: Museum of Fine Arts, 1994), 251n24.

37. Square Piano, Newman, 1831 (pages 82–83)

1. The other two Baltimore piano makers whose pianos follow the Viennese tradition were George Huppmann and Joseph Hisky. It appears likely that Joseph Newman learned his craft from Hisky, who immigrated to Baltimore from Vienna. Surviving pianos with the so-called Viennese action are listed for all three makers in "Clinkscale Online." Hisky's full-page advertisement for his own and imported Vienna pianos appeared in *Matchett's Baltimore Director* of 1831. Joseph Newman did not advertise in the directory but was listed: "Newman Joseph, piano forte manufacturer, Park lane E of Pine st" (279). Cincinnati, Ohio, also had at least one piano maker, Andreas Reuss, who made instruments in this Viennese style, and Charles Pommer and Charles Albrecht, both in Philadelphia, also used the German action.

2. It is possible that Baltimore's rough treatment by the British during the War of 1812 caused lingering distaste for British style. The brief essay on Baltimore history in Matchett's 1831 city directory reveals the wounds were still fresh: "Baltimore suffered as much as any other portion of the confederacy. During nearly the whole of [the British siege of Baltimore] our waters were infested with the enemy's fleets. Our city was denounced as one of the chief objects of his hostility; our commerce was almost annihilated" (*Matchett's Baltimore Director*, 1831, 11).

3. The stenciling used by Baltimore furniture makers typically consists of bronze, brass, silver, gold, or zinc powder brushed or blown onto wet varnish over which stencils have been positioned.

4. For more about the bassoon and moderator stops, see Richard Burnett, *Company of Pianos* (Goudhurst, ENG: Finchcocks Press, 2004), 192–195.

5. For more about the origins of the Turkish fad and its effect on music and musical instruments, see ibid., 120ff and 131n6. See also Harding, *Piano-forte*, part 2, chap. 5. Kenneth Mobbs quotes disparaging remarks about Turkish effects in pianos by composer Carl Czerny and piano historians Franz Josef Hirt, Reginald R. Gerig, and Cecil Clutton. His article is also very informative about the bassoon stop. "Stops and Other Special Effects on the Early Piano," *Early Music* 12, no. 4 (November 1984): 473.

38. Harpsichord, Chickering, 1907–1908
(pages 84–85)

1. "The Revival of a Beautiful Art." This advertisement, a copy of which is in the author's possession, appears to be from *Harper's Monthly Magazine*. It is undated but is likely from an issue ca. 1909.

2. For more about the early music movement, see Harry Haskell, *The Early Music Revival: A History* (London: Thames and Hudson, 1988).

3. Archer Gibson to John D. Rockefeller Jr., 12 January 1948, CWF object file, 1953-1169.

4. Moreland Roller to John Barden (Colonial Williamsburg curatorial assistant), 11 February 1983, CWF object file, 1953-1169.

5. Larry Palmer, *Harpsichord in America: A Twentieth-Century Revival* (Bloomington: Indiana University Press, 1989). This book includes an excellent overview of Dolmetsch's activity in America. See also Margaret Campbell, *Dolmetsch: The Man and His Work* (Seattle: University of Washington Press, 1975).

6. The most likely original disposition is described by Dolmetsch in his essay "The Art of Music before 1750," in *Essentials of Music*, ed. Emil Liebling, vol. 2 of *The American History and Encyclopedia of Music*, ed. W. L. Hubbard (New York: Irving Squire, 1910), 100–105.

GLOSSARY

SPINET

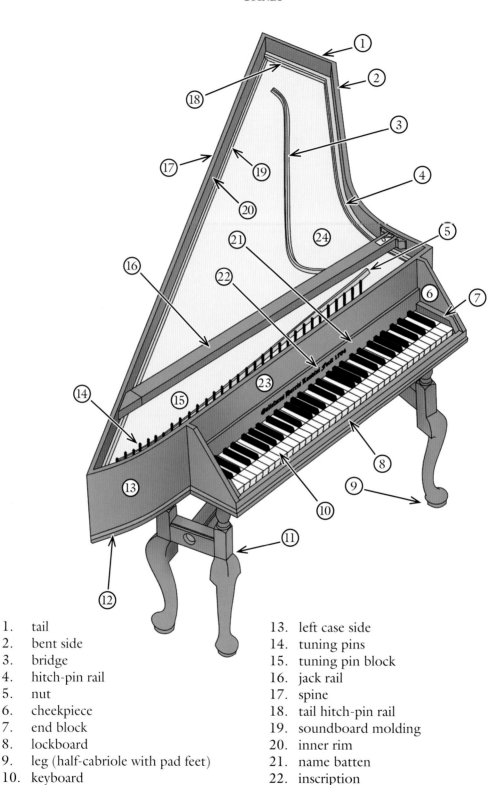

1. tail
2. bent side
3. bridge
4. hitch-pin rail
5. nut
6. cheekpiece
7. end block
8. lockboard
9. leg (half-cabriole with pad feet)
10. keyboard
11. trestle stand
12. bottom molding

13. left case side
14. tuning pins
15. tuning pin block
16. jack rail
17. spine
18. tail hitch-pin rail
19. soundboard molding
20. inner rim
21. name batten
22. inscription
23. nameboard
24. soundboard

Harpsichord

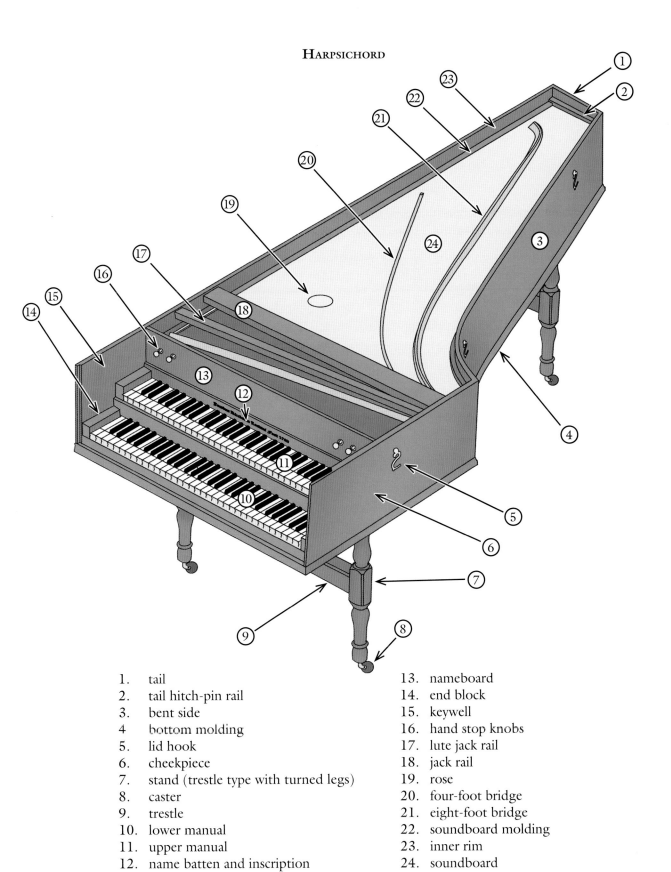

1. tail
2. tail hitch-pin rail
3. bent side
4. bottom molding
5. lid hook
6. cheekpiece
7. stand (trestle type with turned legs)
8. caster
9. trestle
10. lower manual
11. upper manual
12. name batten and inscription
13. nameboard
14. end block
15. keywell
16. hand stop knobs
17. lute jack rail
18. jack rail
19. rose
20. four-foot bridge
21. eight-foot bridge
22. soundboard molding
23. inner rim
24. soundboard

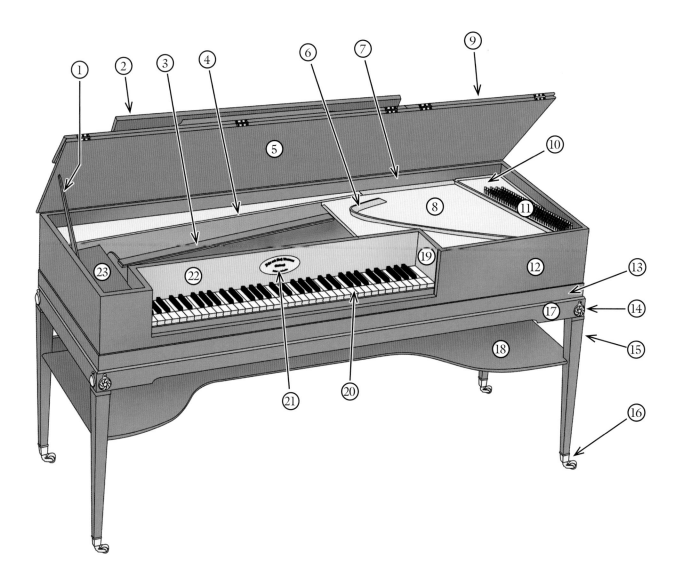

1. lid stick	13. bottom molding
2. lockboard	14. bolt cover
3. hammer rail	15. stand ("French frame")
4. nut	16. caster
5. lid (main section)	17. stand apron
6. bridge	18. music shelf
7. inner rim	19. cheek
8. soundboard	20. keyboard
9. soundboard lid flap	21. nameboard inscription
10. tuning pin block	22. nameboard
11. tuning pins	23. cheek block or left case block
12. case	

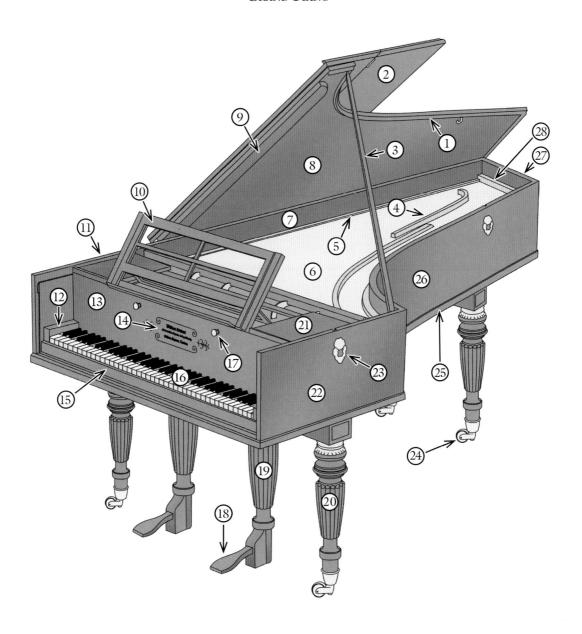

1. lid molding
2. lid flap
3. lid stick
4. bridge
5. soundboard molding
6. soundboard
7. inner rim
8. main lid section
9. cleat
10. music desk
11. spine
12. end block
13. nameboard
14. nameboard inscription
15. key slip
16. keyboard
17. knob-headed nameboard screw
18. pedal
19. pedal column
20. leg (turned and reeded)
21. sliding candle shelf
22. cheekpiece
23. lid hook ring
24. caster
25. bottom molding
26. bent side
27. tail
28. hitch-pin rail (tail section)

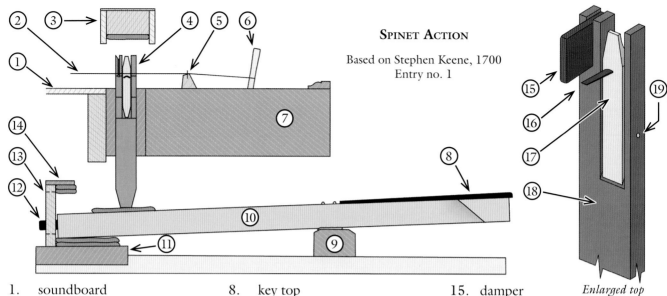

SPINET ACTION

Based on Stephen Keene, 1700
Entry no. 1

Enlarged top portion of spinet or harpsichord jack

1. soundboard	8. key top	15. damper
2. string	9. balance rail and balance pin	16. plectrum
3. jack rail	10. key lever	17. tongue
4. jack	11. key-frame back rail	18. jack body
5. nut	12. rack slip	19. tongue pivot
6. tuning pin	13. rack	
7. tuning pin block	14. stop rail	

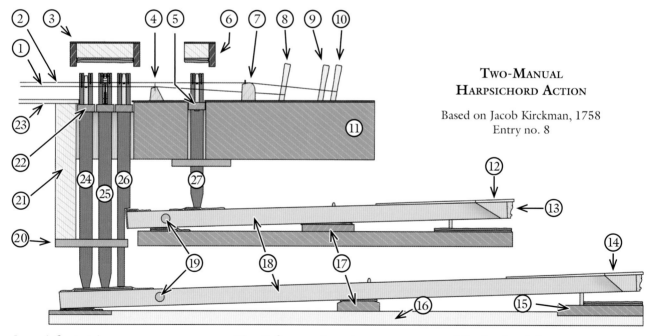

TWO-MANUAL HARPSICHORD ACTION

Based on Jacob Kirckman, 1758
Entry no. 8

1. 4-foot string	10. 8-foot tuning pin	19. lead weights
2. 8-foot string	11. tuning pin block	20. lower jack guide
3. jack rail	12. upper manual key	21. belly rail
4. 4-foot nut	13. key front	22. registers
5. lute stop register	14. lower manual key	23. soundboard
6. lute jack rail	15. front rail and front guide pin	24. 4-foot jacks
7. 8-foot nut	16. key frame	25. 8-foot jacks
8. 4-foot tuning pin	17. balance rails and balance pins	26. dogleg 8-foot jacks
9. 8-foot tuning pin	18. key levers	27. lute jacks

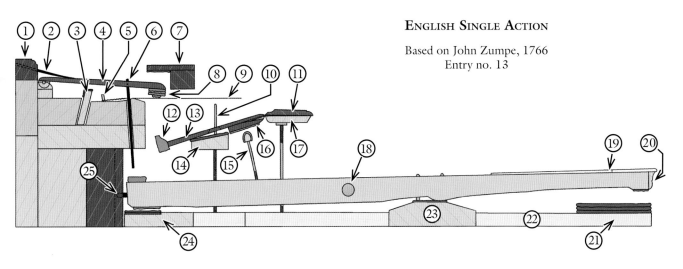

ENGLISH SINGLE ACTION

Based on John Zumpe, 1766
Entry no. 13

1. damper spring rail	10. hammer guide pin	19. key top (ivory)
2. damper spring	11. hammer cap rail	20. key front
3. damper lifter	12. hammer (head)	21. key-frame front rail
4. lever damper	13. hammer (shank)	22. key frame
5. hitch pin	14. hammer rest rail	23. balance rail and balance pins
6. damper sticker	15. jack	24. key-frame back rail
7. damper overrail	16. hammer butt	25. rack slip
8. damper	17. hammer rail	
9. string	18. lead weight	

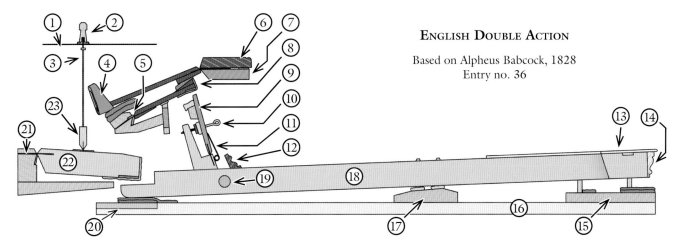

ENGLISH DOUBLE ACTION

Based on Alpheus Babcock, 1828
Entry no. 36

1. string	9. jack (or hopper)	17. balance rail and balance pins
2. wire-mounted damper	10. set-off adjusting screw	18. key lever
3. damper wire	11. jack spring	19. lead weight
4. hammer (head)	12. spring guard	20. key-frame back rail
5. intermediate lever hinge	13. key top (ivory)	21. damper lifter
6. hammer rail cap	14. key front	22. damper underlever
7. hammer rail	15. key-frame front rail	23. damper socket
8. intermediate lever	16. key frame	

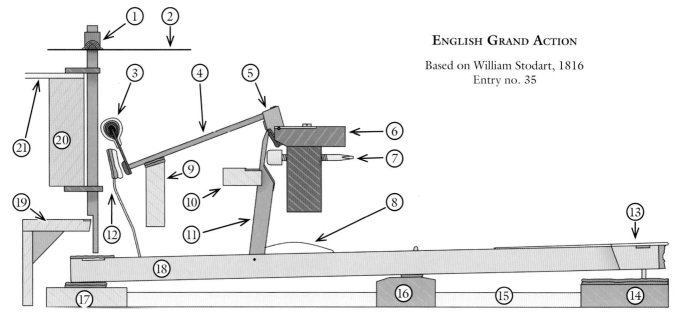

ENGLISH GRAND ACTION

Based on William Stodart, 1816
Entry no. 35

1. damper
2. string
3. hammer (head)
4. hammer (shank)
5. hammer butt
6. hammer rail
7. set-off screw
8. jack spring
9. hammer rest rail
10. jack register
11. jack
12. check
13. key top
14. key-frame front rail
15. key frame
16. balance rail and balance pin
17. key-frame back rail
18. key lever
19. damper lifter
20. belly rail
21. soundboard

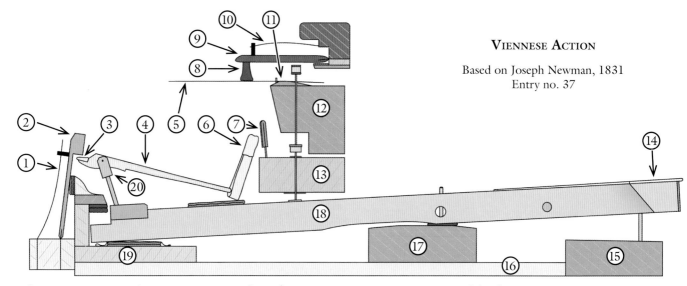

VIENNESE ACTION

Based on Joseph Newman, 1831
Entry no. 37

1. escapement spring
2. escapement
3. hammer beak
4. hammer (shank)
5. string
6. hammer (head)
7. check
8. damper
9. damper lever
10. damper spring
11. nut and nut pin
12. tuning pin block
   (extends to right)
13. check rail
14. key top
15. key-frame front rail
16. key frame
17. balance rail and balance pin
18. key lever
19. key-frame back rail
20. kapsel

PITCH NOTATION

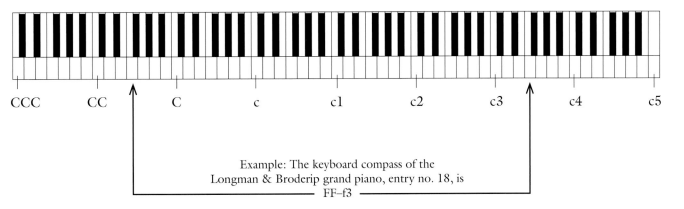

Example: The keyboard compass of the
Longman & Broderip grand piano, entry no. 18, is
——— FF–f3 ———

TECHNICAL INFORMATION

Conventions

- Descriptions of case decoration are omitted. See photographs in main entries.
- All measurements are in millimeters unless otherwise noted.
- Sharp length is front to back overall.
- Net dimensions are in parentheses following overall dimensions and do not include lid, stand, or moldings.
- Scale is the length of the longest c2 string.
- Case side thicknesses include veneer.
- Materials lists omit restoration replacements except where noted.
- CWF is an acronym for the Colonial Williamsburg Foundation.
- Ga. is an abbreviation for gauge.
- The sources for information in this section include the instruments themselves and the object file in the CWF Department of Collections.

1 Spinet, Stephen Keene, London, 1700

Accession number: 1953-876

Markings:
- "Stephanus Keene Londini Fecit" in ink on nameboard
- "54 / E B / 1700" in ink on top key
- "J.S. Morley repaired this / instrument 1925 AD / London S.W. 7" in ink on back of nameboard
- "Date of instrument appears / on last treble key" in ink on back of nameboard

Maker's serial number: none

KEYBOARD

Compass: GG/BB–d3 (4 octaves + 7 notes)

Three-octave measure: 476

Natural coverings: Ebony with three scribe lines including head/tail seam

Sharps: Solid ivory

Key fronts: Trefoil-embossed paper

Sharp length: 52

Head length: 31

Key guide system: Balance pins and rack

CASE/DIMENSIONS

Length: 1,655 (1,637)

Depth: 585 (585)

Height: 790 (170)

Height of keyboard over floor: 665

Notes: There is no provision for a music desk.

Case side thicknesses: Left tail, 11; right tail, 10; bent side, 9; spine, 14

Bottom: Closed; sides nailed to bottom

Soundboard: Quartersawn conifer; grain parallel to spine

Materials: WALNUT: main case, box guide; SPRUCE: soundboard, key levers; SOFTWOODS: nameboard substrate; OAK: key-frame balance rail; PLAIN LIGHT HARDWOODS: stand (stained); BEECH: pin block, nut; FRUITWOOD: jack bodies, bridge(?); EBONY: natural key tops; IVORY: sharps; BRASS: hinges (probably not original), lid closure escutcheon

STRINGS/SCALE

Scale: 270

Strings: String lengths: d3=131; c3=134.5; f2=215; c2=270; f1=408; c1=519; f=777; c=947; F=1,196.5; C=1,349.5; GG/BB=1,380

Bridge and Nut: Scribe line marks center line for nut pins

MECHANICAL

Action: Jacks possibly original but with much added lead

Stops: none

NOTES

Provenance: Purchased in 1953 by CWF from J. George Morley, London

References:
- Donald H. Boalch, *Makers of the Harpsichord and Clavichord 1440 to 1840* (London: George Ronald, 1956), 58.
- ———, *Makers of the Harpsichord and Clavichord 1440–1840*, 2nd ed. (Oxford: Clarendon Press, 1974), 81, #4.
- ———, *Makers of the Harpsichord and Clavichord 1440–1840*, 3rd ed., ed. Charles Mould (Oxford: Clarendon Press, 1995), 414.
- James S. Daring (fortepiano, harpsichord, and spinet), Thomas Marshall (fortepiano and harpsichord), Kevin Bushee (baroque violin), and Herbert Watson (English flute and German flute), *Instrumental Music from the Colonial Williamsburg Collection*, Colonial Williamsburg Foundation, Williamsburg, VA, 1987, WSCD117, compact disc.
- John Watson, "A Catalogue of Antique Keyboard Instruments in the Southeast," *Early Keyboard Journal* 2 (1983–1984): 68 and fig. 5.

2 Spinet, Thomas Hitchcock, London, ca. 1715

Accession number: 2007-56 (L)

Markings:
· "Thomas Hitchcock Londini Fecit" in ink on nameboard
· "471" in ink on front edge of pin block and on key frame in two places, including front of balance rail and top of back rail
· "N° 1 Iuly + 12th 1760" cut into key 2
· "Wm A[?]hor[?]" cut into key 2

Maker's serial number: 471

KEYBOARD

Compass: GG–e3 (4 octaves + 9 notes)

Three-octave measure: 490

Natural coverings: Ivory with two scribe lines including head/tail seam

Sharps: Sandwich of ebony with ivory center

Key fronts: Black-stained molded wood

Sharp length: 69

Head length: 34

Key guide system: Balance pins and rack

CASE/DIMENSIONS

Length: 1,859 (with reproduction lid) (1,829)

Depth: 664 (with reproduction lid) (664)

Height: 830 (with reproduction lid) (160)

Height of keyboard over floor: 709

Notes: There is no provision for a music desk.

Case side thicknesses: Spine, 11; right tail, 9; bent side, 8.5; left tail, 8

Bottom: Closed; grain parallel to register

Soundboard: Quartersawn spruce; grain parallel to register; no apparent coating; average 18 rings per inch

Materials: WALNUT: case, stand, box guide; SPRUCE: soundboard; SOFTWOODS: bottom, spine, inner framing, key levers; FRUITWOOD: bridge; BEECH: nut, pin block, jack bodies; HOLLY(?): jack tongues; OAK: key-frame balance rail; PLAIN LIGHT HARDWOOD: nameboard and inner-rim veneer; EBONY: sharp sides; IVORY: natural key tops; BRASS: tuning pins, bridge pins, nut pins, lock plate (the only case hardware that is probably original)

STRINGS/SCALE

Scale: 268

Strings: Fragments of old wire remain on seven tuning pins and five hitch pins; gauge markings penned on front side of nut (notes, gauge): BB–C, ga. 9; D-sharp–E, ga. 8; G, ga. 7; A-sharp, ga. 6; d-sharp, ga. 5; g-sharp, ga. 4; d1-sharp, ga. 3; a1, ga. 2; f2, ga. 1

Bridge and Nut: Bridge, possibly fruitwood, rounded, with back pins up to b-flat; beech nut

MECHANICAL

Stops: none

Provenance: Thought to have descended in John Crawford family, eventually of Botetourt County, VA; in collection of Botetourt County Historical Society and Museum

References:
· Donald H. Boalch, *Makers of the Harpsichord and Clavichord 1440–1840*, 3rd ed., ed. Charles Mould (Oxford: Clarendon Press, 1995), 387.
· John R. Watson, "A Catalog of Antique Keyboard Instruments in the Southeast, Part IV," *Early Keyboard Journal* 9 (1991): 76–79.

3 Spinet, Cawton Aston, London, 1726

Accession number: 1960-321

Markings:
· "Cawton Aston Londini Fecit No 268 AD 1726" in ink on nameboard
· "Restored at Bayley St. Bedfore Sq. / Oct. 1898 by Arnold Dolmetsch / [illegible]" in pencil on underside of soundboard

Maker's serial number: 286

KEYBOARD

Compass: GG–g3 (5 octaves)

Three-octave measure: 475

Natural coverings: Ivory with three scribe lines including head/tail seam

Sharps: Sandwich of ebony with ivory center

Key fronts: Turned ivory arcades

Sharp length: 74

Head length: 35

Key guide system: Balance pins and vertical rack pins in split key ends

CASE/DIMENSIONS

Length: 1,785 (1,758)

Depth: 680 (670)

Height: 780 (175)

Height of keyboard over floor: 647

Case side thicknesses: Spine, 15; bent side, 10

Bottom: Closed; sides nailed to bottom

Soundboard: 1898 replacement by Arnold Dolmetsch

Materials: WALNUT: case sides (solid), moldings, lid, box guide, rim veneer, pin block veneer, nameboard veneer, end blocks, right jack-rail bracket, stand; SOFTWOODS: spine, bottom, nameboard, keys, jack-rail rim veneer substrate, key frame, belly and other framing, ribs, horizontals of stand; OAK: keyboard rack and overrail, key-frame balance rail; SYCAMORE(?): pin block; BEECH: nut; BOXWOOD: string inlay on case and around inscription, inscription inlay; EBONY: sharp sides, string inlay around inscription; IVORY: natural key tops; BRASS: nut pins, bridge pins, hinges and escutcheons, lid hook, balance-rail pins, rack pins

STRINGS/SCALE

Scale: 291

Strings: No early strings or gauge markings

Bridge and Nut: Bridge probably replaced; back pins used throughout bridge

MECHANICAL

Action: Old jacks, some possibly original; keys guided by rack with key-dip overrail

Stops: none

NOTES

Provenance: Originally from collection of J. Highfield Jones, Esq.; sold at Sotheby's on Dec. 20, 1954, to Leonard Knight Ltd.; sold on Feb. 18, 1955, to Herbert Rothbarth; sold on May 26, 1960, at Christie's (Lot 87) to Leonard Knight Ltd.; sold in 1960 to CWF

References:
- Donald H. Boalch, *Makers of the Harpsichord and Clavichord 1440 to 1840* (London: George Ronald, 1956), 3.
- ———, *Makers of the Harpsichord and Clavichord 1440–1840*, 2nd ed. (Oxford: Clarendon Press, 1974), 6.
- ———, *Makers of the Harpsichord and Clavichord 1440–1840*, 3rd ed., ed. Charles Mould (Oxford: Clarendon Press, 1995), 224.
- Christie, Manson & Woods, *Catalogue of the Highly Important Collection of Fine English Furniture of the 18th Century: Works of Art, Needlework and Persian Carpets Formed by the Late Herbert Rothbarth . . .* (London: Christie, Manson & Woods, 1960), 32, lot 87, and plate 19.
- Sotheby & Co., *Catalogue of Oriental Rugs and Carpets, Including the Property of Lady St. Vincent, Tapestries Including . . . Musical Instrument Including . . . Clocks, English and Continental Furniture Comprising . . .* (London: Sotheby & Co., 1954), lot 97.
- John R. Watson, "Historical Musical Instruments: A Claim to Use, an Obligation to Preserve," *Journal of the American Musical Instrument Society* 17 (1991): 76.
- ———, "A Catalogue of Antique Keyboard Instruments in the Southeast," *Early Keyboard Journal* 2 (1983–1984): 68.

4 Harpsichord, I. N. Cusseneers, Düsseldorf, 1726

Accession number: 1997-227

Markings:
- "CUSSENEERS DUSSELENSIS FECIT MDCCXXVI" in paint on twentieth-century replacement jack rail
- "Faked Jack cover of stained oak." in ink on sticker on back of jack rail, presumably in John Challis's handwriting
- "REBUILT BY / JOHN CHALLIS / 1950" in gilt lettering on front of nameboard
- "Challis / 1949" stamped on top key
- "Rebuilt by / John Challis / Detroit Michigan, 1950" in ink near corner of spine and gap
- "INC" cast into metal rose hole decoration

Maker's serial number: none

KEYBOARD

Compass: C,D–c3 (4 octaves)

Three-octave measure: 474

Natural coverings: Possibly original bone transferred to Challis key levers; contiguous heads and tails; four scribe lines

Sharps: Black-stained oak (probably not original)

Key fronts: Undecorated key end grain (Challis key levers)

Sharp length: 65

Head length: 35

Key guide system: (Challis)

CASE/DIMENSIONS

Length: 1,875 (1,851)

Width: 743 (726)

Height: 890 (213)

Height of keyboard over floor: 724

Case side thicknesses: Cheekpiece, 9.5 (16.5 for raised area); spine, 10.5 (15.5 for raised area); bent side, 9.3

Bottom: Replaced by Challis in 1950; sides nailed to bottom

Soundboard: Quartersawn spruce with decorative painting

Materials: OAK: case, nameboard, stand (with other hardwoods), belly rail, sharps; SPRUCE: soundboard; PLAIN LIGHT HARDWOOD: bridge; PAPER: inner-rim covering; BONE: natural key tops; LEAD ALLOY: rose

STRINGS/SCALE

Scale: 333 (altered)

Strings: No early strings or gauge markings

Bridge and Nut: Back pins used throughout 8-foot and 4-foot bridges

MECHANICAL

Action: Rectangular hole (now plugged) in cheekpiece indicates that registers probably projected from cheekpiece at one time; Challis-era action; three sets of jacks plucking two ranks of 8-foot strings
→ 8-foot leather
← 4-foot leather
→ 8-foot leather (plucking same choir as other 8-foot)

Stops: Challis-era pedals (left to right): back 8-foot, 4-foot, 8-foot buff, and front 8-foot; two 8-foot registers pluck same choir of strings but with different plucking points

NOTES

Provenance: Possibly from Snoeck Collection, Ghent, and Berlin Collection; then belonged to Francis J. H. Byrne of Chickering & Sons during tenure of Arnold Dolmetsch; owned and restored by John Challis of Detroit, MI, and sold to Ray McIntyre in 1950; in 1974 owned by Edward R. McElwee of Hagerstown, MD; sold at McElwee's estate sale on Apr. 22, 1976, to James and Catherine Hollan of Annapolis, MD; given by Catherine Hollan to CWF in 1997; jack rail, original pin block, and another pin block having original top veneer given to CWF by Thomas and Barbara Wolf, who purchased them at McElwee's estate sale

References:
- Donald H. Boalch, *Makers of the Harpsichord and Clavichord 1440–1840*, 2nd ed. (Oxford: Clarendon Press, 1974), 22.
- ———, *Makers of the Harpsichord and Clavichord 1440–1840*, 3rd ed., ed. Charles Mould (Oxford: Clarendon Press, 1995), 30, 263.
- Hal L. Haney, "Harpsichord of Note," *The Harpsichord* 7, no. 4 (Nov., Dec., Jan., 1974–1975): 8–9.

- Illustrated in N. E. Michel, *Historical Pianos, Clavichords, and Harpsichords* (Pico Rivera, CA: printed by author, 1970), 156, 162.
- John R. Watson, "A Catalog of Antique Keyboard Instruments in the Southeast, Part V," *Early Keyboard Journal* 15 (1997): 97–99.

1440–1840, 3rd ed., ed. Charles Mould (Oxford: Clarendon Press, 1995), 684.
- John Watson, "A Catalogue of Antique Keyboard Instruments in the Southeast," *Early Keyboard Journal* 2 (1983–1984): 69.

5 Spinet, John Woolfinden, England, 1725–1740

Accession number: 1937-260

Markings:
- "John Woolfinden Fecit" in ink on nameboard

Maker's serial number: none

KEYBOARD

Compass: GG–g3 (5 octaves)

Three-octave measure: 486

Natural coverings: Ivory with two scribe lines including head/tail seam

Sharps: Black-stained hardwood with ebony veneer on top

Key fronts: Molded light hardwood, all replaced in 1962

Sharp length: 66

Head length: 32

Key guide system: Balance pins and vertical rack pins

CASE/DIMENSIONS

Length: 1,861 (1,854)

Depth: 722 (717)

Height: 873 (174)

Height of keyboard over floor: 656

Case side thicknesses: All case sides, 8 except spine, 13

Bottom: Closed; sides nailed to bottom

Soundboard: Probably replaced; grain parallel to spine

Materials: WALNUT: sides (except spine); BEECH: replacement pin block, box guide, jack tongues, bridge, nut, stand (stained); SPRUCE: soundboard; MAPLE or SYCAMORE: inscription inlay, jack bodies (replacements); SOFTWOODS: nameboard substrate, bottom, spine, key levers; PLAIN LIGHT HARDWOODS: key fronts; ROSEWOOD(?): veneer on nameboard, jack-rail brackets, spine inner rim; EBONY: sharp veneer; IVORY: natural key tops; BRASS: hinges, lid hook, lock escutcheon; IRON: key balance pins, tuning pins (replacements); stand bolts

STRINGS/SCALE

Scale: 307 (probably altered)

Strings: Strings and tuning pins are replacements

Bridge and Nut: Bridge and nut likely replaced

MECHANICAL

Stops: none

NOTES

Provenance: Purchased by CWF in 1937 from New York antiques dealer Frank Partridge, Inc.

References:
- Donald H. Boalch, *Makers of the Harpsichord and Clavichord*

6 Chamber Organ, Unknown, England, ca. 1740

Accession number: 1954-432

Markings:
- No maker's mark
- Pitch markings in ink on pipes

Maker's serial number: none

KEYBOARD

Compass: GG, AA–d3 (4 octaves + 7 notes)

Three-octave measure: 488

Natural coverings: Ebony with one scribe line at head/tail seam

Sharps: Sandwich of ebony with wide ivory center

Key fronts: Wood the color of mahogany without molding

Sharp length: 79

Head length: 36

Key guide system: Balance pins and pins behind sharps and tails

CASE/DIMENSIONS

Depth: 1,018 (968)

Width: 2,134 (1,883)

Height: 3,873 (3,289)

Height of keyboard over floor: 742

Notes: The single wedge feeder bellows raises a wedge reservoir. One telltale is at the left of the key desk for the organist pumping in front, and another is at the rear corner of the case near the side pumping lever.

Materials: MAHOGANY: case; OAK: key levers, stop action, trundles, key-frame rails, sponsils, original table, caps for wooden pipes, pipe stopper handles, sliders and bearers, toe boards, backfalls, pallets; SOFTWOODS: pipes, case secondary woods, back, rack boards, trackers, bellows board, bellows ribs; EBONY: natural key tops, sharp sides, stop knobs; IVORY: sharp centers, telltale indicator marks; LEATHER: bellows (replacement); LEAD ALLOY: pipes; GOLD: pipe gilding; IRON: trundle arms; BRASS: balance pins, key guide pins

MECHANICAL

Action: Tracker action; slider chest; keys raise stickers that rock backfalls that pull trackers that open pallets

Stops: Six left-hand draw knobs operate metal pipes in pairs for divided keyboard (between b and c1): fifteenth (bass), fifteenth (treble), twelfth (bass), twelfth (treble), principal (bass), and principal (treble); three right-hand draw knobs operate wooden pipes: open diapason, flute, and stopped diapason; pedal for machine stop, which removes principal, twelfth, and fifteenth

NOTES

Provenance: Originally at Kimberley Hall, Norwich, England, ancestral home of Wodehouse family; sold in 1953 to Noel

Mander of London, who sold it to CWF in 1954

References:
- John R. Watson, *Artifacts in Use: The Paradox of Restoration and the Conservation of Organs* (Richmond, VA: OHS Press in association with the Colonial Williamsburg Foundation, 2010), 32–34, fig. 5B, 50, fig. 10, 56, fig. 11, 70, fig. 12A, 71, fig. 12B, 77–78, fig. 14, 99, fig. 17, 128, fig. 29, 133, fig. 32, 136, fig. 33, 143, fig. 36, 148, fig. 39, 151, fig. 40, 156–158, fig. 43, 171, fig. 47, 173, fig. 48, 213–214.
- ———, "A Catalogue of Antique Keyboard Instruments in the Southeast," *Early Keyboard Journal* 2 (1983–1984): 71–72.
- ———, "Conservation of Six Historic Organs at Colonial Williamsburg," *The Tracker: Journal of the Organ Historical Society* 46, no. 3 (July 2002): 22–34.
- ———, "Instrument and Document: Balancing Values in the Conservation of Musical Instruments," in *Postprints of the Wooden Artifacts Group, June 2006* (Providence, RI: Wooden Artifacts Group, American Institute for Conservation, 2006), 21–23.
- ———, "Instrument Restoration and the Scholarship Imperative," *Early Keyboard Journal* 19 (2001): 28–29.
- ———, "The Restorative Conservation of Organs: A Conceptual Roadmap," *The Organ Yearbook* 37 (2008): 125–144.
- ———, "Wren Organ Conservation Completed in Williamsburg," *The Tracker: Journal of the Organ Historical Society* 46, no. 1 (2002): 45.
- Michael Wilson, *The English Chamber Organ: History and Development, 1650–1850* (Columbia, SC: University of South Carolina Press, 1968), 111–112 and plate 12.

7 Spinet, John Zopfe, London, 1745–1750

Accession number: 1976-421

Markings:
- "Johannes Balthasar Zopfe Londini Fecit" in ink on nameboard

Maker's serial number: none

KEYBOARD

Compass: GG, AA–g3 (5 octaves)

Three-octave measure: 489

Natural coverings: Ivory with one close pair of scribe lines in addition to head/tail seam

Sharps: Solid ebony or other black wood

Key fronts: Dark hardwood without molding

Sharp length: 77

Head length: 39

Key guide system: Front and balance pins

CASE/DIMENSIONS

Length: 1,831

Depth: 691

Height: 802 (200)

Height of keyboard over floor: 660

Case side thicknesses: Tail, ends, and spine, 16–17; bent side tapers from 14 at tail to 12 at bent end

Bottom: Closed; bottom nailed to sides

Soundboard: Close-grained spruce; grain parallel to spine; 2.8 thick at exposed split near treble end of bridge

Materials: MAHOGANY: case veneer, string inlay on inner rim; OAK: bent side; SOFTWOODS: case sides except bent side; PLAIN LIGHT HARDWOOD: string inlay and inscription cartouche; SYCAMORE: inner-rim veneer; SPRUCE: soundboard; BEECH: bridge, nut, pin block, hitch-pin rail and soundboard molding; LIMEWOOD: key levers; FRUITWOOD(?): jacks, upper jack register; RING-POROUS HARDWOOD: stand; EBONY: sharps; IVORY: natural key tops; BRASS: hinges, lock escutcheon, bridge pins, nut pins; IRON: tuning pins

STRINGS/SCALE

Scale: 288

Strings: Strings absent except fragments on some tuning pins; faint gauge markings visible on nut: ga. 6 between pins 34 and 35, ga. 5 between pins 44 and 45, ga. 4 between pins 53 and 54

Bridge and Nut: Bridge has conventional four-sided cross section; nut partially rounded on side away from bridge

MECHANICAL

Action: Only sixteen surviving jacks; fixed upper and lower guides

Stops: none

NOTES

Provenance: Owned by Bouldin family from ca. 1840s until given to CWF in 1976 by Charlotte Morton

References:
- Donald H. Boalch, *Makers of the Harpsichord and Clavichord 1440–1840*, 2nd ed. (Oxford: Clarendon Press, 1974), 193.
- ———, *Makers of the Harpsichord and Clavichord 1440–1840*, 3rd ed., ed. Charles Mould (Oxford: Clarendon Press, 1995), 689.
- John Watson, "A Catalogue of Antique Keyboard Instruments in the Southeast," *Early Keyboard Journal* 2 (1983–1984): 69.

8 Harpsichord 2M, Jacob Kirckman, London, 1758

Accession number: 1983-236

Markings:
- "Jacobus Kirckman Fecit Londini 1758" in ink on nameboard
- "IV" stamped on front section of stand in two places
- "Rebuilt by / Mr. Arthur P. Kleiner / and / Miss Van Buren / in year / 1931–1932" in ink on underside of soundboard
- "Rebuilt by Arthur P. Kleiner / Van Buren in 1932" in ink on spine liner
- "A P Kleiner / [illegible]" in ink on back of key slip between keyboards

Maker's serial number: none

KEYBOARD

Compass: FF, GG–f3 (5 octaves)

Three-octave measure: 485

Natural coverings: Ivory with two scribe lines including head/tail seam

Sharps: Solid ebony

Key fronts: Molded light hardwood with red paint added later

Sharp length: 79 (upper); 85 (lower)

Head length: 39.5

Key guide system: Front and balance pins

CASE/DIMENSIONS

Length: 2,351 (2,329)

Width: 939 (927)

Height: 898 (297)

Height of keyboard over floor: 666 (+80 to upper)

Case side thicknesses: Spine, 15, tail, 17; bent side, 15–16; cheekpiece, 18.5

Bottom: Closed; bottom nailed to sides

Soundboard: Quartersawn spruce; grain parallel to spine

Materials: WALNUT: case veneer, lid, stand, hitch-pin rail and soundboard molding, pin block veneer; SPRUCE: soundboard; OAK: case substrate; PLAIN LIGHT HARDWOODS: key fronts, inscription inlay; FRUITWOOD: jack bodies, registers; SYCAMORE: veneer string inlay; BOXWOOD and HOLLY: jack tongues; BEECH: bridges, nuts; LIMEWOOD: key levers; EBONY: sharps; IVORY: natural key tops; BRASS: lid hinges, lid hooks, jack-rail hardware, rose, bridge pins, nut pins, hitch pins, stop knobs; IRON: tuning pins, stop levers

STRINGS/SCALE

Scale: 339.5

Strings: 4-foot scale (c2), 165 mm; gauges stamped on 8-foot nut (unison number, gauge marking): 1, ga. 13; 3, ga. 12; 4, ga. 11; 5, ga. 11; 6, ga. 10; 8, ga. 10; 9, ga. 9; 12, ga. 9; 13, ga. 8; 16, ga. 8; 19, ga. 8; 20, ga. 7; 24, ga. 7; 25, ga. 6; 30, ga. 6; 31, ga. 5; 42, ga. 5; 43, ga. 4; 60, ga. 4

Bridge and Nut: 8-foot bridge sawn to shape with back pins up to g1; 4-foot bridge bent to shape with three back pins (up to GG-sharp)

MECHANICAL

Stops: Two hand stops: left for 4-foot and lute and right for 8-foot dogleg and back 8-foot

NOTES

Provenance: Owned by BBC in 1930s; possibly passed to Lotta Van Buren of New York before sale to Alexander Mackay-Smith; given to CWF in 1983 by Joan Mackay-Smith, whose name had changed to Joan Romain by time of transfer

References:
· Donald H. Boalch, *Makers of the Harpsichord and Clavichord 1440 to 1840* (London: George Ronald, 1956), 36, #10.
· ———, *Makers of the Harpsichord and Clavichord 1440–1840*, 2nd ed. (Oxford: Clarendon Press, 1974), 87, #10.
· ———, *Makers of the Harpsichord and Clavichord 1440–1840*, 3rd ed., ed. Charles Mould (Oxford: Clarendon Press, 1995), 428. See also entry for Kirkman, J. 1759(1), p. 429, which appears to be the same instrument.
· Elaine Funaro (harpsichord), *Pietro Domenico Paradisi: Sonate di Gravicembalo (1754)*, Centaur Records, Baton Rouge, LA, CRC 2814, 2006.
· Governor's Musick of Colonial Williamsburg, *A Delightful Recreation—The Music of Thomas Jefferson*, Colonial Williamsburg Foundation, Williamsburg, VA, WSCD-121, 1993, compact disc.
· Michael Monaco (keyboard), *Keys of the Palace*, Colonial Williamsburg Foundation, Williamsburg, VA, WSCD-126, 2002, compact disc.
· John Watson, "A Catalogue of Antique Keyboard Instruments in the Southeast," *Early Keyboard Journal* 2 (1983–1984): 69–70.

9 Harpsichord 2M, Jacob Kirckman, London, 1762

Accession number: 1934-38

Markings:
· "Jacobus Kirckman Londini Fecit 1762" in ink on name batten

Maker's serial number: none

KEYBOARD

Compass: FF, GG–f3 (5 octaves)

Three-octave measure: 485

Natural coverings: Ivory with two scribe lines including head/tail seam

Sharps: Solid ebony

Key fronts: Molded light hardwood

Sharp length: 86 (lower); 79 (upper)

Head length: 39

Key guide system: Front and balance pins

CASE/DIMENSIONS

Length: 2,332 (2,316)

Width: 938 (925)

Height: 889 (295)

Height of keyboard over floor: 663 (+80 to upper)

Case side thicknesses: All case sides, 16

Bottom: Closed; bottom nailed to sides

Soundboard: Quartersawn spruce; grain parallel to spine

Materials: WALNUT: lid, moldings, crossbanding, veneer panels on case; OAK: case substrate, pin block substrate; SOFTWOODS: bottom, inner framing; SPRUCE: soundboard; HOLLY: inscription inlay, case veneer string inlay; IVORY: natural key tops; EBONY: sharps; IRON: tuning pins, pedal hardware; COPPER ALLOY: hinges, hooks, stop knobs, thumb latch

STRINGS/SCALE

Scale: 341

Strings: 8-foot nut original gauge stampings as follows (unison number, gauge stamping): 1, ga. 13; 3, ga. 12; 4, ga. 11; 5, ga. 11; 6, ga. 10; 8, ga. 10; 9, ga. 9; 12, ga. 9; 13, ga. 9; 14, ga. 8; 16, ga. 8; 24, ga. 7; 25, ga. 6; 31, ga. 6; 32, ga. 5; 42, ga. 5; 43, ga. 4; 60, ga. 4

Bridge and Nut: 8-foot bridge sawn to shape with back pins up to g1; 4-foot bridge bent to shape with three back pins (up to GG-sharp)

MECHANICAL

Action:
- ← 4-foot lower keyboard
- → 8-foot lower keyboard
- ← 8-foot upper and lower keyboard (dogleg)
- ← 8-foot lute lower keyboard

Stops: Two hand stops: left for 4-foot and lute and right for 8-foot dogleg and back 8-foot; pedal, added probably later in eighteenth century, turned off 4-foot register

NOTES

Provenance: Purchased by CWF in 1934 from dealer Lenygon & Morant of New York, NY

References:

- Donald H. Boalch, *Makers of the Harpsichord and Clavichord 1440 to 1840* (London: George Ronald, 1956), 63, #19.
- ———, *Makers of the Harpsichord and Clavichord 1440–1840*, 2nd ed. (Oxford: Clarendon Press, 1974), 88.
- ———, *Makers of the Harpsichord and Clavichord 1440–1840*, 3rd ed., ed. Charles Mould (Oxford: Clarendon Press, 1995), 431.
- James S. Daring (fortepiano, harpsichord, and spinet), Thomas Marshall (fortepiano and harpsichord), Kevin Bushee (baroque violin), and Herbert Watson (English flute and German flute), *Instrumental Music from the Colonial Williamsburg Collection*, Colonial Williamsburg Foundation, Williamsburg, VA, 1987, WSCD117, compact disc.
- Governor's Musick of Colonial Williamsburg, *A Delightful Recreation—The Music of Thomas Jefferson*, Colonial Williamsburg Foundation, Williamsburg, VA, WSCD-121, 1993, compact disc.
- *Grove's Dictionary of Music and Musicians*, 5th ed., ed. Eric Blom (London: Macmillan, 1954), s.v. "Kirkman."
- Martha Hamilton-Phillips, "The Magnificent Keyboards of Colonial Williamsburg," *Ovation* 7, no. 6 (July 1986): 26.
- Pipings, *The American Organist* 17, no. 7 (July 1983): 34.
- John Watson, "A Catalogue of Antique Keyboard Instruments in the Southeast," *Early Keyboard Journal* 2 (1983–1984): 70 and fig. 6.
- ———, "An Eighteenth-Century Harpsichord Workshop Contributes Two Important Technologies," in *Eighteenth-Century Woodworking Tools: Papers Presented at a Tool Symposium, May 19–22, 1994*, ed. James M. Gaynor (Williamsburg, VA: Colonial Williamsburg Foundation, 1997), 215–226.
- ———, "Historical Musical Instruments: A Claim to Use, an Obligation to Preserve," *Journal of the American Musical Instrument Society* 17 (1991): 75.

10 Harpsichord 1M, Jacob Kirckman, London, 1762

Accession number: 1997-76

Markings:
- "Jacobus Kirckman Londini Fecit 1762" in ink on 1970s reproduction nameboard by Peter Redstone
- "R[e?]nt[e or a]ul 29" in pencil on key 1 and in chalk on key 60; both in modern lettering
- "IP" scratched into bottom in two places and on inside of spine
- "Lady Cholmeley" in chalk on bottom underside

Maker's serial number: none

KEYBOARD

Compass: FF, GG–f3 (5 octaves)

Three-octave measure: 486

Natural coverings: Ivory with two scribe lines including head/tail seam

Sharps: Solid ebony

Key fronts: Molded light hardwood

Sharp length: 86

Head length: 38.5

Key guide system: Front and balance pins

CASE/DIMENSIONS

Length: 2,282 (2,256)

Width: 932 (915)

Height: 888 (271)

Height of keyboard over floor: 676

Case side thicknesses: All case sides, 16–19

Bottom: Closed; bottom nailed to sides

Soundboard: Quartersawn spruce; grain parallel to spine

Materials: WALNUT: case veneer, hitch-pin rail and soundboard molding, tuning pin block veneer; OAK: case substrate, tuning pin block, key-frame front and balance rails; BEECH: stand (dark stained), bridge, nut; SPRUCE: soundboard; HOLLY: inner-rim and case string inlay; SOFTWOODS: bottom, inner frame, key-frame side rails and back rail, ribs, cutoff bar, liner; FRUITWOOD: jack bodies; PADAUK(?): keywell crossbanding; LIMEWOOD: key levers, lower jack guide; PLAIN LIGHT HARDWOOD: key fronts; HOLLY: some jack tongues; BOXWOOD: some jack tongues; EBONY: sharps; IVORY: natural key tops; IRON: tuning pins, stop levers, caster yokes; BRASS: bridge pins, nut pins, hitch pins, lid hinges, lid hooks, case rose, stop knobs; TINNED BRASS: keyboard front pins, balance pins, jack staples

STRINGS/SCALE

Scale: 349

Strings: 8-foot nut original gauge stampings as follows (unison number, gauge stamping): 1, ga. 13; 2, ga. 12; 3, ga. 12; 4, ga. 11; 5, ga. 11; 6, ga. 10; 8, ga. 10; 9, ga. 9; 12, ga. 9; 13, ga. 8; 18, ga. 8; 19, ga. 7; 24, ga. 7; 25, ga. 6; 30, ga. 6; 31, ga. 5; 42, ga. 5; 43, ga. 4

Bridge and Nut: Bridge has back pins FF–e1

MECHANICAL

Action:
- → 8-foot
- ← 8-foot

Stops: Two hand stops: left for back 8-foot register and right for front 8-foot register

NOTES

Provenance: Owned by Lotta Van Buren; transferred in early 1930s to Lula Gertrude Bagwell, who gave it to Converse College in 1978; in 1997 transferred to CWF

References:

- Donald H. Boalch, *Makers of the Harpsichord and Clavichord 1440–1840*, 2nd ed. (Oxford: Clarendon Press, 1974), 94.
- ———, *Makers of the Harpsichord and Clavichord 1440–*

1840, 3rd ed., ed. Charles Mould (Oxford: Clarendon Press, 1995), 432.
- John Watson, "A Catalog of Antique Keyboard Instruments in the Southeast, Part II," *Early Keyboard Journal* 3 (1984–1985): 65–66.
- ———, "Beyond Sound: Preserving the Other Voice of Historic Organs," in *Organ Restoration Reconsidered: Proceedings of a Colloquium*, ed. John R. Watson (Warren, MI: Harmonie Park Press, 2005), 17–23.

11 Spinet, William Harris, London, 1764

Accession number: 2001-825

Markings:
- "Gulielmus Harris Londini Fecit 1764" in ink on name batten
- "G. W. GOSS, / MUSIC DEALER / 62, BRECKNOOK ROAD, / N / 46 York Rise, Highgate / Restored / July 1898" first four lines are press printed, next line in pencil, and remainder in ink on paper label on back of name batten
- "Fricker 1764" in ink on top of key 1
- "S[l or t]ep[c or i]ons No 6" in ink on key 61

Maker's serial number: none

KEYBOARD

Compass: GG–g3 (5 octaves)

Three-octave measure: 488

Natural coverings: Ivory with two scribe lines including head/tail seam

Sharps: Black-stained hardwood

Key fronts: Molded light hardwood

Sharp length: 85

Head length: 41.5

Key guide system: Balance pins and vertical rack pins between key levers

CASE/DIMENSIONS

Length: 2,015 (1,984)

Depth: 782 (780)

Height: 810 (199)

Height of keyboard over floor: 658

Case side thicknesses: Spine, 14; right tail, 13; bent side, 13; nameboard, 14; left curved case piece, 13

Bottom: Closed; sides nailed to bottom; grain parallel to lockboard

Soundboard: Quartersawn spruce; grain parallel to register; 2.46 thick measured through split between bridge and sharply curved part of bent side

Materials: WALNUT: case, lid; BEECH: bridge, nut, pin block, stand, box guide; PLAIN LIGHT HARDWOOD: inscription inlay; SPRUCE: soundboard; OAK: case substrate, key-frame balance rail; SOFTWOODS: key levers, bottom, key-frame side rails and back rail, rack stop rail, jack-rail substrate; FRUITWOOD: jacks; IRON: balance pins, rack pins; BRASS: lid hinges, lock plate, jack-rail hook; IVORY: natural key tops

STRINGS/SCALE

Scale: 263

Bridge and Nut: Bridge cut from solid beech; bottom twenty-three unisons have back pins on bridge; nut mitered in bass; scribe line marks center line for nut pins

MECHANICAL

Action: Jacks probably original with rectangular lead weights and single damper slot; leather plectra possibly later

Stops: none

NOTES

Provenance: Thought to have been purchased from antiques dealer in New York City in 1941 by family of Courtney Regen, who gave it to CWF in 2001

12 Bureau Organ, Abraham Adcock and John Pether, London, ca. 1760

Accession number: 1958-260

Markings:
- "Abraham Adcock and John Pether Londini Fecit" in ink on batten over keyboard

Maker's serial number: none

KEYBOARD

Compass: C–e3 (4 octaves + 4 notes)

Three-octave measure: 484

Natural coverings: Ivory with two scribe lines including head/tail seam

Sharps: Sandwich of ebony with ivory center

Key fronts: Turned ivory arcades

Sharp length: 78

Head length: 42

Key guide system: Front and balance pins

CASE/DIMENSIONS

Length: 1,163

Depth: 621

Height: 1,170

Height of keyboard over floor: 773 (without dolly)

Notes: The lid and slanted desk can be raised at two positions to allow more sound to get out. Two side doors can also be opened for more volume. The four brass handles permit the upper chest, including the wind-chest, key action, stop action, and pipes, to be lifted off the lower section of the case containing the wind system. A modern dolly fitted to the organ has casters and sliding foot supports. A knob on a rod between the keyboard and the right stop knobs rises and falls with the reservoir to indicate the supply of wind.

Materials: MAHOGANY: case veneer; OAK: pipe stopper handles, rack boards, wind-chest, sliders, table, key frame; SOFTWOODS: case substrate, pipes, bellows boards, bellows ribs, grid dividers, pallets, case secondary woods, stickers; EBONY: sharp sides; IVORY: natural key tops, sharp centers, key fronts, stop knobs; IRON: pumping mechanism, balance pins, front pins; BRASS: case handles, lock escutcheons, pallet springs; LEAD ALLOY: metal pipes, bellows weight, tuning flaps

MECHANICAL

Action: Pin action; keyboard folds into case when not in use; wind-chest below keyboard; far end of keys pull up on trackers that rock backfalls that lower stickers with pins that press through pallet box to open pallets; wind system consists of a wedge feeder bellows and lead weighted wedge reservoir; wind pressure 57 mm; pumping pedals provided for front and side (assistant) use

Stops: Four draw knobs: left two draw knobs for two-rank quint mixture (metal pipes) and stopped diapason 8-foot (wood pipes); right two draw knobs for flute 4-foot (wood pipes) and fifteenth 2-foot (wood and metal pipes); pedal for machine stop removes mixture and fifteenth

NOTES

Provenance: From collection of London-based organist Geraint Jones, who sold it to CWF in 1958

References:
· Reportedly recorded on LP by Geraint Jones on the HMV, Decca, and Deutsche Grammophon labels.
· John R. Watson, *Artifacts in Use: The Paradox of Restoration and the Conservation of Organs* (Richmond, VA: OHS Press in association with the Colonial Williamsburg Foundation, 2010), 99, fig. 17, 121, fig. 25, 122, fig. 26, 124, fig. 27, 126, fig. 28, 129, fig. 30, 130, fig. 31, 159, fig. 44, 218.
· ———, "A Catalogue of Antique Keyboard Instruments in the Southeast," *Early Keyboard Journal* 2 (1983–1984): 71.
· ———, "Conservation of Six Historic Organs at Colonial Williamsburg," *The Tracker: Journal of the Organ Historical Society* 46, no. 3 (July 2002): 22–34.
· Michael I. Wilson, *The Chamber Organ in Britain, 1600–1830* (Aldershot, ENG: Ashgate, 2001), 126 and plate 10.
· ———, *The English Chamber Organ: History and Development, 1650–1850.* (Columbia, SC: University of South Carolina Press, 1968), 51–52 and plate 5.

13 Square Piano, John Zumpe, London, 1766

Accession number: 1968-294

Markings:
· "Johannes Zumpe Londini Fecit 1766 / Princess Street Hanover Square" in ink on nameboard

Maker's serial number: none

KEYBOARD

Compass: GG–f3 (5 octaves - 2 notes)

Three-octave measure: 485

Natural coverings: Ivory with four scribe lines including head/tail seam

Sharps: Black-stained hardwood with ebony veneer on top

Key fronts: Molded softwood

Sharp length: 66

Head length: 39

Key guide system: Balance pins and rack

CASE/DIMENSIONS

Length: 1,239 (1,230)

Depth: 459 (451)

Height: 758 (145)

Height of keyboard over floor: 677

Case side thicknesses: All case sides, 14.5

Soundboard: Laminated three-ply spruce; 3 thick

Materials: WALNUT: case, nameboard, hammer-hinge rail cover, rack; MAHOGANY: hammers, damper levers; SPRUCE: soundboard; BEECH: stand (stained); OAK: hammer-hinge rail, hammer-rest rail, action end brackets; LIMEWOOD: key levers; SOFTWOODS: lower portion of spine, bottom, cheek block, belly rail, key frame, hammer butts; EBONY: sharp key top veneer; IVORY: natural key tops; BALEEN: rack slips, damper springs, damper stickers; BRASS: nut pins, bridge pins, hitch pins, jack wires, hammer guide pins; IRON: tuning pins

STRINGS/SCALE

Scale: 304

Strings: Bichord throughout; GG–G overspun

Bridge and Nut: No back pins on nut or bridge

MECHANICAL

Action: English single action with lever dampers hinged on continuous wire axle; hammer heads probably had single layer of leather, eventually three layers; damper sticker of baleen hinged to damper lever

Stops: One hand stop: for dampers

NOTES

Provenance: Purchased by CWF from Pro Musica Instrument Co. of Annapolis, MD, in 1968

References:
· Martha Novak Clinkscale, *Makers of the Piano*, vol. 1, *1700–1820* (1993; repr., New York: Oxford University Press, 1995), 330, #2.
· Martha Hamilton-Phillips, "The Magnificent Keyboards of Colonial Williamsburg," *Ovation* 7, no. 6 (July 1986): 26.
· Malcolm Rose and David Law, eds., *A Handbook of Historical Stringing Practice for Keyboard Instruments, 1671–1856* (Lewes, ENG: printed by authors, 1991), 58.
· John Watson, "A Catalogue of Antique Keyboard Instruments in the Southeast," *Early Keyboard Journal* 2 (1983–1984): 74.
· ———, "Beyond Sound: Preserving the Other Voice of Historic Organs," in *Organ Restoration Reconsidered: Proceedings of a Colloquium*, ed. John R. Watson (Warren, MI: Harmonie Park Press, 2005), 24–26.
· ———, "Instrument and Document: Balancing Values in the Conservation of Musical Instruments," in *Postprints of the Wooden Artifacts Group, June 2006* (Providence, RI: Wooden Artifacts Group, American Institute for Conservation, 2006), 18, 20–21.

14 Harpsichord, John Kirshaw, Manchester, 1769

Accession number: 2003-57

Markings:
· "John Kirshaw Manchester 1769" in ink on nameboard
· "Jno. Kirshaw Apr 19th 1769" in ink on bottom jack
· "Alfred Reeve Restituit / Maidenhead / 1961" in ink on key bed under front rail of keyboard
· "Alfred Reeve Restituit 1961" in ink on side of bottom key
· "Octave" and "Buff Stop" in ink on nameboard under left two hand stops
· "2 Unison" and "1 Unison" in ink on nameboard under right two hand stops

Maker's serial number: none

KEYBOARD

Compass: FF, GG–f3 (5 octaves)

Three-octave measure: 484

Natural coverings: Ivory with two scribe lines including head/tail seam

Sharps: Solid ebony

Key fronts: Molded light hardwood, all replaced

Sharp length: 82

Head length: 39

Key guide system: Balance pins and vertical rack pins between key levers

CASE/DIMENSIONS

Length: 2,226 (2,213)

Width: 976 (961)

Height: 922 (278)

Height of keyboard over floor: 700

Case side thicknesses: All case sides, 16–17

Bottom: Closed; bottom nailed to sides

Soundboard: Quartersawn spruce; average 12 rings per inch

Materials: DIMPLE-FIGURED DARK HARDWOOD: case exterior veneer panels; MAHOGANY: case crossbanding(?), lid, carved legs, apron veneer; OAK: spine and probably other case side substrates, key frame, apron substrate, drawer sides and bottom; ROSEWOOD: name batten (solid), crossbanding, apron veneer; SYCAMORE: molded key fronts; BEECH: nuts; SPRUCE: soundboard; HOLLY: nameboard inscription inlay, stop label inlays, possibly light string inlay; SOFTWOOD: bottom; FRUITWOOD: jacks, registers; LIMEWOOD: key levers; EBONY: sharps; IVORY: natural key tops; BRASS: stop knobs; IRON: stop levers; LEATHER: jack pads; CLOTH: key frame, dampers

STRINGS/SCALE

Scale: 344

Bridge and Nut: Back pins used on bridge up to c1/c1-sharp

MECHANICAL

Action:
→ 8-foot
← 8-foot
Jacks confirmed to be original; closed rectangular damper mortises

Stops: Four hand stops: left pair for 4-foot and buff and right pair for back 8-foot and front 8-foot; one pedal (now removed but surviving) turned off back 8-foot and 4-foot

NOTES

Provenance: Possibly belonged to vicar of Snodland, Kent, early in twentieth century; then owned by Alan Legg of Cirencester, who sold it to Michael Thomas in 1961; sold to Norman Paulu of Madison, WI; given to CWF by Pamela Seekins Paulu in 2003

References:
· Donald H. Boalch, *Makers of the Harpsichord and Clavichord 1440–1840*, 2nd ed. (Oxford: Clarendon Press, 1974), 95.
· ———, *Makers of the Harpsichord and Clavichord 1440–1840*, 3rd ed., ed. Charles Mould (Oxford: Clarendon Press, 1995), 460.
· "Rebuilder of Harpsichords: The Art of Michael Thomas," *The Guardian* (Manchester, ENG), April 3, 1962.

15 Square Piano, John Zumpe and Gabriel Buntebart, London, 1770

Accession number: 1980-94

Markings:
· "Johannes Zumpe / et Buntebart / Londini Fecit 1770, / Princes Street Hanover Square" in ink on nameboard
· "XXIIII" chisel cuts on top key, right side rail of key frame, key bed near belly rail, and spine
· "WI" chisel cuts on spine

Maker's serial number: none

KEYBOARD

Compass: FF–f3 (5 octaves)

Three-octave measure: 486

Natural coverings: Ivory with two scribe lines including head/tail seam

Sharps: Black-stained hardwood with ebony veneer on top

Key fronts: Molded softwood

Sharp length: 72

Head length: 41

Key guide system: Balance pins and rack

CASE/DIMENSIONS

Length: 1,282 (1,265)

Depth: 475 (469)

Height: 797 (with reproduction stand) (159)

Height of keyboard over floor: 704 (with reproduction stand)

Case side thicknesses: All case sides, 15–17

Bottom: Grain parallel to spine and built up of four planks; prominent cleat in center appears original

Soundboard: Probably replaced in 1780s modernization; quartersawn spruce; diagonal grain; 12–15 rings per inch; triangular area in right rear corner has grain parallel to spine and is probably part of original soundboard

Materials: MAHOGANY: case, stand, damper levers, damper overrail, hammers, action brackets, hammer-rail cap; SPRUCE: soundboard; BEECH: hitch-pin plank; HOLLY: inscription cartouche; SYCAMORE: nameboard veneer; OAK: hammer rail, spine; PURPLEHEART(?): nameboard banding; SOFTWOODS: key frame (including balance rail), nameboard substrate, key fronts; LIMEWOOD: key levers; IVORY: natural key tops; EBONY: sharp veneer; LEATHER: hammer heads; IRON: tuning pins, stand hardware; BRASS: lid hinges

STRINGS/SCALE

Scale: 294

Strings: Bichord throughout; all strings replaced; no gauge markings

Bridge and Nut: Bridge probably dates to ca. 1780s modernization; nut has small triangular cross section

MECHANICAL

Action: English single action; jack head with one layer of leather on heavy, threaded brass wire

Stops: Three hand stops (now missing): for buff, bass dampers, and treble dampers

NOTES

Provenance: Purchased by CWF at Sotheby's in London, May 22, 1980, lot no. 87

References:
- Martha Novak Clinkscale, *Makers of the Piano*, vol. 1, *1700–1820* (1993; repr., New York: Oxford University Press, 1995), 331, #13.
- John Watson, "A Catalogue of Antique Keyboard Instruments in the Southeast," *Early Keyboard Journal* 2 (1983–1984): 75.

16 Chamber Organ, W. H. (William Holland?), England, 1782

Accession number: 1980-187

Markings:
- "W-H 1782" "W-H" cut into and "1782" stamped on bung board

Maker's serial number: none

KEYBOARD

Compass: CC–e3 (5 octaves + 4 notes)

Three-octave measure: 479

Natural coverings: Ivory with two scribe lines including head/tail seam

Sharps: Solid ebony

Key fronts: Light hardwood without molding

Sharp length: 77

Head length: 39

Key guide system: Parchment key hinge only

CASE/DIMENSIONS

Depth: 488

Width: 977

Height: 2,050

Height of keyboard over floor: 770 (without dolly)

Notes: The case encloses (from bottom to top) the wedge feeder bellows, reservoir, pallet box, wind-chest, keyboard, and pipes. Some of the treble 2-foot pipes are perched above others on an offset toe board.

Materials: MAHOGANY: case; SOFTWOODS: pipes, secondary wood; OAK: caps for wooden pipes, pallets; EBONY: sharps; IVORY: natural key tops; LEATHER: bellows joints and gussets, pallet covers; PARCHMENT: hinges for keys, covering for conductor boards; LEAD ALLOY: tuning flaps; BRASS: pallet springs, case handles, stop knobs; GOLD: facade pipe gilding; IRON: pumping hardware

MECHANICAL

Action: Pin action; grid made from solid oak in which tone channels were cut (grid and table board of one piece)

Stops: Four draw knobs: left pair for 8-foot stopped diapason and fifteenth (bass) and right pair for fifteenth (treble) and flute (4-foot); echo pedal removes stopped diapason and flute stops

NOTES

Provenance: Belonged to Arthur Ackerman & Son, Inc., Chicago, in 1930; purchased by CWF in Chicago from Sotheby Parke Bernet, Inc.

References:
- John Watson, "A Catalogue of Antique Keyboard Instruments in the Southeast," *Early Keyboard Journal* 2 (1983–1984): 72 and fig. 8.

17 Square Piano, Frederick Beck, London, 1785

Accession number: 1930-414

Markings:
- "Fredericus Beck Londini Fecit 1785 / No 10 Broad Street Soho" in ink on nameboard

Maker's serial number: none

KEYBOARD

Compass: FF, GG–f3 (5 octaves)

Three-octave measure: 483

Natural coverings: Ivory with two scribe lines including head/tail seam

Sharps: Black-stained hardwood

Key fronts: Molded light hardwood, all replaced in 1962

Sharp length: 83

Head length: 38.5

Key guide system: Front and balance pins

CASE/DIMENSIONS

Length: 1,469 (1,456)

Depth: 504 (495)

Height: 807 (95)

Height of keyboard over floor: 703

Notes: There is no provision for an internal music desk.

Case side thicknesses: Ends, 18.3–18.6; front, 19.4; spine, 19.9

Bottom: Two layers of softwood; lower layer with grain parallel to spine; upper layer with grain parallel to strings

Soundboard: Spruce; extends to right case side obscuring pin block beneath; grain parallel to spine; 2.9 thick at exposed edge

Materials: MAHOGANY: case, lid, damper levers, hammer-rail cap, hammer shanks; SPRUCE: soundboard; BEECH: bridge, hitch-pin plank; OAK: key-frame front and balance rails; MAPLE or SYCAMORE: nameboard veneer; SOFTWOODS: bottom, belly rail; PLAIN LIGHT HARDWOOD: molded key fronts; HOLLY: inscription inlay, veneer string inlay; LIMEWOOD: key levers; IVORY: natural key tops; LEATHER: jack tops, key pads; PARCHMENT: damper-lever hinges; BALEEN: damper springs; IRON: stop levers, tuning pins; BRASS: stop knobs, lid hooks, lid hinges, jack wires (tinned), lock plate

STRINGS/SCALE

Scale: 303.5

Strings: Bichord throughout; all strings replaced

Bridge and Nut: Bridge has simple undercutting in bass end; crest is angled giving bridge five-sided cross section

MECHANICAL

Action: English single action with tinned and threaded brass jack wires topped with hard brown and soft white leather buttons; horizontal lever dampers lifted by vertical stickers topped with leather buttons; dampers of soft white leather (probably original)

Stops: Two hand stops: for buff and dampers

NOTES

Provenance: Purchased by CWF in 1930 from H. C. Valentine & Co., Richmond, VA

References:
- Martha Novak Clinkscale, *Makers of the Piano*, vol. 1, *1700–1820* (1993; repr., New York: Oxford University Press, 1995), 20, #9.
- John Watson, "A Catalogue of Antique Keyboard Instruments in the Southeast," *Early Keyboard Journal* 2 (1983–1984): 75–76.

18 Grand Piano, Longman & Broderip/ Culliford & Co., London, 1790

Accession number: 2012-80

Markings:
- "Culliford & Co / Makers Jan. 7 / 1790" in ink on back of nameboard
- "[illegible]" in ink on back of nameboard
- "166" stamped on top of pin block yoke

Maker's serial number: 166

KEYBOARD

Compass: FF–f3 (5 octaves)

Three-octave measure: 488

Natural coverings: Ivory with two scribe lines including head/tail seam

Sharps: Solid ebony

Key fronts: Molded light hardwood

Sharp length: 82

Head length: 40.5

Key guide system: Front and balance pins

CASE/DIMENSIONS

Length: 2,321 (2,282)

Width: 978 (947)

Height: 915 (287)

Height of keyboard over floor: 705

Case side thicknesses: All case sides, 22

Bottom: Closed

Soundboard: Quartersawn; grain parallel to spine; light coating from ca. 1890s rebuilding

Materials: MAHOGANY: exterior veneer, stand, pedals; OAK: case substrate, pin block; SYCAMORE: inner-rim veneer, jack-rail veneer, bridge, nut, pin block veneer; SPRUCE: soundboard; LIMEWOOD: key levers; SOFTWOOD: nameboard substrate; FIGURED LIGHT HARDWOOD: keywell veneer; EBONY: sharps; IVORY: naturals; BRASS: lid hooks, lid hook rings, lid hinges, damper overrail hook, bridge pins, nut pins, hitch pins, lock escutcheon; IRON: tuning pins, pedal rods, pedal trapwork, trestle bolts and other screws, gap spacer arcs

STRINGS/SCALE

Scale: 286.5

Strings: Trichord throughout; gauge numbers stamped on nut: ga. 14 between notes 3 and 4, ga. 13 between notes 5 and 6, ga. 12 between notes 7 and 8, ga. 11 between notes 10 and 11, ga. 10 between notes 24 and 25, ga. 9 between notes 37 and 38

Bridge and Nut: Bridge undivided; double pinned throughout; no undercutting in bass end; nut one piece in single arc

MECHANICAL

Action: English grand action; damped to top note; three screws in key bed for vertical key-frame balance rail adjustments

Stops: Two pedals: for keyboard shift and dampers; hand stop in right end block limits keyboard shift for una corda or due corde

NOTES

Provenance: Owned by Russell Mackinnen prior to 1968, at which time piano was at Pro Musica Instrument Co. in Annapolis, MD; eventually purchased by John Cook of Hollywood, MD, who sold it to CWF in 2012

19 Square Piano, Longman & Broderip, London, 1788–1789

Accession number: 1971-577

Markings:
· "LONGMAN & BRODERIP / MUSICAL INSTRUMENT MAKERS / No. 26 CHEAPSIDE & No. 13 HAYMARKET / LONDON" in enamel on nameboard
· "1478" stamped on cheek block
· "No 3" in pencil on back of nameboard
· "London 1788 Manf[?] / New York 1904 Repaired" in pencil on bottom under key frame

Maker's serial number: 1478

KEYBOARD

Compass: FF–f3 (5 octaves)

Three-octave measure: 483

Natural coverings: Ivory with no scribe lines

Sharps: Solid ebony

Key fronts: Molded light hardwood

Sharp length: 80

Head length: 40

Key guide system: Front and balance pins

CASE/DIMENSIONS

Length: 1,570 (1,553)

Depth: 550 (547)

Height: 831 (215)

Height of keyboard over floor: 702

Notes: Supports remaining on the inner rim indicate the former presence of a dust board. A folding music desk is attached to the back of the nameboard.

Case side thicknesses: Ends, 16; spine, 19

Bottom: Slab-sawn conifer wood with grain parallel to spine; two access hatches not original

Soundboard: Quartersawn spruce; 3 thick at belly; modern clear coating; extension on right rear corner beyond pin block probably original and without fretwork

Materials: MAHOGANY: case, legs, apron veneer, damper levers, hammer shanks, hammer-rail cap, action brackets, folding internal music desk; OAK: spine, hammer rail, key-frame front and balance rails; BEECH: bridge; SOFTWOODS: soundboard, bottom, nameboard substrate, stand aprons, belly rail; PLAIN LIGHT HARDWOOD: key fronts; HOLLY: nameboard banding; LIMEWOOD: key levers; MAPLE: nameboard veneer (stained); EBONY: sharps; IVORY: natural key tops; LEATHER: jack caps; ENAMELED COPPER: inscription plaque; BRASS: inscription bezel, lid hinges, lock plate; IRON: hand-stop levers, tuning pins

STRINGS/SCALE

Scale: 308

Strings: Bichord throughout; no gauge markings; tuning pins on right

Bridge and Nut: Bridge has decorative profile on treble end and "shark's-mouth" undercutting on bass end; evidence of back pins on bridge, probably not from original construction

MECHANICAL

Action: English single action; hammers with guide pins and wood heads with three to four layers of leather; tinned brass jack wires topped with rawhide block covered with soft white leather and a thinner, darker layer of leather; damper stickers hang from leather collars

Stops: Three hand stops: two for bass and treble dampers, split between b and c1, and third for buff

NOTES

Provenance: Given to CWF by Mr. and Mrs. Howard Van Vleck in 1971

References:
· Martha Novak Clinkscale, *Makers of the Piano*, vol. 1, *1700–1820* (1993; repr., New York: Oxford University Press, 1995), 186, #29.
· Martha Hamilton-Phillips, "The Magnificent Keyboards of Colonial Williamsburg," *Ovation* 7, no. 6 (July 1986): 26.
· John Watson, "A Catalogue of Antique Keyboard Instruments in the Southeast," *Early Keyboard Journal* 2 (1983–1984): 75.

20 Square Piano, George Garcka, London, ca. 1792

Accession number: 1996-810

Markings:
· "George Garcka London Fecit / PATENT" in ink on nameboard
· "J.BLAND No45 / HOLBORN LONDON" stamped on soundboard
· "1335" in ink on soundboard below Bland stamping; may be serial number or Bland's retail ledger transaction or stock number
· "George Garcka / Patent" in pencil on back of nameboard; probably instructions for calligrapher

Maker's serial number: 1335(?)

KEYBOARD

Compass: FF–c4 (5 octaves + 7 notes)

Three-octave measure: 477

Natural coverings: Ivory with two scribe lines including head/ tail seam

Sharps: Solid ebony(?)

Key fronts: Molded light hardwood

Sharp length: 80

Head length: 39

Key guide system: Front and balance pins

CASE/DIMENSIONS

Length: 1,697 (1,677)

Depth: 601 (593)

Height: 821 (casters missing) (219)

Height of keyboard over floor: 721 (casters missing)

Case side thicknesses: Ends and front, 20; spine, 24.5

Bottom: Corner blocks glued to bottom position piano on stand and protect trapwork when piano off stand

Soundboard: Quartersawn spruce(?); grain parallel to spine; no apparent coating; 20–25 rings per inch; unusual extended soundboard patented by Garcka (patent no. 1849 dated February 4, 1792) reaches from pin block to left end of case extending over key levers; entire area functions as vibrating soundboard due to existence of second soundboard positioned 5 mm below upper one; lower soundboard glued to belly rail; both soundboards about 4 thick with 5 spacer between them around perimeter

Materials: MAHOGANY: case, legs, damper levers, hammer shanks, hammer-rail cap; SPRUCE: soundboard; MAPLE(?): nameboard veneer; BEECH: bridge; LIMEWOOD: key levers; PLAIN LIGHT HARDWOODS: inscription inlay, hammer rail, hitch-pin plank veneer, molded key fronts; OAK: key-frame balance and front rails, spine; SOFTWOODS: key-frame side rails, belly rail, bottom, stand aprons, sled to raise key frame; EBONY(?): sharps; IVORY: natural key tops; BALEEN: damper springs; LEATHER: jack heads, hammer covers; IRON: tuning pins, spring on damper system, pedal trapwork; BRASS: lid hinges, caster cups, jack wires, hitch pins, nut pins, bridge pins

STRINGS/SCALE

Scale: 307

Strings: Bichord throughout; unisons 1–12 overspun, 13–18 solid brass, 19–top iron; about 20% of strings missing but remaining strings likely original or very early

Bridge and Nut: Bridge of one piece with single curve in treble; "shark's-mouth" undercutting in bass end; treble end heavily cantilevered; decorative molded profile at treble end

MECHANICAL

Action: English single action raised on sled to permit removal under double soundboard; hammers have three layers of leather and guide pins; lever overdampers hinged on pivoting portion of spine; original baleen springs replaced with brass; damper overrail (now missing)

Stops: Two pedals (now missing): left for dampers and right for lid swell; buff stop and buff stop mechanism (now missing) may have been controlled by hand stop

NOTES

Provenance: Descended in family of Henry S. Wilson of Augusta County, VA; after Wilson's death in 1950, passed to his niece Elizabeth Calhoun Montgomery; Eugene Wetherup, Elizabeth's son, gave piano to CWF in 1996

References:
· John R. Watson, "A Catalog of Antique Keyboard Instruments in the Southeast, Part V," *Early Keyboard Journal* 15 (1997): 146–147.

21 Square Piano, James Ball, London, ca. 1791

Accession number: 1997-117

Markings:
· "Jacobus Ball Londini Fecit Patent / Duke Street Grosvenor Square" in ink on nameboard
· "[illegible]" in ink on top key

Maker's serial number: none

KEYBOARD

Compass: FF–f3 (5 octaves)

Three-octave measure: 484

Natural coverings: Ivory with two scribe lines including head/tail seam

Sharps: Black-stained hardwood with ebony veneer on top

Key fronts: Molded light hardwood

Sharp length: 80

Head length: 42

Key guide system: Front and balance pins

CASE/DIMENSIONS

Length: 1,597 (1,570)

Depth: 556 (538)

Height: 868 (236)

Height of keyboard over floor: 730

Notes: Unusual shelves for candles are hinged to either end of the nameboard and extend backward over the key levers when not in use. There is no evidence that the piano ever had a dust board.

Case side thicknesses: Ends and front, 15; spine, 19

Bottom: Grain parallel to spine

Soundboard: Quartersawn spruce(?); grain parallel to spine; 3.7 thick

Materials: MAHOGANY: case, stand, hammer shanks, damper levers, end brackets, internal folding music desk, candle shelves, hammer-rail cap; LIMEWOOD: key levers; BEECH: bridge; SPRUCE: soundboard; SYCAMORE or MAPLE: nameboard veneer; PLAIN LIGHT HARDWOOD: molded key fronts; SOFTWOODS: bottom, belly rail; OAK: upper stand horizontals; IVORY: natural key tops; EBONY: Sharp veneer; LEATHER: jack tops, hammer covers; BALEEN: damper springs; BRASS: jack wires, casters (probably replaced), lid hinges; IRON: tuning pins

STRINGS/SCALE

Scale: 297

Strings: Bichord throughout; no gauge markings

Bridge and Nut: Bass end of bridge has simple undercutting; treble section greatly cantilevered towards nut

MECHANICAL

Action: English single action with lever overdampers and wood stickers with small leather buttons at top; damper system swivels upward for access to hitch pins

Stops: none

NOTES

Provenance: From collection of Ian Pleeth in England; transferred in late twentieth century to Tim Hamilton, who brought piano to America and sold it to Nicholas and Shelley Schorsch, who gave it to CWF in 1997

References:
- John Watson, "Instrument and Document: Balancing Values in the Conservation of Musical Instruments," in *Postprints of the Wooden Artifacts Group, June 2006* (Providence, RI: Wooden Artifacts Group, American Institute for Conservation, 2006), 18–20.

22 Grand Piano, James Ball, London, 1794–1805

Accession number: 1999-236

Markings:
- "Jacobus Ball . . ." on nameboard (now missing)

Maker's serial number: 166

KEYBOARD

Compass: FF–c4 (5 octaves + 7 notes)

Three-octave measure: 489

Natural coverings: Ivory with two scribe lines including head/tail seam

Sharps: Solid ebony

Key fronts: Molded light hardwood

Sharp length: 82

Head length: 42

Key guide system: Front and balance pins

CASE/DIMENSIONS

Length: 2,260 (2,220)

Width: 1,058 (1,040)

Height: 925 (296)

Height of keyboard over floor: 700

Case side thicknesses: All case sides, 23–24.5

Soundboard: Quartersawn; grain parallel to spine

Materials: MAHOGANY: stand, case veneer, damper heads, hitch-pin rail, hammer butts; OAK: case substrate, hammer rail, upper belly rail, action brackets; CEDAR: hammer shanks; BEECH: jacks; SOFTWOODS: bottom, lower belly rail, damper lifter; PLAIN LIGHT HARDWOODS: molded key fronts, damper register, setoff buttons, bridge; LIMEWOOD: key levers; FRUITWOOD: damper jacks; PURPLEHEART(?): keywell banding; EBONY: sharps; IVORY: natural key tops; LEATHER: damper pads on key levers, hammer covers, back-check pads, butt pads; IRON: tuning pins, back-check wires, setoff screws, gap spacer arcs, pedal trapwork; BRASS: lid hinges, lid hooks, lid hook rings, hammer-rail cap plates, jack springs, balance pins, front pins (tinned), nut pins, bridge pins, hitch pins (tinned)

STRINGS/SCALE

Scale: 277

Strings: Trichord throughout

Bridge and Nut: Bridge divided for brass and iron sections; back pins throughout bridge

MECHANICAL

Action: English grand action; entire compass damped

Stops: Two pedals: for keyboard shift and dampers; hand stop in right end block limits keyboard shift for una corda or due corde

NOTES

Provenance: Probably originally at Woodville, a plantation of Coles family of Albemarle County, VA; purchased in 1963 at estate auction at Woodville by Willard Agee of Charlottesville, VA; by 1989 in the possession of Robert Self, who sold it that year to John R. Watson; purchased by CWF in 1999

References:
- Martha Novak Clinkscale, *Makers of the Piano*, vol. 1, *1700–1820* (1993; repr., New York: Oxford University Press, 1995), 16–17, #3.
- John R. Watson, "A Catalog of Antique Keyboard Instruments in the Southeast, Part IV," *Early Keyboard Journal* 9 (1991): 82.
- ———, "Historical Musical Instruments: A Claim to Use, an Obligation to Preserve," *Journal of the American Musical Instrument Society* 17 (1991): 72.

23 Square Piano, John and Archibald Watson, Edinburgh, ca. 1797

Accession number: 2011-76

Markings:
- "John and Archd. Watsons / Edinburgh / Makers from London" in ink on nameboard
- "Robt. Stephenson" in ink in right rear corner of soundboard
- "Watson" in ink (in period hand) at top center of back of nameboard
- "Restored 1982 John Watson" in ink on business card attached to back of nameboard

Maker's serial number: none

KEYBOARD

Compass: FF–c4 (5 octaves + 7 notes)

Three-octave measure: 485

Natural coverings: Ivory with no scribe lines

Sharps: Solid ebony

Key fronts: Molded light hardwood

Sharp length: 83

Head length: 44

Key guide system: Front and balance pins

CASE/DIMENSIONS

Length: 1,632 (1,615)

Depth: 583 (571)

Height: 839 (235)

Height of keyboard over floor: 726

Notes: There is no evidence that there was ever a dust board or a folding music desk behind the nameboard.

Case side thicknesses: Ends and front, 17.5; spine, 21.5

Bottom: Two layers of pine; upper layer with grain parallel to strings

Soundboard: Quartersawn spruce; 4 thick at exposed edge

Materials: MAHOGANY: case sides, lid, stand, music shelf, soundboard moldings, belly rail, hammer rail and shanks, action brackets; SPRUCE: soundboard; SOFTWOODS: bottom, spine; OAK: key-stop rail; LIMEWOOD: key levers; MAPLE: belly cap molding; PURPLEHEART(?): nameboard banding; PLAIN LIGHT HARDWOODS: nameboard veneer, inscription cartouche, key fronts; EBONY: sharps; IVORY: natural key tops; BRASS: underdampers, hinges, bolt covers (replacements); TINNED BRASS: front pins, balance pins, bridge pins, nut pins, hitch pins

STRINGS/SCALE

Scale: 296.5

Strings: Bichord throughout

Bridge and Nut: Beech bridge with simple undercutting; nut also beech

MECHANICAL

Action: English single action with brass underdampers; old, but probably not original, lead weights added to key levers near jack wires

Stops: none

NOTES

Provenance: Descended in family of Joan Metcalf who immigrated with piano to Gainesville, FL, from United Kingdom; sold in 2011 to John R. Watson and Linda Baumgarten, who gave it to CWF the same year

References:
- Martha Novak Clinkscale, *Makers of the Piano*, vol. 1, *1700–1820* (1993; repr., New York: Oxford University Press, 1995), 318, #7.
- John Watson, "A Catalogue of Antique Keyboard Instruments in the Southeast," *Early Keyboard Journal* 2 (1983–1984): 76.
- ———, "Three Examples of Keyboard Restoration in the Southeast," *Early Keyboard Journal* 1 (1982–1983): 16.

24 Square Piano, George Dettmer, London, mid-1790s

Accession number: 1997-228

Markings:
- "George Dettmar London / Patent Action Piano Forte Manufacturer" in ink on nameboard
- "C Norman / Little Bentley / Essex / 1837" scratched into underside of dust board

Maker's serial number: none

KEYBOARD

Compass: FF–c4 (5 octaves + 7 notes)

Three-octave measure: 485

Natural coverings: Ivory with two scribe lines including head/tail seam

Sharps: Black-stained hardwood with ebony veneer on top

Key fronts: Light hardwood without molding

Sharp length: 79

Head length: 42.5

Key guide system: Front and balance pins

CASE/DIMENSIONS

Length: 1,636 (1,617)

Depth: 595 (587)

Height: 845 (226)

Height of keyboard over floor: 714

Notes: A dust board extends the entire width of the piano. It is undecorated bare wood of a design typically covered in green silk. Green stains on the board indicate green silk was probably once present.

Case side thicknesses: Ends, 20; front and spine, 19

Bottom: 43 thick measured at end where facing is missing

Soundboard: Quartersawn; 3.1 thick at break near bass end of pin block

Materials: MAHOGANY: case (solid), lid (solid), hoppers, hammer shanks, hammer rail (top), damper levers, action brackets, sharps (black stained and topped with fruitwood), portion of tuning pin block above soundboard, soundboard fretwork; SATINWOOD: perimeter banding around case sides and lid; nameboard veneer; LIMEWOOD: key levers; SPRUCE: soundboard; SOFTWOODS: dust board (originally covered with green silk), nameboard substrate, keyboard back rail, bottom; OAK: key-frame front and balance rails; FRUITWOOD: plain key fronts, sharp key tops (stained, veneer only); IRON: hand-stop lever; BRASS: hand-stop knob, hinges; IVORY: natural key tops; LEATHER and VELLUM: hammer hinges, hammer-head covering, sticker pads on key levers, hopper-jack tops, front-rail pads under sharps; BALEEN: damper lever springs

STRINGS/SCALE

Scale: 304

Strings: Bichord throughout; no gauge markings

Bridge and Nut: Bridge of one piece; slight back curve at c; no back pins; "shark's-mouth" undercutting in bass end; bottom three unisons have back pins on hitch-pin plank to mitigate sharp side bearing

MECHANICAL

Action: English double action with lever overdampers

Stops: One hand stop: for dampers

NOTES

Provenance: Purchased by James Hollan of Annapolis, MD; given to CWF by Catherine Hollan in 1997

References:
- John R. Watson, "A Catalog of Antique Keyboard Instruments in the Southeast, Part V," *Early Keyboard Journal* 15 (1997): 125–127.

25 Square Piano, Charles Albrecht, Philadelphia, 1800–1805

Accession number: 2004-20

Markings:
- "CHARLES ALBRECHT / Maker / Philadelphia." in gold lettering on nameboard
- "Joshua Baker Maker" in pencil on key bed
- "Restoration 1983–84 / Osborne Piano Shop, Carlisle PA. / Technicians: / Mark Showers / Keith Bowman" in pencil on bottom under key frame

Maker's serial number: 166

KEYBOARD

Compass: FF–f3 (5 octaves)

Three-octave measure: 483

Natural coverings: Ivory with no scribe lines

Sharps: Solid ebony

Key fronts: Molded light hardwood

Sharp length: 86

Head length: 42

Key guide system: Front and balance pins

CASE/DIMENSIONS

Length: 1,601 (1,583)

Depth: 567 (558)

Height: 799 (234)

Height of keyboard over floor: 665

Notes: There is no provision for an internal folding music desk.

Case side thicknesses: Ends, 21.5; spine, 24

Soundboard: Section to right of pin block not fretted

Materials: MAHOGANY: case, stand, hammer-rail cover, over-dampers, damper overrail; WHITE PINE: key levers; SOFTWOODS: soundboard, nameboard substrate, bottom, belly rail, spine; OAK: key-frame balance and front rails; PLAIN LIGHT HARDWOODS: keywell veneer, case inlay, hammers, key fronts; MAPLE: pin block, bridge, hitch-pin plank; STRIPED DARK WOOD: crossbanding veneer on keywell; IVORY: natural key tops, lockboard key-hole surround; EBONY: sharps; LEATHER: hammer covers; IRON: stop lever, tuning pins; BRASS: bolt covers, casters, lid hinges, stop-lever knob, hitch pins, balance pins; TINNED BRASS: bridge pins, nut pins

STRINGS/SCALE

Scale: 296

Strings: Bichord throughout; all strings replaced

Bridge and Nut: No back pins except to reduce angles at bass hitch pins

MECHANICAL

Action: English single action with mop-stick dampers on hinged rack; dampers raised by means of hand stop; hammers on guide pins; damper overrail padded but too high for contact with damper levers

Stops: One hand stop: for dampers

Provenance: Descended in family of Jeannette Hamner, who gave it to CWF in 2004

26 Square Piano, John Huber, Harrisburg, 1805–1809

Accession number: 2009-34

Markings:
- "John Huber / MUSICAL INSTRUMENT MAKER / HARRISBURG" copper-plate-printed on oval paper label under glass on nameboard

Maker's serial number: none

KEYBOARD

Compass: FF–f3 (5 octaves)

Three-octave measure: 471

Natural coverings: Ivory with three scribe lines including head/tail seam

Sharps: Black-stained hardwood with ebony veneer on top

Key fronts: Light hardwood without molding

Sharp length: 88

Head length: 46

Key guide system: Front and balance pins

CASE/DIMENSIONS

Length: 1,666 (1,652)

Depth: 589 (563)

Height: 843 (213)

Height of keyboard over floor: 732

Notes: The tuning pins are filed to shape at the top and not forged. There is no provision for an internal folding music desk, including any provision for a rack when the keyboard flap is folded back. The hitch-pin rail terminates with a large ogee profile extending over the soundboard. The portion of the case in front of the keys is attached to the key frame rather than the case and slides out with the keyboard. The lockboard therefore latches horizontally into the case at the treble end of the keyboard.

Case side thicknesses: Ends, 17.3; front, 14.7; spine, 20

Bottom: Solid with grain parallel to spine

Soundboard: Quartersawn white pine; passes under pin block cap to right end of case

Materials: MAHOGANY: case veneer, damper levers; PLAIN LIGHT HARDWOOD: nameboard veneer, string inlay, arris string inlay, hammer shanks, key fronts; WALNUT: hitch-pin rail, case veneer, inner rim, left case block, hammer rail; WHITE PINE: bottom, soundboard, damper system overrail, case substrate including front and sides, key levers, key frame (all rails), belly rail; CORK: hammer heads; LEATHER: hammer coverings, damper sticker buttons; IVORY: natural key tops; PAPER: inscription; GLASS: inscription cover; IRON: stop lever, tuning pins, stand bolts

STRINGS/SCALE

Scale: 303

Strings: Unichord and overspun, 1–12; bichord and brass, 13–24; bichord and iron, 25–top; gauge markings on key levers:

25, ga. 1; 31, ga. 2; 37, ga. 3; 46, ga. 4

Bridge and Nut: Black-stained, one-piece bridge with single curve; bass ends in indented taper and no undercutting; treble section cantilevered to increase distance from belly; crest notched along length to keep wood away from speaking length of wire

MECHANICAL

Action: English single action; jack wires topped with round buttons with leather tops; light hardwood hammers hinged to massive hammer rail fixed to belly and case rather than to key frame; hammers guided by long, thin guide wires in long slots; hammer heads made of cork with thick white leather on top plus thin dark layer and thick white leather outside; walnut lever overdampers, leather-hinged at rear; damper springs of steel wire and protected by white pine cover; damper levers guided by thin wire guides and raised by wire stickers with circular buttons at top

Stops: One hand stop: for dampers

NOTES

Provenance: Purchased at auction in ca. 1940s by Sandy Welch's mother; sold by Sandy and Andrew Welch to CWF in 2009

---

27 Square Piano, Joseph Kirckman, London, 1804

Accession number: 2003-72

Markings:
· "Joseph Kirckman / Piano Forte Maker / to her Majesty / London 1804" in ink on nameboard
· "IIIV" stamped on top of right stand apron

Maker's serial number: 2707

KEYBOARD

Compass: FF–c4 (5 octaves + 7 notes)

Three-octave measure: 482

Natural coverings: Ivory with no scribe lines

Sharps: Solid ebony

Key fronts: Molded light hardwood

Sharp length: 83

Head length: 44

Key guide system: Front and balance pins

CASE/DIMENSIONS

Length: 1,655 (1,645)

Depth: 573 (562)

Height: 867 (228)

Height of keyboard over floor: 742

Notes: The dust board supports survive, but no dust board.

Case side thicknesses: Ends, 17; front, 18.2; spine, 20

Soundboard: Quartersawn spruce; 4 thick

Materials: MAHOGANY: case (solid), lid (solid), stand apron facings and legs, hammer shanks, damper levers, hammer-rail cap, key slip, action brackets; BEECH: bridge; SPRUCE: soundboard;

SYCAMORE: nameboard veneer; OAK: hitch-pin rail veneer, key frame, spine; SOFTWOODS: stand apron substrate, nameboard substrate, bottom; LIMEWOOD: key levers; PURPLEHEART: keywell banding; EBONY: sharps; IVORY: natural key tops; IRON: tuning pins (blued); BRASS: lid hooks, bridge pins, nut pins, balance pins

STRINGS/SCALE

Scale: 301

Strings: Bichord throughout; tuning pins on right

Bridge and Nut: Sycamore or maple bridge with single curve in treble, decorative undercutting in bass end, and unusual stepped undercut near treble where bridge comes close to belly

MECHANICAL

Action: English single action with arched jack wires topped with a hard-leather block and soft white leather; mahogany hammers with leather head covering; lever dampers with baleen springs

Stops: One pedal (now missing): raised dampers by sliding wedged support under buff leather-topped batten that lifted damper levers

NOTES

Provenance: Sold to Dr. and Mrs. Thomas Sears Jr. via another dealer on Apr. 4, 1981, by S. Nager, a dealer in Massachusetts

---

28 Square Piano, George Astor & Co., London, 1800–1810

Accession number: 1994-49

Markings:
· "New Patent / Astor & Compy / No. 79 Cornhill, London" in gold lettering on nameboard
· "2707" stamped on cheek block
· "86" stamped in left rear corner of hitch-pin rail and on back of nameboard
· "I F" cut into top key lever

Maker's serial number: 2707

KEYBOARD

Compass: FF–c4 (5 octaves + 7 notes)

Three-octave measure: 481

Natural coverings: Ivory with no scribe lines

Sharps: Black-stained hardwood with ebony veneer on top

Key fronts: Molded light hardwood

Sharp length: 81

Head length: 43.5

Key guide system: Front and balance pins

CASE/DIMENSIONS

Length: 1,671 (1,643)

Depth: 593 (588)

Height: 866 (216)

Height of keyboard over floor: 748

Notes: A folding music desk is attached to the back of the nameboard. A dust board (now missing) had been hinged to the spine. The soundboard fretwork vent is missing.

Case side thicknesses: Ends and front, 21; spine, 30

Soundboard: Quartersawn spruce; 3 thick at exposed edge; heavy clear coating from later restoration

Materials: MAHOGANY: case, lid, stand, hammer rail; SPRUCE: soundboard; BEECH: bridge, nut; PLAIN LIGHT HARDWOODS: case veneer banding, nameboard veneer, inner-rim veneer, hitch-pin rail veneer; LIMEWOOD: key levers, hammers, damper blocks; EBONY: sharp veneer; IVORY: natural key tops; BRASS: casters, some strings, hinges; IRON: pedal trapwork, tuning pins

STRINGS/SCALE

Scale: 300

Strings: Bichord throughout

Bridge and Nut: One-piece, double-curve beech bridge undercut in bass end with straight slant profile; no back pins

MECHANICAL

Action: English double action with captive "Irish" dampers; additional keys passing under soundboard also English double action but without dampers

Stops: One pedal (now missing): raised dampers by pressing down on keys just behind nameboard

NOTES

Provenance: Owned in mid-twentieth century by Mrs. George P. Bissell; given to CWF by Mrs. Alfred E. Bissell in 1994

29 Grand Piano, John Broadwood & Son, London, 1806

Accession number: 1979-240

Markings:
· "1806. / John Broadwood and Son, / Makers to His Majesty, / and the Princesses. / Great Pulteney Street Golden Square / London." in ink on nameboard
· "N3541" in ink on left end of pin block top; also faintly in pencil on back of nameboard, under treble end of pin block, and stamped on top surface of keyboard section of stand
· "41" (end of serial number) in chalk on diagonal frame piece
· "T" in chalk on inside of spine under soundboard
· "J.H.G. Ball" stamped on top of right end of pin block
· "Thorndick" in pencil on cheekpiece under pin block
· "Cochran[e?]" in ink at treble end of hammer/setoff rail

Maker's serial number: 3541

KEYBOARD

Compass: FF–c4 (5 octaves + 7 notes)

Three-octave measure: 489

Natural coverings: Ivory with two scribe lines including head/tail seam

Sharps: Solid ebony

Key fronts: Molded light hardwood

Sharp length: 85

Head length: 42

Key guide system: Front and balance pins

CASE/DIMENSIONS

Length: 2,276 (2,245)

Width: 1,076 (1,056)

Height: 898 (294)

Height of keyboard over floor: 663

Notes: The folding, adjustable music desk survives intact.

Case side thicknesses: Bent side, 21.5; spine, 20; tail, 22.5

Bottom: Closed

Soundboard: Quartersawn spruce; 7.5 thick in treble; 4.5 thick near center; 14–30 rings per inch

Materials: MAHOGANY: case veneer, crossbanding, lid, stand, pedals, hammer butts, action brackets; OAK: case substrate, key-frame balance rail; SPRUCE: soundboard; SOFTWOODS: nameboard, internal framing; SATINWOOD: nameboard veneer; SYCAMORE: key fronts; BEECH: nut, bridge, jacks; PLAIN LIGHT HARDWOODS: molded key fronts, pin block veneer; MAPLE(?): inscription cartouche; LIMEWOOD: key levers; PURPLEHEART(?): key well banding; EBONY: sharps; IVORY: natural key tops; LEATHER: pads on keys for dampers, covering on damper register; IRON: gap spacer arcs, tuning pins, pedal trapwork, setoff pins, backcheck wires; BRASS: lid hinges, damper rail hooks, lid hooks, lid hook rings; TINNED BRASS: nut pins, bridge pins, hitch pins, balance pins, front pins

STRINGS/SCALE

Scale: 270

Strings: Trichord throughout

Bridge and Nut: Bridge and nut divided for separate brass and iron sections

MECHANICAL

Action: English grand action; entire compass damped

Stops: Three pedals (left to right): una corda, bass dampers (FF–b), and treble dampers (c1–c4); hand stop in right end block limits keyboard shift for una corda and due corde

NOTES

Provenance: Delivered in 1806 to Mrs. Mosely in Norfolk, England; eventually owned by Rodman Rockefeller of New York, who gave it to CWF in 1979

References:
· Martha Novak Clinkscale, *Makers of the Piano*, vol. 1, *1700–1820* (1993; repr., New York: Oxford University Press, 1995), 48, #51.
· James S. Daring (fortepiano, harpsichord, and spinet), Thomas Marshall (fortepiano and harpsichord), Kevin Bushee (baroque violin), and Herbert Watson (English flute and German flute), *Instrumental Music from the Colonial Williamsburg Collection*, Colonial Williamsburg Foundation, Williamsburg, VA, 1987, WSCD117, compact disc.
· Martha Hamilton-Phillips, "The Magnificent Keyboards of Colonial Williamsburg," *Ovation* 7, no. 6 (July 1986): 26.
· Malcolm Rose and David Law, eds., *A Handbook of Historical Stringing Practice for Keyboard Instruments, 1671–1856* (Lewes, ENG: printed by authors, 1991), 29.
· John Watson, "A Catalogue of Antique Keyboard Instruments in the Southeast," *Early Keyboard Journal* 2 (1983–1984): 77.

30 Square Piano, John Broadwood & Son, London, ca. 1808

Accession number: 1994-109

Markings:
- "John Broadwood & Son, / Makers to His Majesty, / and the Princesses. / Great Pulteney Street, Golden Square, / London." in ink on nameboard
- "N 12,598" in ink at right end of tuning pin block
- "[J H?]" in ink on bass end of pin block
- "Hodges" in ink on top of d3 key
- "L W M," "E R E," "M D M," "L W," and similar but illegible marks on soundboard
- "N. 12598" in pencil on back of nameboard
- "W" in pencil on back of nameboard in two places
- "12533 Hunter" in ink on underside of dust board
- "12679 / B[a?]ll" in pencil on right key-frame side rail

Maker's serial number: 12598

Keyboard

Compass: FF–c4 (5 octaves + 7 notes)

Three-octave measure: 489

Natural coverings: Ivory with two scribe lines including head/tail seam

Sharps: Solid ebony

Key fronts: Molded light hardwood

Sharp length: 81

Head length: 41.7

Key guide system: Front and balance pins

Case/Dimensions

Length: 1,679 (1,654)

Depth: 620 (617)

Height: 823 (237)

Height of keyboard over floor: 675

Notes: There is an internal folding music desk in addition to the one formed by the lid flap. The cheek block houses a storage box with a lid. A slab-sawn spruce dust board has white paint on top with two thin black border lines and is pierced for the dampers.

Case side thicknesses: Ends and front, 20–22; spine, 24

Bottom: Slab-sawn conifer wood with grain parallel to spine

Soundboard: Quartersawn white pine; 5 thick at visible front edge near belly

Materials: MAHOGANY: case veneer, hammer-rail cap, action brackets, intermediate levers, internal folding music desk; OAK: case substrate, key-frame balance and front rails, damper underlevers; BEECH: bridge; PLAIN LIGHT HARDWOODS: key fronts, damper blocks, nameboard veneer (slightly figured); LIMEWOOD: key levers; SOFTWOODS: dust board, bottom, key-frame back and side rails; EBONY: sharps, IVORY: natural key tops; IRON: tuning pins; BRASS: bottom molding, leg ferrules, casters, lid hinges; TINNED BRASS: damper wires

Strings/Scale

Scale: 304

Strings: Bichord throughout; unisons 1–11 overspun, 12–24 brass; no gauge markings; tuning pins on left

Mechanical

Action: English double action with wire-mounted dampers on underlevers; mahogany-shanked hammers have white leather-wrapped heads and no guide pins; top half octave has separate key frame and strikes through slot at edge of soundboard

Stops: One pedal (now missing): for dampers; pedal column also missing

Notes

Provenance: Bought by James Thomas Marshall at courthouse auction in Charlottesville, VA, for daughter Eliza Ellen Marshall (m. Norris) ca. 1861–1862; given to CWF by James Marshall's great-granddaughter Ellen S. Wyant of Charlottesville in 1994

References:
- John R. Watson, "Instrument Restoration and the Scholarship Imperative," *Early Keyboard Journal* 19 (2001): 22–23.

31 Square Piano, George Dettmer, London, 1805–1810

Accession number: 2011-67

Markings:
- "George Dettmer Piano Forte / Maker / By his Majesty's Royal Letter Patent / No 7 Gresse Street, Rathbone Place / London" in ink on nameboard
- "Eigen[missing] / Hertha Sp[?][?][?][n or h]y / Wien X1/79 / Hauilgasse Nr. 10 / Ruf B-57-9-23" stamped on ca. mid-twentieth-century paper sticker on inside of right keywell end

Maker's serial number: none

Keyboard

Compass: FF–c4 (5 octaves + 7 notes)

Three-octave measure: 483

Natural coverings: Ivory with two scribe lines including head/tail seam

Sharps: Black-stained hardwood with ebony veneer on top

Key fronts: Light hardwood without molding

Sharp length: 85

Head length: 43

Key guide system: Front and balance pins

Case/Dimensions

Length: 1,818 (1,789)

Depth: 619 (610)

Height: 868 (with reproduction casters) (227)

Height of keyboard over floor: 744 (with reproduction casters)

Notes: A folding music desk (now missing) was originally attached to the back of the nameboard.

Case side thicknesses: Ends and front, 24; spine, 21

Soundboard: Quartersawn spruce; grain parallel to spine

Materials: MAHOGANY: case exterior, jack hoppers, spring guards, stand, hammer-cap rail, lid, spine; TULIPWOOD: keywell crossbanding; MAPLE or SYCAMORE: keywell ends; SATINWOOD(?): nameboard veneer, case banding; BEECH: bridge; SOFTWOODS: bottom, nameboard substrate, spine substrate; SPRUCE: soundboard; HOLLY: nameboard veneer; LIMEWOOD: key levers; EBONY: sharp veneer; IVORY: natural key tops; MARBLE: oval inlays on case exterior; LEAD: key weights; BRASS: hopper springs, lid hinges, lockboard thumb latch; TINNED BRASS: balance pins, front pins, bridge pins, nut pins, hitch pins

STRINGS/SCALE

Scale: 295

Strings: Bichord throughout; all strings replaced

Bridge and Nut: Beech bridge and nut; bridge undercut in bass

MECHANICAL

Action: English double action originally with captive wire-mounted dampers (now missing)

Stops: none

NOTES

Provenance: Paper sticker on inside of right key cheek suggests ownership in Vienna, Austria, in mid-twentieth century; sold Dec. 7, 2010, as lot 191 at William H. Bunch Auctions, Chadds Ford, PA; 2011, purchased by Mitchell Manger, Beverly Hills, CA; purchased by CWF, 2011

---

32 Square Piano, John Geib & Son, New York, 1808–1809

Accession number: T115-2011

Markings:
· "Patent, / John Geib & Son. / NEW-YORK" in gold lettering on black oval cartouche on nameboard
· "D. Thomas" stamped on rear-facing end of bass keywell end
· "5360" stamped on left case block
· "to be bordered with flowers" in pencil on underside of dust board
· "to have roses" in pencil on back of nameboard under music desk
· "No. 7" in pencil on back of nameboard under music desk
· "B" in pencil on front of damper block 1
· "Aug 12 / 1789" in pencil on inner belly rail facing top key lever; possibly a restorer's prank
· "Aug" in pencil on back wall of treble action well; in same hand as previous mark

Maker's serial number: 5360

KEYBOARD

Compass: FF–c4 (5 octaves + 7 notes)

Three-octave measure: 484

Natural coverings: Ivory with no scribe lines

Sharps: Solid ebony

Key fronts: Molded light hardwood

Sharp length: 77

Head length: 46.5

Key guide system: Front and balance pins

CASE/DIMENSIONS

Length: 1,757 (1,746)

Depth: 618 (613)

Height: 908 (232)

Height of keyboard over floor: 800

Notes: A spruce dust board is painted green on top with a single thin, painted line border. It is hinged to the spine with a catch on the lid to hold it up when necessary. Horizontal fretwork at the top of the case under the lid flanking the keyboard has white paint that was added later. A folding music desk is attached to the back of the nameboard.

Case side thicknesses: Ends and front, 22; spine, 32

Bottom: Solid softwood

Soundboard: Quartersawn spruce; 3.5 thick at exposed edge; modern clear coating

Materials: MAHOGANY: main case veneer, key frame, hopper assemblies, internal music desk, lid, horizontal fretwork vents flanking keywell under lid; SATINWOOD(?): case and stand border banding; PURPLEHEART: nameboard banding; BASSWOOD: hammer heads and shanks, damper heads, possibly nameboard fretwork; MAPLE: central nameboard veneer (curly), bridge, nut, pin block; SPRUCE: soundboard, dust board; LEATHER: hammer and damper underlever coverings; BRASS: casters, caster cups, leg ferrules, drawer pulls, lid swell riser, hinges, front pins, balance pins; LEAD: key weights; IRON: trapwork, leg bolts

STRINGS/SCALE

Scale: 302

Strings: Bichord throughout; all strings replaced

Bridge and Nut: Maple bridge and nut; one-piece bridge with flat top lubricated with graphite

MECHANICAL

Action: English double action with wire-mounted dampers on underlevers; keys from d3 upwards pass under soundboard

Stops: Two pedals (now missing): left for dampers and right for lid swell; pedal columns also missing

NOTES

Provenance: Owned by Anna Dunbar of Falmouth, Stafford County, VA, in the nineteenth century; then transferred through a succession of owners to Chloe Tyler Winterbotham, who gave the piano to the College of William and Mary, which loaned it to CWF

---

33 Vertical Piano, Robert Wornum Jr., London, 1813–1820

Accession number: 1986-98

Markings:
· "Harmonic" in pencil on back of nameboard
· "Made by Rt Wornum Wigmore Street London" in pencil on underside of d1 key
· "M27545" stamped on plastic label on action; possibly applied by dealer Morley
· "15" stamped in large numbers on top center of tuning pin block

- "18" stamped in small numbers on right end of action in three places, including action support, damper rail, and vertical action frame

Maker's serial number: 15

KEYBOARD

Compass: FF–c4 (5 octaves + 7 notes)

Three-octave measure: 489

Natural coverings: Ivory with no scribe lines

Sharps: Solid ebony

Key fronts: Molded light hardwood

Sharp length: 86

Head length: 44.5

Key guide system: Front and balance pins

CASE/DIMENSIONS

Width: 1,127 (1,072)

Depth: 559 (523)

Height: 1,242 (1,178)

Height of keyboard over floor: 711

Case side thicknesses: All case sides, 27

Bottom: 33 thick

Soundboard: Quartersawn white pine; close, even grain

Materials: ROSEWOOD: case exterior veneer; SYCAMORE: key-well panels, pin block; MAHOGANY: action frame, damper rail, stickers, secondary wood in upper front panel; LIMEWOOD: key levers; WHITE PINE: soundboard; SOFTWOODS: substrate of back board (under rosewood veneer), vertical framing columns; BEECH: nut, bridge, bottom; BRASS: string inlay on case exterior

STRINGS/SCALE

Scale: 277

Strings: Bichord, FF–BB; trichord, C–f3; no gauge markings

Bridge and Nut: Beech bridge with flat top and no graphite; bridge pins arranged so strings of each unison same length; beech nut with flat top and graphite

MECHANICAL

Action: Stickers action with escapement adapted from English double action; hammers on wire pivots similar to contemporaneous grand pianos; dampers extend up to d3

Stops: Two pedals: for keyboard shift and dampers; hand stop in right end block limits keyboard shift for una corda or due corde

NOTES

Provenance: Purchased in 1986 from Robert Morley & Co. of London with funds given by David L. Peebles

References:
- Martha Novak Clinkscale, *Makers of the Piano*, vol. 1, *1700–1820* (1993; repr., New York: Oxford University Press, 1995), 326–327, #3.
- John R. Watson, "A Catalog of Antique Keyboard Instruments in the Southeast, Part III," *Early Keyboard Journal* 5 (1986–1987): 58, 69, fig. 8.

34 Grand Piano, John Broadwood & Sons, London, 1816

Accession number: TL2004-24

Markings:
- "John Broadwood & Sons. / Makers to His Majesty & the Princesses / Great Pulteney Street, Golden Square, / London." in ink on nameboard
- "6942" in pencil on back of nameboard, in pencil on underside of damper register, in ink on top of lower damper guide rail at bass end, in chalk on inside of spine under pin block, and stamped onto top of pedal lyre
- "Finkson No. 6942" in pencil on back of nameboard
- "Murray" in ink on front of setoff rail treble end
- "Finkson" in ink on CC key
- "Murray 6872" in pencil on right top side of key frame
- "6942 / Russell / Mar. '16 A.C." in pencil under bass end of upper damper guide

Maker's serial number: 6942

KEYBOARD

Compass: CC–c4 (6 octaves)

Three-octave measure: 491

Natural coverings: Ivory with no scribe lines

Sharps: Solid ebony

Key fronts: Molded light hardwood

Sharp length: 81

Head length: 42

Key guide system: Front and balance pins

CASE/DIMENSIONS

Length: 1,468 (1,437)

Width: 1,149 (1,128)

Height: 905 (289)

Height of keyboard over floor: 700

Notes: The original sliding adjustable music desk survives.

Case side thicknesses: All case sides, 24–26

Bottom: Closed; solid softwood with grain parallel to spine

Soundboard: Quartersawn white pine; grain at 10-degree angle to spine (gap/spine corner to tail/bent side corner)

Materials: MAHOGANY: exterior case veneer, legs, pedal lyre, pedals, music desk, hammer rail, action brackets; OAK: case substrate; LIMEWOOD: key levers; ROSEWOOD: case crossbanding veneer, keywell veneer; BEECH: bridge, nut; SOFTWOOD: bottom, WHITE PINE: soundboard; HOLLY: inscription inlay, inner-rim string inlay; FRUITWOOD: damper jacks; EBONY: sharps; IVORY: natural key tops; IRON: tuning pins, pedal trapwork, gap spacer arcs; BRASS: inlays on case and keywell, leg ferrules, casters, cast bosses above legs, cast molding around bottom and at vertical corners of case, pedal lyre rods, nameboard screw knobs, lid hinges, lid hook rings; TINNED BRASS: bridge pins, nut pins, hitch pins, key-frame pins

STRINGS/SCALE

Scale: 269

Strings: Trichord throughout; first twenty-one strings (CC–G-sharp) brass on own bridge and nut

Bridge and Nut: Beech bridge and nut; both divided between G-sharp and A for brass and iron sections; bridge double pinned throughout; notched to allow unison strings to have same speaking length

MECHANICAL

Action: English grand action mounted on oak, mahogany, and conifer key frame; mahogany hammer rail has a brass comb securing continuous pivot wires; leather-faced setoff buttons of light hardwood are adjusted by threaded iron pins shaped like tuning pins; fruitwood(?) damper jacks are topped with red leather; cloth is replaced; dampers for g2–d#3 are offset so cloth approaches string very near nut; notes e3–c4 have dummy damper jacks (without damper cloth)

Stops: Two pedals: for keyboard shift and dampers; right pedal split for bass and treble dampers (between b and c1); hand stop in right end block limits keyboard shift for una corda or due corde

NOTES

Provenance: July 16, 1816, shipped to George Balls of Norfolk, VA, presumably an agent for Lady Skipwith of Prestwould Plantation in Mecklenburg County; descended in Skipwith family to Dr. and Mrs. John W. Price, who gave piano to the College of William and Mary in 1946; on loan to CWF

References:
· Martha Novak Clinkscale, *Makers of the Piano*, vol. 1, *1700–1820* (1993; repr., New York: Oxford University Press, 1995), 53, #89.
· John Watson, "A Catalogue of Antique Keyboard Instruments in the Southeast," *Early Keyboard Journal* 2 (1983–1984): 78.
· ———, "Instrument and Document: Balancing Values in the Conservation of Musical Instruments," in *Postprints of the Wooden Artifacts Group, June 2006* (Providence, RI: Wooden Artifacts Group, American Institute for Conservation, 2006), 23–24.

35 Grand Piano, William Stodart, London, 1816

Accession number: 2000-67

Markings:
· "William Stodart, / Maker to their Majesties & Royal Family, / Golden Square, London" in gold calligraphy on nameboard
· "1672" in ink on top of pin block near cheekpiece and nut
· "1672" in pencil on bottom underside
· "Stephens N 71 / July 10th 1816 / GB [?]36 No 1672" in pencil on back of nameboard; readable only under infrared examination
· "[illegible]" in ink on key 1
· "[illegible]" in ink on key 2
· "A. Reid" stamped on top of right keyboard bracket
· "Eiloart / No. 30" in pencil on underside of right candle stand of music desk
· "G B" stamped on end grain of tenons visible on underside of front leg-mounting cleat

Maker's serial number: 1672

KEYBOARD

Compass: CC–c4 (6 octaves)

Three-octave measure: 487

Natural coverings: Ivory with no scribe lines

Sharps: Solid ebony

Key fronts: Molded light hardwood

Sharp length: 80

Head length: 45.8

Key guide system: Front and balance pins

CASE/DIMENSIONS

Length: 2,290 (2,261)

Width: 1,131 (1,111)

Height: 919 (296)

Height of keyboard over floor: 692

Notes: The original sliding adjustable music desk survives.

Case side thicknesses: Cheekpiece, 24; spine, 22 at cheekpiece end and 25 at tail end; tail, 25

Bottom: Closed; appears never to have been removed

Soundboard: Quartersawn spruce; clear coating; 12–16 rings per inch; hitch-pin rail replaced

Materials: ROSEWOOD: exterior veneer; MAHOGANY: action brackets, hammer rail, music desk; PLAIN LIGHT HARDWOODS: inner-rim veneer, pin block and damper overrail veneer, molded key fronts, nut, bridge; OAK: case substrate, upper belly rail, key-frame front and balance rails; SOFTWOODS: bottom, lower belly rail, key bed, damper overrail substrate; SPRUCE: soundboard; LIMEWOOD: key levers; FRUITWOOD: damper jacks; EBONY: sharps; IVORY: natural key tops; LEATHER: hammer covers, back-check pads, jack register cover, butt pads; IRON: tuning pins, pedal trapwork, gap spacer arcs; BRASS: lid hooks, lid hook rings, lid hinges, bottom molding, corner moldings, case and lid inlays, bosses above legs, leg rings, leg ferrules, leg casters, lid screw knob heads, hammer-rail cover plates

STRINGS/SCALE

Scale: 278

Strings: Trichord throughout except bichord in three lowest notes

Bridge and Nut: Bridge and nut divided for brass and iron sections; bridge slightly cantilevered in treble and undercut on bass end; back pins used throughout bridge

MECHANICAL

Action: English grand action; mahogany hammers have original leather covers; top twelve notes not damped

Stops: Two pedals: for keyboard shift and dampers; hand stop in right end block limits keyboard shift for una corda or due corde

NOTES

Provenance: Originally owned by Thomas Rutherfoord of Richmond, VA; remained in family until 2000 when it was given to CWF by descendant Irene Bernard Hilliard

References:
· John R. Watson, "Instrument Restoration and the Scholarship Imperative," *Early Keyboard Journal* 19 (2001): 24–25.

36 Square Piano, Alpheus Babcock, Boston, 1828

Accession number: 2000-94

Markings:
· "Made by A. Babcock, / for C. Hall, / NORFOLK." engraved in rectangular brass nameplate on nameboard
· "475" stamped on left nameboard support, stamped and in pencil on key bed, in pencil on left key end block, in pencil on each of five rails connecting balance rail to front rail of key frame, and stamped on keys 34 and 65
· "[W?] Clark [illegible] / July 8th 1828" in pencil on right key frame member
· "Clark" in pencil on right key frame member of main and treble key frames and along front edges of both front rails

Maker's serial number: 475

KEYBOARD

Compass: FF–f4 (6 octaves)

Three-octave measure: 484

Natural coverings: Ivory with no scribe lines

Sharps: Solid ebony

Key fronts: Molded light hardwood

Sharp length: 82

Head length: 45

Key guide system: Front and balance pins

CASE/DIMENSIONS

Length: 1,710 (1,675)

Depth: 660 (654)

Height: 860 (246)

Height of keyboard over floor: 742

Case side thicknesses: Ends and front, 20; spine, 52

Bottom: 83 thick

Soundboard: Quartersawn spruce; grain parallel to spine; 6 thick; triangular area in right rear corner beyond tuning pin block filled with solid mahogany

Materials: MAHOGANY: case veneer, hammer shanks, intermediate levers, spring guards, internal folding music desk; SPRUCE: soundboard; ROSEWOOD: nameboard veneer, case crossbanding; PLAIN LIGHT HARDWOODS: action brackets, key levers, hoppers, jacks, molded key fronts, hammer-rail cap (stained); BEECH: damper blocks, bridge; EBONY: sharps; IVORY: natural key tops; LEATHER: hammer covering, intermediate lever covers; IRON: tuning pins, harmonic swell hardware, pedal trapwork; BRASS: inscription plaque, string inlay, drawer pulls, leg ferrules, leg casters, bridge pins, nut pins, hitch pins, lock plate

STRINGS/SCALE

Scale: 291

Strings: Bichord throughout; first sixteen unisons overspun, all others iron; tuning pins bored

MECHANICAL

Action: English double action with wire-mounted dampers on underlevers; hammer heads have embedded lead weights on all but top half octave (patented by John Mackay in 1828)

Stops: Two pedals: left for dampers and right for harmonic swell

NOTES

Provenance: Given to CWF in 2000 by Kenneth McFarland, who purchased piano from a private owner in Durham, NC

References:
· Martha Novak Clinkscale, *Makers of the Piano,* vol. 2, *1820–1860* (New York: Oxford University Press, 1999), 19 (EP4458).

---

37 Square Piano, Joseph Newman, Baltimore, 1831

Accession number: 2010-62

Markings:
· "Joseph Newman, / BALTIMORE." printed on nameboard
· "E. NEWMAN" in pencil on D-sharp key (note 11)
· "Wm R Talbott / August 27, 1831" in pencil on underside of soundboard; observed through fiberscope
· "EN" stamped on trapwork pivot block under piano
· "EN" stamped on bottom within two inches of dovetail block that holds pedal lyre

Maker's serial number: none

KEYBOARD

Compass: FF–f4 (6 octaves)

Three-octave measure: 482

Natural coverings: Ivory with no scribe lines

Sharps: Solid ebony with rounded fronts

Key fronts: Light hardwood without molding

Sharp length: 91

Head length: 41

Key guide system: Front and balance pins

CASE/DIMENSIONS

Length: 1,722 (1,693)

Depth: 811 (803)

Height: 915 (333)

Height of keyboard over floor: 778

Notes: The strings run at an angle from right rear to left front with the tuning pins on the left and an all-wood hitch-pin plate, which is veneered with mahogany.

Case side thicknesses: Ends and front, 18.5; spine, 28

Soundboard: Quartersawn spruce; grain at 25-degree angle to spine (left rear to right front)

Materials: MAHOGANY: case veneer (crotch figure), stand; PLAIN LIGHT HARDWOODS: nameboard veneer (some with buryl figure), bridge, key fronts, hammers, hammer shanks; SOFTWOODS: bottom; BASSWOOD(?): key levers; BEECH: nut; SPRUCE: soundboard; EBONY: sharps; IVORY: natural key tops; BRASS: pedals, lid hinges, lock plate; IRON: tuning pins, damper and escapement springs

STRINGS/SCALE

Scale: 289

Strings: Unichord and open overspun brass on brass, FF–GG; bichord and brass, GG-sharp to F-sharp; bichord and iron, G–b1; trichord and iron, c2–f4

Bridge and Nut: Bridge undivided; bass end of bridge undercut about 75 mm

MECHANICAL

Action: Viennese action with nonadjustable escapement

Stops: Four pedals: for bassoon (FF–f1), dampers, moderator, and Janissary (drum and bell)

NOTES

Provenance: Probably in or near Aberdeen or Baltimore, MD, prior to 1950 when owned by a Mrs. Goodenough of Aberdeen; given to her grandson's college roommate, Walter Penn-field Boyd, between 1949 and 1953; following Walter Boyd's death, consigned to Harlowe-Powell Auction Gallery where purchased by CWF in May 2010

---

38 Harpsichord, Chickering & Sons, Boston, 1907–1908

Accession number: 1953-1196

Markings:
· "CHICKERING & SONS BOSTON USA MCMVIII / No 53" in paint on nameboard
· "Made by Chickering & Sons / under the direction of / Arnold Dolmetsch / Boston, USA / MCMVII / No 53" in paint on pin block

Maker's serial number: 53

KEYBOARD

Compass: FF–f3 (5 octaves)

Three-octave measure: 476

Natural coverings: Ivory with four scribe lines including head/tail seam

Sharps: Black-stained hardwood with ivory veneer on top

Key fronts: Turned and gilded arcades

Sharp length: 72 (upper); 71 (lower)

Head length: 38

CASE/DIMENSIONS

Length: 2,399 (2,384)

Width: 970 (965)

Height: 887 (268)

Height of keyboard over floor: 704 (+46 to upper)

Notes: The original folding music desk and the presumed original tuning T-hammer survive.

Case side thicknesses: Spine and cheekpiece, 28; bent side, 18

Bottom: Open (exposed internal framing and underside of soundboard)

Soundboard: Quartersawn spruce; no rose; grain direction from top jack to tail/spine joint

Materials: MAHOGANY: case veneer; SPRUCE: soundboard; MAPLE: pin block veneer; MAPLE or BEECH: bridges, nuts, registers; FRUITWOOD: jacks; BOXWOOD(?): tongues; EBONY: natural key tops; IVORY: sharp key tops; LEATHER: plectra; BRASS: lid hardware, pedals; IRON: tuning pins

STRINGS/SCALE

Scale: 381

Strings: Brass strung, FF–G; remainder of compass in steel; not determined if strings are Dolmetsch period

MECHANICAL

Action: As altered by Challis
← 8-foot hard leather; lower keyboard (probably originally *peau de buffle* leather)
← damper; lower keyboard (probably originally right plucking hard leather)
← 4-foot hard leather; lower keyboard (probably unaltered)
→ 8-foot upper keyboard (probably originally crow quills)

Stops: Six pedals (from left to right; four registers numbered from near side to far side):
1. upper manual 8-foot as altered by Challis; originally, down position turned register 1 off and register 3 on
2. 8-foot lower manual (moves register 4 to left)
3. 4-foot lower manual
4. buff stop, lower manual 8-foot
5. buff stop, upper manual 8-foot
6. manual coupler

NOTES

Provenance: Sold in 1916 by Chickering & Sons to Archer Gibson of New York; bequeathed to John D. Rockefeller's sister Alta Rockefeller Prentice, who gave harpsichord to CWF in 1953

ACKNOWLEDGMENTS

This book exists first of all through the generosity and advocacy of Dordy and Charlie Freeman, whose support over the past twenty-five years has cultivated the Colonial Williamsburg Foundation collection of keyboard instruments. For allowing me time to write, and for trusting the effort would be worthwhile, I thank David Blanchfield, Colonial Williamsburg director of conservation, and Ronald L. Hurst, vice president for collections, conservation, and museums and the Carlisle H. Humelsine Chief Curator.

My neighbor and friend and Foundation librarian Juleigh Clark assisted with some of the most challenging research. For including me in their stimulating discussions, I thank the widely scattered troop of enthusiasts who populate my e-mail folder with exchanges about the inventive competition and occasional skulduggery among the historical instrument makers. Their names appear in various endnotes.

For her heroic efforts to set my prose right and her resolute determination in verifying sources, I thank Colonial Williamsburg book editor Amy Z. Watson (no relation). No one had a more constructive influence on this book. Paul Aron, director of publications, deftly and gently kept the ball rolling in spite of my many distractions and was willing to take a chance when I asked to design the book myself.

Many coworkers in the Department of Conservation collaborated with me on the treatment of the instruments. Intern Astrid Smith cheerfully handled most of the conservation treatments in the past year. Other Foundation conservators who assisted with conservation of the instruments include Christine Gessler, Albert Skutans, Shelley Svoboda, Chris Swan, Emily Williams, Pam Young, and intern Kesha Talbert.

Several skilled, loyal, and remarkably generous volunteers and interns came cross-country at their own expense to serve short-term residencies to work with me on major conservation treatments. These include James Collier, Lou Dolive, Ian Gillis, Lucy Gwynn, Tom Winter, Jesse Moffet, Nick Waanders, Frederic Smith, and Joseph Kirby. Local volunteers Bill Wallis, Dean Couch, and Coleman Hutchins helped with the fabrication of missing parts. Jim Bowers patiently digitized photo archives, Sterling Murray gave valuable guidance on the opening historical essay, and Dominic Gwynn generously provided much-needed expertise on organs. The enthusiasm and support of these friends will always be a source of inspiration.

Finally, I thank Linda Baumgarten, who steadily supported this project as a professional colleague, as a peer reviewer, and, not the least, as my wife. I could not ask for a better companion.

PHOTO CREDITS

All drawings and most photos are by the author. Some overall instrument photos are by Craig McDougal, CWF Collections photographer. Entry no. 1, photo of Keene virginal by permission of the Edinburgh University Collection of Historic Musical Instruments and photo of Blanchet spinet courtesy of the Charleston Museum, Charleston, South Carolina. Entry no. 4, Challis photo from Hal Haney, "Harpsichord of Note," *Harpsichord* 7, no. 4 (Nov., Dec., Jan., 1974–1975): 8. Entry no. 6, Kimberley Hall photo courtesy Robert V. Buxton. Entry no. 15, photo of the Smithsonian example courtesy of the Smithsonian Institution. Entry no. 17, portrait of Lucy Randolph Burwell courtesy of the Virginia Historical Society (1951.35). Entry no. 23, the document with signature is in the Edinburgh University Collection of Historic Musical Instruments. Entry no. 28, the detail photo of the Broderip & Wilkinson piano is by Kenneth Mobbs, 1976; used by permission. Entry no. 34, photo of Lady Jean Skipwith's music book by permission of the Prestwould Foundation.

OBJECT DONORS

The strength of the Colonial Williamsburg
Foundation keyboard instrument collection owes
a great deal to the following friends who have
given instruments.

Jeannette S. Hamner (entry no. 25)
Irene Bernard Hilliard (entry no. 35)
Catherine B. Hollan (entry nos. 4 and 24)
Kenneth McFarland (entry no. 36)
Charlotte Morton (entry no. 7)
Pamela Seekins Paulu (entry no. 14)
David L. Peebles, Ferguson Engerprises, Inc.
(funding for entry no. 33)
Courtney Regen (entry no. 11)
Rodman Rockefeller (entry no. 29)
Joan Romain (entry no. 8)
Nicholas and Shelley Schorsch (entry no. 21)
Thomas H. and Sara Sears (entry no. 27)
John R. Watson and Linda Baumgarten
in memory of Robert A. Watson (entry no. 23)
Carolyn Weekley in honor of Lida Duke
Stokes Brock (funding for entry no. 37)
Eugene Wetherup (entry no. 20)
Tom and Barbara Wolf (parts of entry no. 4)
The Friends of Colonial Williamsburg
Collections (funding for entry no. 26)

LOANS

Hitchcock spinet, entry no. 2, on loan from the
Botetourt County Historical Society and Museum,
Fincastle, Virginia.

Geib square piano, entry no. 32, on loan from the
Muscarelle Museum of Art, College of William and
Mary, Williamsburg, Virginia, and gift of Chloe Tyler
Winterbotham in memory of her mother, Chloe Tyler
French (Mrs. John R. Winterbotham).

Broadwood & Sons grand piano, entry no. 34,
on loan from the College of William and Mary,
Williamsburg, Virginia.

INDEX

129

About the Author

After receiving his undergraduate degree in music education, John R. Watson began a career split between church music and keyboard instrument making. Thirty-two instruments bear his name, including three in daily use at the Colonial Williamsburg Foundation where he became conservator of instruments and mechanical arts in 1988 and associate curator of musical instruments in 2008. His research on issues in musical instrument conservation resulted in numerous lectures and articles and two books, *Artifacts in Use: The Paradox of Restoration and the Conservation of Organs,* copublished in 2010 by the Organ Historical Society and the Colonial Williamsburg Foundation, and *Organ Restoration Reconsidered: Proceedings of a Colloquium,* published in 2005 by Harmonie Park Press in association with the Colonial Williamsburg Foundation.

About the Colonial Williamsburg Foundation

The Colonial Williamsburg Foundation is the not-for-profit center for history and citizenship, encouraging audiences at home and around the world to learn from the past.

Colonial Williamsburg is dedicated to the preservation, restoration, and presentation of eighteenth-century Williamsburg and the study, interpretation, and teaching of America's founding principles. In the 301-acre restored eighteenth-century capital of Virginia, Colonial Williamsburg interprets the origins of the idea of America. The Foundation actively supports history and citizenship education through a wide variety of outreach programs.

Colonial Williamsburg also operates the DeWitt Wallace Decorative Arts Museum, the Abby Aldrich Rockefeller Folk Art Museum, Bassett Hall, and the John D. Rockefeller, Jr. Library.